Ukraine in Conflict

An Analytical Chronicle

DAVID R. MARPLES
UNIVERSITY OF ALBERTA

E-INTERNATIONAL RELATIONS PUBLISHING

E-International Relations
www.E-IR.info
Bristol, England
2017

ISBN 978-1-910814-29-1 (paperback)
ISBN 978-1-910814-30-7 (e-book)

This book is published under a Creative Commons CC BY-NC 4.0 license. You are free to:

- **Share** – copy and redistribute the material in any medium or format
- **Adapt** – remix, transform, and build upon the material

Under the following terms:

- **Attribution** – You must give appropriate credit, provide a link to the license, and indicate if changes were made. You may do so in any reasonable manner, but not in any way that suggests the licensor endorses you or your use.
- **Non-Commercial** – You may not use the material for commercial purposes.

Any of the above conditions can be waived if you get permission. Please contact info@e-ir.info for any such enquiries, including for licensing and translation requests.

Other than the terms noted above, there are no restrictions placed on the use and dissemination of this book for student learning materials/scholarly use.

Production: Michael Tang
Cover Image: Nomadsoul1

A catalogue record for this book is available from the British Library

E-IR Open Access

Series Editor: Stephen McGlinchey
Editorial Assistance: Janja R. Avgustin and Agnieszka Pikulicka-Wilczewska

E-IR Open Access is a series of scholarly books presented in a format that preferences brevity and accessibility while retaining academic conventions. Each book is available in print and e-book, and is published under a Creative Commons CC BY-NC 4.0 license. As E-International Relations is committed to open access in the fullest sense, free electronic versions of all of our books, including this one, are available on the E-International Relations website.

Find out more at: http://www.e-ir.info/publications

About E-International Relations

E-International Relations is the world's leading open access website for students and scholars of international politics, reaching over three million readers per year. E-IR's daily publications feature expert articles, blogs, reviews and interviews – as well as student learning resources. The website is run by a non-profit organisation based in Bristol, England and staffed by an all-volunteer team of students and scholars.

http://www.e-ir.info

Abstract

Through a series of articles written between 2013 and 2017, this book examines Ukraine during its period of conflict – from the protests and uprising of Euromaidan, to the Russian annexation of Crimea and the outbreak of war in Ukraine's two eastern provinces Donetsk and Luhansk. It also looks at Ukraine's response to Russian incursions in the form of Decommunisation – the removal of Lenin statues, Communist symbols, and the imposition of the so-called Memory Laws of the spring of 2015. The book places these events in the context of the 1991 collapse of the Soviet Union, and Ukraine's geostrategic location between Russia and the European Union. It seeks to provide answers to questions that are too often mired in propaganda and invective and to assess whether the road Ukraine has taken is likely to end in success or failure.

About the Author

David R. Marples is a Distinguished University Professor of Russian and East European History and currently Chairman of the Department of History and Classics, University of Alberta, Canada. He is the author of fourteen single-authored books, including *Our Glorious Past: Lukashenka's Belarus and the Great Patriotic War* (2014), and *Heroes and Villains: Creating National History in Contemporary Ukraine* (2008). He has published over 100 articles in peer-reviewed journals. He has also co-edited three books on nuclear power and security in the former Soviet Union, contemporary Belarus, and most recently, *Ukraine's Euromaidan: Analyses of a Civil Revolution* (Stuttgart: ibidem-Verlag, 2015).

Acknowledgements

I owe a debt to a number of people who have helped me in various ways over the past four years when these articles were written. The initial ones appeared on the Stasiuk Blog, part of the Program for the Study of Contemporary Ukraine, Canadian Institute of Ukrainian Studies, at the University of Alberta. I directed this programme for about ten years between 2004 and 2014, courtesy of CIUS directors Zenon Kohut (2004-June 2014) and Volodymyr Kravchenko (from July 2014).

The remainder of the articles appeared on my personal blog, starting from the end of October 2015. I have benefited from the wonderful assistance of my PhD students, and single out particularly Ernest Gyidel and Shona Allison. Ernest's assistance was provided in part by the Research Initiative on Democratic Reforms in Ukraine (RIDRU) at the University of Alberta, funded by the Kule Institute of Advanced Studies. I am grateful to the leader of the initiative, Olenka Bilash, for her assistance in this regard. Myroslava Uniat, an MA student at the University of Alberta originally from Kyiv, provided me with some insights into events in Ukraine and co-wrote two of the articles.

I would like to express my appreciation to *Open Democracy Russia* for granting permission to reprint the following articles:

'Ukraine: The View from the West,' 20 February 2014, https://www.opendemocracy.net/od-russia/david-marples/ukraine-view-from-west ;
'Igor Strelkov—Moscow Agent or Military Romantic,' 13 June 2014, https://www.opendemocracy.net/od-russia/david-marples/igor-strelkov-moscow-agent-or-military-romantic;
'Long live the Donetsk People's Republic,' 8 July 2014, https://www.opendemocracy.net/od-russia/david-marples/long-live-donetsk-people%E2%80%99s-republic;
'The Ukrainian Army is Unprepared for War,' 6 August 2014, https://www.opendemocracy.net/od-russia/david-marples-myroslava-uniat/ukrainian-army-is-unprepared-for-war;
'@FuckingPutin,' 22 August 2014, https://www.opendemocracy.net/od-russia/david-marples/fuckingputin
'Poroshenko's Choices,' 11 November 2014, https://www.opendemocracy.net/od-russia/david-marples/poroshenko%27s-choices

I am also grateful to one other journal for permission to republish the original article: *Krytyka* for 'Volodymyr Viatrovych and Ukraine's Decommunisation Laws' (2 May 2015), and especially to my publisher E-International Relations and to Stephen McGlinchey and Agnieszka Pikulicka-Wilczewska in particular.

A number of scholars have helped in various ways, sometimes by organising workshops and conferences, at other times with advice, and lastly in regular discussions about the events discussed in this collection, most often on social networks: Tarik Cyril Amar, William Risch, Serhii Yekelchyk, Oleksandr Melnyk, Serhii Plokhy, Dominique Arel, Andrii Portnov, Rory Finnin, Marta Dyczok, Bohdan Harasymiw, Svitlana Krasynska, Oliver Carroll, Volodymyr Kulyk, Taras Kuzio, and Jared McBride. The opinions expressed are at all times my own, as are any errors herein.

David R. Marples
Edmonton, Alberta, Canada
23 February 2017

TRANSLITERATION AND FOOTNOTES

In general I have rendered the transliteration of names based on the nationality of the people in question, thus Viktor Yushchenko (Ukrainian), but Aliaksandr Lukashenka (Belarusian). Russian names end in -iy and Ukrainian names in -ii. I have removed the soft sign throughout. All city and town names of places in Ukraine are in the Ukrainian format.

Many of the footnotes are internet links as almost all sources were available online. All footnotes were accessed during the period 1-23 February 2016 and on the odd occasion when the link is no longer available, I have made that clear. I have used subheadings if the articles were over 1,000 words in length.

Contents

INTRODUCTION		1
1.	PROSPECTS FOR 'PUTINISM' IN UKRAINE	9
2.	UKRAINE'S ASSOCIATION AGREEMENT WITH THE EU: ACCEPTABLE COMPROMISES AND SHARED HYPOCRISIES	13
3.	WHAT DO UKRAINIANS WANT?	22
4.	EUROMAIDAN: IS THERE AN END GAME?	25
5.	THE PEOPLE AND THE OPPOSITION	29
6.	ANALYSING EUROMAIDAN FROM THE WEST	33
7.	INSIDE THE HEAD OF V.V. PUTIN	37
8.	CRIMEA: RECAPPING FIVE MONTHS OF CHANGE IN UKRAINE	41
9.	ODESA AND THE ESCALATING WAR	47
10.	KING COAL AND THE FUTURE OF THE UKRAINIAN DONBAS	52
11.	IGOR STRELKOV: MOSCOW AGENT OR MILITARY ROMANTIC?	57
12.	PUTIN'S DWINDLING OPTIONS IN UKRAINE	63
13.	LONG LIVE THE DONETSK PEOPLE'S REPUBLIC!	68
14.	THE AFTERMATH OF MH-17	72
15.	THE UKRAINIAN ARMY IS UNPREPARED FOR WAR	77
16.	@FUCKYOUPUTIN	81
17.	ASSESSING UKRAINE'S OPTIONS	88

18.	PREPARING FOR NEW PARLIAMENTARY ELECTIONS IN UKRAINE	92
19.	THE SNIPERS' MASSACRE IN KYIV	97
20.	THE PEOPLE'S REPUBLICS CAST THEIR VOTES	101
21.	POROSHENKO'S CHOICES AFTER THE PARLIAMENTARY ELECTIONS	106
22.	MINSK-2	111
23.	ONE YEAR AFTER EUROMAIDAN	115
24.	COMPARING MAIDAN 2004 WITH EUROMAIDAN 2014	119
25.	ETHNIC AND SOCIAL COMPOSITION OF UKRAINE'S REGIONS AND VOTING PATTERNS	122
26.	UKRAINIAN PARLIAMENT LEGALISES 'FIGHTERS FOR INDEPENDENCE IN THE 21ST CENTURY'	131
27.	VOLODYMYR VIATROVYCH AND UKRAINE'S DECOMMUNISATION LAWS	134
28.	KYIV REVISITED	139
29.	WHAT TO DO WITH DONBAS: PHASE 3	143
30.	UKRAINE AT 24	147
31.	PEACE AT LAST IN UKRAINE? ANALYSING RUSSIAN GOALS	153
32.	COMMUNIST HEROES OF UKRAINE	157
33.	THE DNR, 'GRISHA PHILLIPS', AND SPEAKING THE TRUTH	160
34.	RUSSIANS AS TERRORIST VICTIMS	164
35.	DECENTRALISATION: PROS, CONS, AND PROSPECTS	169
36.	THE 'IMMINENT COLLAPSE OF RUSSIA': A RESPONSE TO ALEXANDER J. MOTYL	177

37. POROSHENKO, POLLS, AND THE RISE OF THE 'GAS PRINCESS'   181

38. UKRAINE AND RUSSIA: REWRITING HISTORIES   185

39. THE DONALD ON CRIMEA   191

40. DEATH OF A SEPARATIST LEADER   196

41. THE DESTRUCTION OF 'COLONIAL REMNANTS'   199

BIBLIOGRAPHY   204

NOTE ON INDEXING   211

Introduction

This is a book in an unusual format. Like many other scholars working on Ukraine, I followed the events of Euromaidan and its aftermath daily. In my case, I wrote frequent analyses intended for an obscure blog site anticipating that the duration would be relatively short like the Orange Revolution of 2004. As events escalated, however, it became something of a habit. Occasionally I published the pieces in various places, like *Open Democracy Russia* or *New Eastern Europe*. But for the most part the articles remained limited to a very small audience.

My original blog site was linked to the Canadian Institute of Ukrainian Studies (CIUS)' Stasiuk Program for the Study of Contemporary Ukraine. My commitment was voluntary since I was not employed there full-time, but it was an arrangement of mutual satisfaction and I was supplied with an office and a computer. Earlier I had commissioned others to write articles, such as the Ukrainian publicist Mykola Riabchuk, who focused on the endemic corruption and crime during the presidency of Viktor Yanukovych (2005-2010). But with the coming of Euromaidan, I was too intrigued by events to allow much space for my fellow scholars and writers.

In 2014, I was appointed Chair of the Department of History and Classics at the University of Alberta, signifying that I could no longer continue to assist at CIUS. Along with teaching duties, my time was more limited. In the summer of that year, however, before taking over as Chair, I was a Visiting Professor at the Centre for Russian and East European Studies at the University of Hokkaido, in Sapporo, Japan. Suddenly I had the time to study more closely (though not literally) the events in Ukraine and the personalities involved. Above all I had time to write.

From June to August 2014, and slightly beyond, I was able to produce more in-depth articles (10-17 in this book) at leisure in an ideal working environment, and once I returned to Canada, I continued to write even under the pressure of a difficult administrative post, often completing items I had begun in Sapporo.

The topic really has no end, but it seems to me that the onset of decommunisation in Ukraine, involving the removal of Lenins and ban placed on the Communist Party and Communist symbols and monuments, is a conclusion of sorts. The war in the east continues in spasms, with no substantial gains by the Ukrainian government or the separatist regimes, but in the remainder of Ukraine the transformation is readily apparent to any visitor. Ukraine is casting off its Soviet heritage, at least the physical manifestations of the Leninist past and creating something new, largely based on what is termed the struggle for independence in the 20th century. For me, this marks an end of sorts to the phenomenon known as Euromaidan.

There were two options at this juncture: either to restructure the articles or to leave them in their current form. I selected the latter for a variety of reasons. They seem more authentic and natural this way. Although there is inevitably some overlap between them, they provide a narrative from the beginning to a logical end point. At times, the conjectures therein were obviously incorrect, but those reflect prevailing opinions or my own thoughts at the time of writing.

As analyses rather than news stories, there are also some discussions with or about the interpretations of other scholars. Perhaps here I should make my own position clear. As Euromaidan developed I tried to maintain a distance from events, which was possible for a scholar of Ukraine who is not of Ukrainian ancestry. Many of my colleagues wholeheartedly supported the protests and condemned Russian actions. Others adopted a concerned and sometimes scathing attitude to what they perceived as the rise of extreme ethnic nationalism in some parts of Ukraine.

By the spring of 2015, when Ukraine introduced its so-called Memory Laws, together with James Sherr of Chatham House, I sent a letter to Ukrainian president Petro Poroshenko, which advised against accepting them. We argued that they would place prospective shackles on scholars, especially in Ukraine, who might question the reputations of the 'fighters for independence in 20th century Ukraine', who include some controversial figures, especially from the period of the Second World War. One of the initiators of the laws declared that we were all (over 70 Western scholars from North America, Europe and Ukraine) agents of the Kremlin. It was a sign of the polarisation of society. No criticism was palatable, even from those who thought they were friends of Ukraine.

Both the Russian and Ukrainian governments indulged in propaganda. In Russia, the propaganda was part of the hybrid conflict and was quite effective. It took some time for the Western world to comprehend and respond. In Ukraine, those who had always distrusted Vladimir Putin were strengthened in their beliefs, while many who had not expected an invasion were heavily shaken.

I visited Ukraine in both 2015 and 2016 and was able to talk to some of the participants of the events. I have corresponded with many others, including people who fought on both sides of the border in Donbas. I have attended local, national, and many international conferences on the problems engendered by Euromaidan, and gained the impression that an analytical chronicle of events as they appeared at the time would not only be useful, but might also help readers acquire a clearer perspective.

That is what I have tried to do in this collection. It begins just prior to the aborted signing of an EU-Ukraine Association Agreement, during a summit in Vilnius, Lithuania in November 2013. It ends with a discussion of decommunisation and the programmes and policies of the Ukrainian Institute of National Remembrance, tasked with introducing and monitoring the changes of city and street names and removals of statues and memorials dedicated to Soviet figures. The last entry is actually by way of a conclusion.

Throughout, it should be clear that Ukraine has been placed in a position of crisis, partly by Russia and partly by its own leadership – starting with President Viktor Yanukovych, but also by its own business elites that remain in place today and wield strong influence.

The book is aimed at an academic audience in part but framed so that it is accessible to the wider section of the population that became fascinated and horrified by what occurred. At the time of writing, the death toll in the war that followed Euromaidan is over 10,000 – with tens of thousands wounded and several million displaced from their homes. And, these events followed 22 peaceful years following the declaration of independence in 1991.

What has occurred might be perceived as the long-term consequences of that independence and the efforts of some Ukrainian leaders to distance Ukraine from its Russian neighbour. No doubt, some scholars would assert that the West is more responsible than Russia, by trying to attract Ukraine into its structures – particularly the EU and NATO. At the annual convention of the Association for Slavic, East European and Eurasian Studies in Washington, DC (November 2016), both former US Ambassador to the USSR, Jack Matlock and Professor Emeritus of Princeton University Stephen F. Cohen expressed this view to what appeared to be a large and sympathetic audience.

My goal herein has not been to answer these questions but to provide a depiction of a society in a state of upheaval and change, and in which major players like Russia and the EU have played important roles. Above all, it is about change and upheaval in Ukraine – one of the largest countries in Europe – which after more than two decades has run into difficulties and faces opponents that even question its right to exist.

The articles cover a period of over three years, arguably the most traumatic in the history of independent Ukraine. They begin with the prelude to the signing (or non-signing) of the Association Agreement between Ukraine and the European Union. Yanukovuch's sudden change of mind was the spark for the first protests in the square, now familiarly and better known as 'the Maidan'. The name given to the demonstrations, Euromaidan, was based on these initial protests.

The articles in the volume are mainly concerned with Ukrainian politics, with some emphasis on economic, social and historical questions. Some are academic, and others are commentaries, but usually founded on a wide reading of the Ukrainian media and government outlets. The goal in every case is to make the content comprehensible to the general reader as well as the specialist. The articles are 'frozen in time' in that they have not been revised, but in almost every respect they remain relevant today. The overall goal is to elucidate a complex and divisive period, which is still evolving a quarter century after the collapse of the Soviet Union. In many respects questions shelved in 1991, thanks partly to the peaceful demise of the Communist state, are re-emerging – and for Russia, no question is more crucial than the future of Ukraine.

Euromaidan elicited a dramatic and ruthless response from Russia, namely the annexation of Crimea, which narrowly preceded the departure of Viktor Yanukovych and the imposition of a temporary government of Ukraine that excluded representatives of the former Regions Party, of which the ex-president had been the leader. Most of the articles focus on these events and what followed in the eastern regions, where the disillusionment with the Euromaidan took on extreme forms.

In the spring of 2017 it is possible to reflect on these events. Some clashes are still taking place in the Donetsk and Luhansk regions, but the intensity has not reached the level of 2014 or early 2015. Several related questions appear constantly in academic discussions and social media: Firstly, was the removal of President Viktor Yanukovych a coup d'etat and did extremist forces hijack the protests to further the installation of what Russia has termed a Nazi regime in Kyiv? Secondly, was the eventual outbreak of war in the east a civil war or simply a Russian invasion of Ukraine, following on from the takeover of Crimea?

On the first question, I think there is enough evidence that although the far right forces played an important role in the later stages of Euromaidan, they were unable to dictate their will. They carried out acts of violence, but the temporary government installed after the president left office was not in any way Nazi, neo-Nazi, or even particularly right wing. Moreover, Yanukovych opted to leave Kyiv. He was not physically attacked or threatened even during the final stages of the uprising. The temporary government established by the demonstrators was soon replaced by a newly elected president, and shortly by a new parliament. While certain parties, most notably the Regions Party, were dismantled, the extremist forces did not benefit much from these events. That explains in part why they remain so disaffected today.

Incidentally, Yanukovych continues to deny that he gave an order for the Berkut police forces to fire on demonstrators. Thus, we are still left with the question – addressed further in this collection – of who were the snipers who fired on protesters killing the 'Heavenly Hundred' who are commemorated in Ukraine today? The government inquiry has been inconclusive and unsurprisingly the question has elicited much speculation. Though Yanukovych was in many respects a tyrant, he was a weak leader who seemed afraid to order a complete crackdown on the protestors. He was unlikely, in other words, to have authorised extreme force. But, an order to use lethal force may have come from another government agency.

Concerning the second question, the simple answer is that Ukraine experienced a civil war, but the separatist forces were relatively weak until bolstered by Russian military materiel and 'volunteers' – including many of the initial leaders of the regimes in Donetsk and Luhansk. But, it would be facile and incorrect to state that these two 'people's republics' were creations of Russia. They expressed a deep discontentment within the region with Euromaidan and the new government in Kyiv. Within a matter of weeks, the Donetsk region, which had boasted the president, prime minister and most of the Cabinet of Ukraine, had lost all its power. And, many felt detached from the events in the centre and west of the country. Thus, long nurtured desires for more autonomy came to the fore. One can term these sentiments pro-Russian, pro-Soviet or pro-separatist. More accurately they were a reflection of the mind-set of many residents.

Several further points can be made three years on.

Firstly, Ukraine has moved away from the Russian orbit. This statement applies easily to the western regions and to central Ukraine around the capital

Kyiv. But more important, it is clear that industrial regions that were formerly in the Soviet Communist heartland, like Dnipropetrovsk (the city is now called Dnipro) and Kharkiv have no desire to separate from Ukraine. Even in the distant east, in the coal mining and steel towns of the Ukrainian part of Donbas, opinion polls indicate that there is no longing for a Russian invasion or to join the Russian Federation. Rather, the population would prefer more autonomy and local power. In this sense, the new Ukraine is here to stay, even if it is not yet clearly defined. I believe the articles herein help to explain why. After 25 years, there is a general satisfaction within the country with the concept of an independent Ukraine.

Secondly, the quasi-messianic phase of the conflict, the quest for the so-called Russkiy Mir (Russian World), initiated in Moscow has failed. Indeed, it is rarely mentioned by the Russian leadership and is confined to eccentric academics like Aleksandr Dugin and some of the wilder separatist leaders – most of whom have now left Donetsk and Luhansk, or been killed in action. This fact should not surprise us. The idea of a Greater Russia – Rossiya – did not take root in any of the prior places in which it was attempted. This can be seen in the examples of Abkhazia, South Ossetia (the breakaway parts of Georgia) and above all Transnistria, which separated from Moldova thanks to Russian intervention in 1992. In the place of a New Russia, there is disorder and a lack of security. The host countries are suffering a form of internal cancer that they cannot eradicate because they do not have the force to do so. The government and separatists coexist unhappily and with occasional outbreaks of violence. From the Russian perspective, the consolation is that the lack of unification precludes these states from entering Western structures such as NATO or the EU.

Thirdly, Ukraine's response to Euromaidan has been ambivalent and at times questionable. Had I written this book in 2011 or 2012, the focus would without doubt have been corruption in the Yanukovych presidency, though it was also present in the administrations of the previous two presidents, Leonid Kuchma and Viktor Yushchenko. Corruption was one factor behind the Euromaidan protests. Yet it remains as much of a problem today as it was in 2010-13. Indeed Ukraine's current president, Petro Poroshenko, has become even richer since he entered office – partly through his chocolate company, Roshen. But, Poroshenko is far from the worst of these Ukrainian oligarchs who control valuable resources and, in some respects, dictate state policy.

There have been no radical reforms to take Ukraine in a different direction. That is not to say there have not been *any* reforms, but they have yet to make an impact on corruption. Instead, as I show in this book, the focus has been on erasing the past, most notably the physical manifestations of the Soviet period: Lenin statues, city and street names linked to Communism, monuments to Soviet heroes and architecture that appeared during the Soviet period. The campaign has not been without its critics, mainly for the way in which it is being conducted – 'Communist style' according to one observer. Volodymyr Viatrovych, who is leading the process, received a death threat in early March in the form of a wreath with the prospective date of his future death (9 May 2017) on the doorstep of the Ukrainian National Institute of Memory.

For this author, the biggest concern is the nature of the programme to move Ukraine away from the Communist period. It is healthy to remove the Lenins that have adorned Ukraine for the past 90 years or so. However, the quest to replace Soviet heroes with new versions based on a nationalist interpretation of the past seems unwise. In some parts of Ukraine it could be seen as provocative and the key question is one of direction. Of what is the new Ukraine composed? How should one remember the past? Must it always be one set of heroes or another reflecting fundamentally opposed ideologies, or would it be wiser to facilitate national healing by focusing more on forgiving and acknowledging past indiscretions or crimes? Such questions spark heated debates within and outside Ukraine today. Alongside these debates has been a propaganda campaign in Russia against what it maintains is a neo-Nazi takeover of Ukraine. The vitriol extends to anyone who appears sympathetic to the cause of Ukraine. Russian propaganda has even targeted Canadian Foreign Minister Chrystia Freeland because her maternal grandfather edited a newspaper in Krakow when it was under Nazi occupation. Freeland had earlier been banned from travelling to Russia because of her strong support of Ukraine during the conflict and support for sanctions imposed by the EU and United States in response to the taking of Crimea. Thus, Russian focus on Ukrainian nationalism has become an integral part of its foreign policy.

In turn, some Ukrainians refuse to accept any Western critiques of their country. They accuse such critics of being 'Kremlin agents' who are working for Vladimir Putin and the Russian government. The accusation is usually inaccurate and induced by fear and suspicion. One should always recall that a very real danger of their country disintegrating and falling a victim to violence of outside forces influences public opinion. We in the West are not in this position and it is very difficult to comprehend the sort of decisions facing leaders in Ukraine. Still, many Ukrainian scholars have also taken the view that for Ukraine to pursue a democratic path, an official revanchist nationalist policy is hardly the best option. At present, these scholars are rather isolated.

My goal in this book has been to take a more distant approach, though I have at times offered some examples of what I perceive as hyperbole or innate bias from Western commentators on Ukraine. The events have spurned a number of 'instant critics' – scholars who had not hitherto focused on Ukraine but have been willing to comment on social media or television about a country they have perhaps never visited. Invariably, they have taken the Russian side, arguing that Vladimir Putin is simply responding to Western – particularly American – intrusions into the former Soviet space. Most scholars of Ukrainian background in the West have been, conversely, fiercely supportive of Ukraine. One offered on YouTube a list of those scholars he had 'uncovered' as Russophiles. None appeared immediately to fit that description.

As a historian by training, I recognise that the events analysed in this volume will likely not be understood fully for several decades. Nevertheless, the temptation to comment – and to comment frequently – was too hard to resist.

1

Prospects for 'Putinism' in Ukraine

12 August 2013

Co-authored with Myroslava Uniat

Late July and early August provided examples of the application of 'Putinism' in Ukraine: a foreign policy based on a combination of ruthlessness and pressure. The Russian president made a visit to Kyiv, which was calculated to bring to heel Ukrainian leader Viktor Yanukovych and dissuade Ukraine from signing the Association Agreement with the European Union at the November summit in Vilnius.

Vladimir Putin's diplomacy is sometimes skilful and calculated. But, with regard to Ukraine, it appears crude and blinkered. It failed manifestly in 2004 when he tried to influence the Ukrainian presidential elections, on the eve of the Orange Revolution. In the 2010 elections he was more careful. But today he appears to have reverted to his former policy of overt pressure and persuasion, now accompanied by a contemptuous attitude to his Ukrainian counterpart, Viktor Yanukovych.

Putin visited Kyiv on 27-28 July, and behaved like a headmaster dealing with errant pupils. Ostensibly, he came to take part in the celebrations of the 1025th anniversary of Kyivan Rus', along with Russian Patriarch Kirill I, a man who frequently delves into secular affairs. In 2010, for example, he effusively congratulated Belarusian leader Aliaksandr Lukashenka for his electoral victory, despite its electoral improprieties. Putin and Kirill emphasised Slavic unity and the common past of the East Slavic nations. The celebrations culminated with a visit to the Kyevo Pecherska Lavra monastery and a procession carrying the cross of St. Andrew, the Apostle of Jesus Christ believed to have introduced Christianity to Eastern Europe.[1]

Also in Kyiv, the Russian president attended a round-table conference entitled 'Orthodox-Slavic Values: The Foundation of Civilised Choice of Ukraine'[2] organised by the Ukrainian Choice Movement, led by Viktor Medvedchuk, the former head of the presidential administration for Leonid Kuchma. A powerful oligarch, Medvedchuk supports Ukraine joining the Common Economic Space customs union with Russia, Belarus, and Kazakhstan. He is an active opponent of the Association Agreement with the EU.

While Putin's presence at the conference was not entirely unexpected, it contrasted with his peremptory chat with Ukrainian president Yanukovych. The bilateral meeting between the two presidents lasted for only fifteen minutes and contained only platitudes on the part of Putin about a common motherland and past cooperation.[3] Former Regions Party deputy Taras Chornovil feels that Putin's presence at the meeting organised by Medvedchuk indicates his aversion to dealing with the Ukrainian president, who is 'a nobody' to him. In Chornovil's opinion, such behaviour was more likely to push Ukraine toward the EU than herald a return to the Russian camp.[4]

The celebrations were marked by dissension. Members of the Svoboda Party protested the visit of the two Russian leaders, as did the radical women's organisation Femen, whose leader Anna Hutsol received a savage beating from a man in a Kyiv cafe on this same day, the latest of several attacks on members of the group over the course of the week. Yanukovych's speech appeared defensive and he seemed irritated that the guests would use a spiritual occasion for political purposes: 'We will not allow the use of churches and religious organisations by some political powers to serve their own narrow interests'.[5]

The following day, the Kyiv Patriarchate of the Orthodox Church organised its own commemoration with a procession and prayer service on St. Volodymyr's Hill and the Ukrainian Patriarch Filaret encapsulated the event as follows:

---

[1] https://www.rt.com/news/russia-ukraine-christianity-celebrations-670/
[2] http://ura-inform.com/ru/society/2013/08/01/argumenty-i-fakty-putin-i-medvedchuk-schitajut-chto-soglashenie-s-es-ne-smozhet
[3] http://www.pravda.com.ua/news/2013/07/27/6995061/
[4] http://www.pravda.com.ua/news/2013/08/8/6995688/
[5] http://www.rferl.org/a/ukraine-russia-belarus-moldova-serbia-kievan-rus/25058270.html

'Yesterday at this location the Patriarch of the Moscow Orthodox Church prayed for the leaders and representatives of the government, and today the Kyiv Patriarchate gathers to pray for the Ukrainian people'.[6] The implication was clear: the event attended by Putin and Kirill had little to do with Ukraine and Ukrainians.

Russia's response was prompt. On 29 July, it placed a ban on imports of Ukrainian chocolate, affecting four Roshen factories owned by the pro-European oligarch and former foreign minister Petro Poroshenko.[7] On 8 August, the ban was expanded to all Roshen confectionary, along with cheese, reportedly because of the antibiotics contained in Ukrainian products. As pointed out in one report, however, Russian factories owned by the same cheese producers were operating as normal.[8]

The Russian measures seem blatantly political in nature. They are reminiscent of the 2009 ban on Belarusian dairy products at a time when Belarus resisted deeper integration with Russia.[9] This is not to say, however, that Russia has no leeway. Despite the failure of 'Putinism' and its overt pressure on this occasion, other problems may lie ahead for the Ukrainian leaders. Support for the Russian-led Customs Union is evident in some quarters, in addition to the above-mentioned Medvedchuk and his Ukraine's Choice movement. The Communist Party of Ukraine can be expected to provide solid backing, but more important, pro-Russian factions within the Regions Party are also emerging.

One such supporter, Regions' deputy and Dnipropetrovsk businessman Oleh Tsarov, declared in an interview with the American *Forbes* magazine that in his view the six points of the EU Association Agreement are in conflict with the Constitution of Ukraine and that theoretically a group of Regions' deputies could appeal to the Constitutional Court concerning its legality. In addition the Customs Union would provide important benefits, including loans to offset Ukraine's substantial budget deficit (now at $2.7 billion) and offset the costs of expensive energy imports. Tsarov also noted that Russia previously had expressed willingness to create a reserve fund of $15 billion for Ukraine if it rejected the EU package and created a consortium with Russia. Further, if the Ukrainians went ahead and signed the agreement in Vilnius, Russia would impose a total ban on Ukrainian products prior to the 2015 presidential

---

[6] http://www.pravda.com.ua/inozmi/svoboda/2013/07/30/6995198/
[7] http://www.pravda.com.ua/inozmi/svoboda/2013/07/30/6995198/
[8] https://economics.unian.net/industry/821506-chem-zakonchatsya-ukrainsko-rossiyskie-torgovyie-voynyi.html
[9] https://www.euractiv.com/section/trade-society/news/trade-war-poisons-russia-belarus-relations/

elections.[10]

Tsarov's comments demonstrate that opinion in Ukraine is divided on its future direction. Its leaders can reject outright the bullying of Putin and Kirill – it is difficult to refer to their visit in any other terms. They can also use the Association Agreement as a means to increase their fading popularity. On the other hand, the economic situation poses serious concerns. Tsarov correctly noted Ukraine's lack of GDP growth, and its dire need for loans. In his view also, there is no guarantee that under the agreement's terms, the EU would open up its markets to Ukrainian products.[11]

Putin's visit to Ukraine has demonstrated the official Russian view: Ukraine faces a choice between two options and that it can no longer choose a middle route between them. Putin perceives Ukraine as a neighbour of common heritage, and with the same spiritual and historical roots. But more important he needs Ukraine as a geo-strategic partner firmly in the Russian orbit. Thus far, his policies have had little impact. But he has some powerful economic weapons at his disposal and, equally significant, support from some influential oligarchs in the Ukrainian parliament.

Yanukovych in turn faces several dilemmas. He cannot afford to alienate Russia completely. He is under pressure from prominent Europeans to free former Prime Minister Yulia Tymoshenko, most recently from the Chairman of the European Parliamentary Committee on Foreign Affairs Elmar Brok, who has called the latter's sentence an example of selective justice.[12] And he must fend off critiques from within his own party members who favour closer integration with Russia.

To date his strategy has been to support the Association Agreement while keeping doors open to Russia and strengthening internal control over Ukraine. It has worked in part, but the economic downturn and the deteriorating relationship with Russia, as well as the personal coolness toward him of Putin, suggest that its days are numbered.

---

[10] https://www.unian.net/politics/819828-v-pr-zayavlyayut-chto-shest-punktov-soglasheniya-s-es-protivorechat-konstitutsii.html
[11] https://www.unian.net/politics/819828-v-pr-zayavlyayut-chto-shest-punktov-soglasheniya-s-es-protivorechat-konstitutsii.html
[12] http://www.pravda.com.ua/news/2013/08/6/6995552/

2

Ukraine's Association Agreement with the EU: Acceptable Compromises and Shared Hypocrisies

5 October 2013

This paper will examine the prospects for Ukraine signing the Association Agreement (AA) with the EU and provide an assessment of the potential pitfalls and advantages of potential cooperation, as well as the responses of the leadership of the Russian Federation, which has made great efforts to persuade Ukraine to commit itself to the more closely intertwined Customs Union. It will also analyse the political and economic situation in Ukraine and offer some perspectives of the likely impact on them of the association with the Europeans.

Early Steps

Ukraine entered a Partnership and Cooperation Agreement (PCA) with the EU in 1998. In May 2009, it then joined the Eastern Partnership Project – an initiative of Poland and Sweden that also encompassed six of the EU border states: Armenia, Azerbaijan, Georgia, Belarus, Moldova, and Ukraine. Ironically, aside from Moldova, all of them were founding states of the Soviet Union in December 1922, though at that time the three Caucasian states formed a single bloc. In December 2011, at the 15th EU-Ukraine summit, the two sides entered final negotiations to establish a political association and economic agreement to replace the original PCA, namely the Association Agreement.

On 30 March 2012, the partners initialled the AA, which included a Deep and Comprehensive Free Trade Agreement (DCFT). The EU requested a number of reforms in Ukraine to be in place before the final signing. They included improvements to the legal and juridical systems, prison confinement, changes to the election laws, and positive steps toward the release of former Prime Minister Yulia Tymoshenko, whose arrest the EU perceives as politically motivated and based on 'selective justice'.

The release earlier this year of another high profile political prisoner, the former Minister of Interior Yurii Lutsenko, on 7 April 2013, appeared to be a major step in the right direction, but his case was less problematic for the Ukrainian leadership. Still, the stage seems set for three of the states in the Eastern Partnership – Ukraine, Moldova, and Georgia – to sign Association and DCFT agreements with the EU at the Vilnius Summit on 28-29 November.

Political Situation in Ukraine

Ukraine's political situation was only made more complicated by the parliamentary elections of 2012, in which the ruling Regions Party attained a plurality, but overall a clear minority of votes, and five parties attained the minimum percentage required to enter the parliament: Batkivshchyna (Fatherland), UDAR (literally The Blow; the acronym stands for the Ukrainian Democratic Alliance for Reform), the Communist Party of Ukraine, and Svoboda (Freedom). Western observers pointed out several flaws in the election and considered it 'not completely free'. The Ukrainian Cabinet today is under the firm control of ministers from Donetsk region, which is also the home base of the country's president, and Regions Party member, Viktor Yanukovych. In July 2012, at the latter's behest, parliament accepted a controversial language law, guaranteeing regional status of languages where 10% of more of the population speaks them. Specifically, the law empowered Russian speakers in the southern and eastern regions of Ukraine, where they predominate. Though the president had long threatened to introduce such a law, he was not necessarily expected to do so because of the polarising impact it was likely to have.

Notably over recent weeks, Yanukovych has also quelled dissidence in his own party ranks on the issue of signing the Association Agreement, though earlier in the summer of 2013 opinion polls highlighted substantial opposition to it within the parliamentary party. The Communists unsurprisingly are even more adamantly opposed. On 17 September, however, the Ukrainian Central Election Commission refused permission to the Communists and the Ukraine Choice movement, which is led by pro-Putin oligarch Viktor Medvedchuk, permission to hold a meeting concerning a referendum on whether Ukraine should sign the Agreement. Yanukovych has thus eliminated protests and exploited support from Ukraine's oligarchs for closer cooperation with the EU. In so doing, he has taken away from the opposition its key policy, which will leave the three parties more vulnerable in the next elections unless they turn to an alternative platform.

Such a move leaves Yanukovych in a good position to contest the presidential election of 2015, though the move westward will leave space for a pro-Russia candidate to fill. In that case, the president may form a temporary alliance with the opposition – a situation similar to that in 1999 when Leonid Kuchma ran against the Communist leader Petro Symonenko, and received most of his votes in regions that traditionally opposed him.

One problem for the president currently is that he is losing support in the main party strongholds of the east and south because of economic difficulties and a failure to fulfil election promises. In turn his predicament may benefit the Communists or even the UDAR, a party that has some support in these regions. Thus, the goal for the Regions is to ensure that the signing of the Agreement pays quick dividends before the presidential elections.

Opinion polls suggest that support in Ukraine for closer ties with the EU has finally surpassed that for the Russian-led Customs Union. Minister of the Economy Petro Poroshenko has declared that the gap is over 50% compared to 30%. Other polls suggest the gap is smaller: joint Ukrainian-Russian public opinion polls have 36% supporting the EU and 38% the Customs Union with Russia, Belarus, and Kazakhstan. The regional divide is itself deeply worrisome, though it is evident in each member state of the Eastern Partnership.

Relations with Russia

Ukraine's relations with Russia are difficult and strained. In Moscow, there are three people who deal with Ukraine. The first is Vladimir Putin himself, who has made Ukraine his key target in relations with what used to be termed the 'Near Abroad'. In this respect, particularly revealing was the Russian president's visit to Ukraine on 27-28 July, in conjunction with the 1025th anniversary of Kyivan Rus', when Russian Patriarch Kirill I accompanied him in attending celebrations at the Pecherska Lavra. Also in Kyiv, President Putin attended a round-table conference entitled 'Orthodox-Slavic Values: the Foundation of Civilised Choice of Ukraine', organised by the Ukrainian Choice Movement of Medvedchuk, who was formerly head of the presidential administration of Leonid Kuchma. A powerful oligarch (though only the 57th richest!), Medvedchuk supports Ukraine joining the Common Economic

Space customs union and is an active opponent of the Association Agreement with the EU.

The second figure is economist Sergey Glazyev, the advisor of the Russian president for Customs Union issues and relations with Ukraine, who has been particularly outspoken and aggressive, declaring that if the AA is signed, Russia will exclude Ukraine from the Free Trade area of the CIS. He also stated that the Eurasian Commission would impose a single customs tariff on Ukrainian products, particularly as goods from the EU that are no longer subject to import duties, would likely flood the Ukrainian market. In this way, Glazyev continued, Ukraine will be pushed toward default; hence signing the agreement will be tantamount to 'euthanasia'. He was believed to be responsible for the ban on Ukrainian products that started with the Roshen chocolate company in the summer of 2013, which extended to Moldovan wines last month. Though outspoken, many analysts regard Glazyev as a peripheral statesman.

The third figure is a familiar one to Russia watchers, namely Vladislav Surkov, a 49-year old English-speaking businessman and ideologue with enormous influence over the Russian government and Putin in particular. His impact has been compared with that of Mikhail Suslov, the so-called 'grey cardinal' for many years in the Soviet leadership from Stalin to Brezhnev. On 20 September, Surkov received the appointment of presidential aide. In a recent paper, analyst Roman Rukomeda speculated that his installation was specifically for future relations with Ukraine. The position returns him to his former prominence following his earlier spell as Deputy Chief of Staff to Putin in 2004. Surkov is the architect of the prevailing economic system in Russia that has been termed 'sovereign democracy' and he is close to extremist factions such as *Nashi*. Many regard him as the Kremlin's chief ideologue.

The current prominence of these strongly nationalist leaders suggests that Russia will put considerable pressure on Ukraine both before the Vilnius Summit – though the Russian side expects the agreement to be signed – and especially afterward. Most important will be the 2015 presidential election campaign, though Russia's past attempts to influence Ukrainian elections have been spectacularly unsuccessful.

Economic Situation in Ukraine

Ukraine's economic situation is very difficult. One can begin with the catastrophic decline in population since independence from 52.5 to the present 44.5 million, a drop of over 15% in 22 years. Its GDP fell by 1.3% in the second quarter of 2013, though over the entire year a modest growth of

0.5% is anticipated. The Russian scenario that Ukraine will face a serious crisis after signing the Association Agreement is not exaggerated. In the short term, Ukraine faces continued depletion of its hard currency reserves, which fell by 30% over the past year, and now has barely enough to cover 2-3 months of imports. The inflow of European goods expected after the agreement may reduce current export of Ukrainian products to Russia.

The issue is whether the largely unreformed Ukrainian economy can compete. That is not to say that there have been no attempts at reform. One year ago, Poroshenko announced that 1,200 factories would be removed from the list of strategic assets that could not be privatised. The list was assumed to include coalmines, oil and gas pipelines, and grain silos among other assets. On 11 September 2013, the Ukrainian State Property Fund announced that 45 coalmines belonging to various state-owned enterprises would be privatised in an effort to raise coal production through modernisation of mines using private capital.

This sector is perhaps the best example of Ukraine's current economic dilemmas: the state mining sector ran up losses of over $1 billion in the first seven months of 2013: 70% of the mines are state-owned and 80% of them reply on subsidies to stay afloat. Thus, the question needs to be asked: why would private businesses risk investing in an industry with falling productivity and for which demand is weak? The law of 2012 also stipulates that any privatisation must come with guarantees of the social security of the coalminers through creation of trade unions and other safeguards.

Despite the passage of the law, there has been little movement on privatisation in Ukraine; rather, companies have been auctioned off to the main financial backers of the Regions Party – oligarchs Rinat Akhmetov and Dmytro Firtash. These business leaders, intent on building personal empires – Akhmetov's net worth is estimated at 15.4 billion – have continued to exploit Ukraine's assets following a similar pattern to that in Russia in the 1990s.

The recent lowering of Ukraine's credit rating by Moody's to Caa1 and the current need for foreign loans may put pressure on currency. All these factors, added to the very real threat of Russian economic responses to Ukraine signing the AA, suggest that over next five years Ukraine will undergo deep economic recession – we have already seen the lowering of GDP forecasts for next year. Some of the demands of the Europeans will have immediate and distressing effects – two analysts pointed out earlier this week that the requirements needed for large combustible plants would cost about half of Ukraine's current annual budget to implement. But with reforms, over the long term the country can recover and will do better outside the Russian orbit, which is based largely on non-renewable resources and demands for closer integration.

Moreover, the EU is prepared to make some compromises. It may permit the benefits of free trade to begin at once rather than waiting for ratification of the AA by all 28 member-states. In other words, the EU link may be the best way to introduce a form of shock therapy in Ukraine that can reduce past dependence on Russian goods and, even more important, bring in economic reforms that have been almost fatally delayed in the entire period of independence. Finally, trade with the EU will eventually be more useful and profitable for Ukraine, than trade with the oil and gas dependent Russia.

The EU Perspective

Concerning the EU's attitude to signing the Association Agreement with Ukraine, one can start with recent quote from president of Gorshenin Institute in Kyiv, Vadym Omelchenko, that the AA might become the main geopolitical accomplishment for current leaders of European structures. The statement illustrates the fate of several EU initiatives and their general failure to have an impact in two of the countries of the Eastern Partnership where the issue of human rights violations has precluded close cooperation, namely Belarus and Azerbaijan.

Conversely, the EU has opted to ignore some of the glaring issues in domestic Ukraine and may circumvent some problems by choosing, as suggested earlier, to ratify the AA separately at a later date – it has already been accepted by the Ukrainian Cabinet – as well as allowing Ukraine to make some token gestures without following up with meaningful reforms.

From the EU perspective let us focus for a moment on the most critical issue concerning relations with the Ukrainian government, namely the continuing incarceration of opposition leader and former Prime Minister, Yulia Tymoshenko, jailed for seven years in 2011 for negotiating a 2009 deal with Vladimir Putin on gas prices that, according to the court, brought harm to Ukraine. The sentence also banned her from any role in politics for a 10-year period. The EU has hardly presented a united front on the issue – though at the recent economic summit in Yalta Lithuanian president, Dalia Grybauskaite, stated that: 'the request from the European Union on Tymoshenko's case is still on the table and, without a solution, I do not see a possibility for the signature'. The issue has divided Western analysts, whereas Tymoshenko's erstwhile Orange partner, former president Yushchenko has called for the Agreement to be signed whether or not Tymoshenko is released first.

As Taras Kuzio pointed out in a recent commentary, it is impractical for the Ukrainian president to release Tymoshenko either fully or for medical treatment in Germany, Canada has also offered to assist her. Given a direct choice between her release and pardon – and there are further impending charges about her involvement in the 1996 murder of businessman Yevhen Shcherban – and a potential failure of the Vilnius summit, Yanukovych would opt for the latter, whatever its implications for Ukraine's integration with the Russian-led Customs Union.

Yanukovych is not a politician in the Western sense of the word. He does not care particularly about his place in history, or taking a dramatic westward step. Rather like the Regions Party leaders with whom he keeps company and rules Ukraine, the Ukrainian president puts survival and his personal future ahead of that of the national interest.

In short, after many meetings at different levels, it is still not apparent to the EU leaders that their Ukrainian counterparts are more concerned about power than a European future. British analyst Andrew Wilson has stated that Yanukovych is ignorant of how the EU works, believing that the crucial matter is a balance of power and that the EU's concern for Tymoshenko is ritualistic. The agreement with the EU is simply a business solution that will keep Russian oligarchs out of their domain. In turn, the Ukrainian opposition perceives its task as supporting what it terms the 'criminal government' in its path toward Europe before defeating it in the elections. Implicitly, the EU is for the moment at least enhancing the re-election chances of the Regions leader simply by dealing with him.

At the same time, the potential of Ukraine and its $330 billion economy for the Europeans seems obvious. Yet they fear the creation of two hostile trading blocs, using high tariffs, quotas and other restrictive measures that will impede the free flow of goods. And many European leaders are wary of such an impasse, including newly re-elected German Chancellor Angela Merkel. On the other hand, the Europeans have shown great patience in keeping the agreement afloat in the face of the Ukrainian government's painfully slow progress on the suggested reforms – most of which were rushed through parliament hurriedly in September as the summit approached, though they remain more on paper than reality.

Conclusion

In the long term, can Ukraine become a potential member of the EU?

Questions arise over the expedience of further EU expansion given the recent crises in member states. There are fears also over the likely impact of adding a country of over 40 million to the mix, one with deep internal problems and divisions. The irony is that an anti-Orange and in many respects anti-Ukrainian government is leading the way toward western integration and for reasons that may have little to do with any form of commitment to democracy and economic reforms. In the future, it will be necessary to ensure several things for success:

1. Fundamental economic reforms, including privatisation (without restrictive conditions attached) and revamping of obsolete industries that require subsidies to survive.
2. Oligarch investment in the Ukrainian economy rather than in private bank accounts abroad, which may require a fundamental assault on corruption.
3. Ensuring that the presidential elections of 2015 are free and fair – it will require careful monitoring of election commissions, likely lowering the minimum percentage required to get seats in parliament (the new quota of 5% would likely mean that even the Communists or Svoboda may not get seats after the elections, and many smaller parties would be excluded), the first past the post system would likely favour the Regions Party. There is a need also to maintain a national vote for president rather than a parliamentary one and to reassess the ways in which election commissions are put together.
4. Monitoring of human rights in Ukraine must be made a priority for the EU, especially given the increased chances for a continuation of Yanukovych in office.
5. As noted, the signing of the AA and subsequent deeper integration that may ultimately end with EU membership will undermine the purpose and tactics of the Ukrainian opposition, which taken together won the majority of votes in the last election. On the other hand, a united opposition with a single leader running in the next presidential election might profit from the declining economic fortunes of Ukraine in 2014 and early 2015.

Finally, if one can separate the Association Agreement from economic and human rights issues, it will mark a fundamental turning point for the Ukrainian state, and a path oriented away from the Soviet legacy toward a European future. In itself, this will be a significant achievement, one that has been attained in a stumbling and often uncertain manner, and in spite and in part because of Russian truculence and threats. When the Orange Revolution occurred in late 2004, many observers felt that this might be the logical direction for Ukraine to take.

For a variety of reasons, the Orange presidency of Viktor Yushchenko failed in a spectacular fashion. The corruption pervasive during the time of Leonid Kuchma's leadership not only remained in place; it became deeper and more endemic under Yushchenko. It is markedly worse under Yanukovych. And yet the paradox is that it is this government and president who may take Ukraine into Europe. It is a mixed blessing that has resulted from compromises on the side of Brussels, and intransigence on the part of Kyiv. But it may happen, and in the long term, despite all the caveats cited, it may be for the best.

3

What Do Ukrainians Want?

28 November 2013

The mass protests in Ukraine that began last Sunday brought back memories of the Orange Revolution of 2004. But to what extent do they reflect sentiment throughout Ukraine?

Many media accounts have reduced the impasse to a simplistic equation: the people of Ukraine wish to remove the country from the dominion of the Russian bully (Putin) and commit to the free society of the European Union. President Viktor Yanukovych appeared to have taken the correct path, but halted on the brink of the summit in Vilnius where he was to have signed an Association Agreement with the EU for two reasons: pressure from Russia and refusal to release former Prime Minister Yulia Tymoshenko.

Some reporters have cited a recent press release from the company GfK Ukraine, which conducted an opinion poll in October, suggesting that support for the EU agreement has risen sharply among Ukrainian residents (to 45%) while that for the Russian-led Customs Union has fallen dramatically to (14%). Earlier the tallies were more or less even. Ottawa-based analyst Ivan Katchanovski, however, points out that the GfK polls have been unreliable in the past and have tended to exaggerate support for affiliation with Europe and ask questions that were not very clear to the respondents.

The complexity of the situation in Ukraine today is exemplified in a new poll conducted by the Kyiv International Institute of Sociology between 9 and 20 November 2013, i.e. on the eve of the protests in many Ukrainian cities. The first question was framed as follows: If there were to be a referendum on the question should Ukraine join the Customs Union with Russia, Belarus, and Kazakhstan, would you vote for it, against it, or decline to vote? The results showed 40.8% in favour and 33.1% opposed.

Broken down by region, support for joining the Customs Union was very high in the East (64.5%), high in the South (54%), moderate in the Centre (29.6%), and lowest in the West (16.4%). Looking at the age demographics, it is the older generation that is mainly in favour, including almost half of those over 70, and decreasing with each age group to 32.1% among those aged 18-29.

Turning to the results for a referendum on Ukraine joining the European Union, 39.7% were in favour and 35.1% opposed. Support came chiefly from the west (66.4%) and the centre (43.4%), while only 18.4% of those living in the east were supportive. Over 50% of those aged 18-29 backed the idea, but only 28% of those aged over 70.

Thus, it is fair to say that Ukraine is divided not only regionally, which has been evident since independence in 1991, but also demographically by age group. One cannot take these results as definitive because the question of Ukraine joining the European Union is purely speculative. The GfK poll had asked only about support for signing an Association Agreement with the EU. But if one accepts that those who support the AA would also be likely to favour full EU membership for Ukraine at a future time, then one can make several conclusions from these polls.

First, it is the younger generation that is most committed to the EU and in turn comprises the vast majority of demonstrators in Kyiv's Independence Square, as well as in other cities. But they do not necessarily reflect the sentiments of the older generation (over 40), and are contrary to the views of those over the age of 55, a group that comprised over 28% of Ukraine's population last year.

Second, it is Western Ukraine that is the main supporter of the EU, as one might expect given its geographical location and history, especially the strongly anti-Soviet sentiments in the past, and anti-Russian perspective today.

Third, those who would prefer Ukraine to join the Customs Union live in the key industrial centres, comprising such cities as Donetsk, Odesa, Dnipropetrovsk, Kharkiv, and Luhansk, though not the capital Kyiv. These regions are facing an economic crisis with faltering industries, as well as negative birth rates and declining living standards.

The East, however, is the heartland of the ruling Regions Party and President Yanukovych. By signing the Association Agreement in Vilnius, Yanukovch would have incurred a rupture within his own party and lost the support of others, such as the Communists, who have long favoured closer integration with Russia.

Given such a dangerous divide in society, the best option for the government might have been to do nothing, the policy of long-time president Leonid Kuchma (1994-2004) and of Yanukovych until the Europeans raised the stakes by offering the Association Agreement. That option disappeared when Russia made it clear that the possibility of a parallel 3+1 membership of the Customs Union was not on the table and that Ukraine must make its choice.

As analyst Oles Oleksiyenko put it in an article of 22 November, 'Yanukovych has outwitted himself'. He believed to the last minute that he could gamble on the stakes being raised and getting a better deal from either the EU or Russia. Unfortunately, despite the mass protests that appear so vividly on our TV screens, there is no overwhelming support in Ukraine for either option.

4

Euromaidan: Is There an End Game?

16 December 2013

Is Euromaidan going to change the face of Ukraine irrevocably or can the forces of the government and President Viktor Yanukovych recover? Is this Ukraine's version of an Arab Spring or something that ultimately will change little?

We have observed with fascination the development of events in Kyiv over the past three weeks but the outcome remains uncertain. Although the protesters have demonstrated the ability to attain crowds in excess of 200,000 on a regular basis and have established emphatically their presence in the square, the presidency and government remain in place. Aside from the largely symbolic toppling of the small Lenin statue on Taras Shevchenko Boulevard, there have been few discernible changes to date.

Generally, the Western world has watched with benign detachment, with EU leaders offering some platitudes of encouragement and expressions of satisfaction that so many people support the country's links to Europe and away from Russia. Few souls could watch without emotion the titanic encounter on 1 December between the demonstrators and the Berkut when the latter attempted but failed to clear the square in the early hours. That event demonstrated the commitment of the civic uprising.

But looked at from the perspective of the president, and that is not something that is especially easy to do, how should the situation be assessed?

For the moment, government buildings and the president's residency are secure. There has been no attempt to storm them. Thus, while a renewed attempt to clear the square is currently not feasible, daily business can continue. Indeed, the president will visit Vladimir Putin in Moscow tomorrow, ostensibly to return waving the paperwork for a substantial new loan and proclaiming: 'It is financial peace in our time'.

Prime Minister Mykola Azarov has survived for now. At the somewhat unpalatable round table of the current and past presidents, there was a suggestion that he should be the first sacrifice. Yanukovych baulked at the notion. Azarov and his Donetsk-based cabinet are still in authority.

Western leaders have not come down unequivocally on the side of the revolution. Senator John McCain (R-Arizona) does not represent Barack Obama. In fact, he is a 'loose cannon', known for his savage attacks on authoritarian governments, but not for bringing about their removal. Ukrainian American nationalist leader Askold Lozynskyj, who has also addressed the crowd in the Maidan, is another. For Yanukovych, nothing could be better than having right-wing demagogues express their support for the opposition cause.

European leaders are another matter. Some have spoken of improving the terms of the Association Agreement. But no one has stated overtly that future discussions will be limited to the opposition. Thus, in theory, the Azarov government could still go to a future meeting at some point, providing it is firmly committed to signing.

The Europeans have gone further than they did in 2004-05, when the Yushchenko presidency was affirming its commitment to the EU. But for the sentiment in Ukraine to retain momentum, a guarantee of future membership would be an astute step, whatever the current state of the Ukrainian economy or democratic processes.

Russia, like Yanukovych, is doing little other than encouraging its media to make disparaging remarks about the protests, deflating numbers, and highlighting extremist elements. Few in the Moscow leadership will have endured sleepless nights because of musical concerts in central Kyiv.

Is the opposition leading or following the Euromaidan? It is difficult to tell. Certainly, the opposition leaders are present, and often. They make speeches, they are defiant, but they urge caution, peaceful protests, which is what one would expect of democratic politicians. What else can they do?

It is unlikely that they can effect change through Parliament. They do not have sufficient delegates. It is uncertain whether a call for a general strike would meet with approval, particularly in the eastern industrial regions, where there is much, justifiable fear over what a deep and comprehensive free trade agreement with the EU would bring.

Their best hope would be early presidential or parliamentary elections. In the latter case, they might include a motion to eliminate the office of the presidency altogether. But how are they going to enforce this demand? What further pressures can be brought on the government to resign? The round-table discussions continue, now including the opposition, but that is a small concession for Yanukovych to make, as is the suspension of Kyiv city officials who authorised the crackdown on 1 December.

It also raises another issue: who really controls Ukraine? No other country in Europe is so dominated by oligarchs, figures who have amassed grotesque wealth but lack political ambitions other than to be left alone in their wealthy playground.

Most of these oligarchs would like the door to the EU to be wide open. But that does not mean closing the one to Russia either, particularly for figures like Dmytro Firtash, the president of the Federation of Employers of Ukraine, who has exploited the gas conflict between the two countries. Oddly, there have been few protests against the inequalities manifest in Ukrainian society. Yet the Regions Party is, if nothing else, visible proof of the power of the wealthy, in this case Donetsk and Kyiv-based businessmen.

And oddly, Yanukovych might reflect, despite the portrait of Tymoshenko on the Maidan Christmas tree, there is no overwhelming chorus screaming that the first step must be her immediate release. One reason might be the vested interests of other leaders in spearheading the revolutionary cause, which could be undermined by her formidable presence in the square. But it was Tymoshenko's continued imprisonment that ultimately destroyed the prospects of the Vilnius summit. And she is a more dangerous foe than any other leader.

The best allies of the president, in addition to a Russian loan, are cold weather and shortage of supplies to the Maidan. Ultimately, he must reason, the crowds will dwindle, and the Berkut can retake the square, preferably without violence – or at least, anything that can appear on camera. He retains the support of a solid third of the country. His oligarchs have not rejected him, though perhaps they could wish for a more assertive and self-confident leader.

Thus, while his credibility as president is seriously in doubt, Yanukovych may not be entirely crestfallen with the development of events to date. The Euromaidan is looking increasingly like the July Days of 1917 in Petrograd: a mass uprising without leaders and without an end game in sight.

5

The People and the Opposition

28 January 2014

As the protests that started in Ukraine last November continue, it seems worthwhile to consider their goals and leaders, some of which have evolved or changed since the initial fury at President Viktor Yanukovych's change of heart about signing an Association Agreement with the EU.

Over the course of the Yanukovych presidency there have been some contentious issues. One of them was his decision to promote minority languages in areas of the country in which more than 10% of the population speaks them. The language law, sanctioned in August 2012, effectively advanced Russian to the status of a second state language in the eastern and southern regions.

Though divisive and contested, however, language issues have been notably absent from the Euromaidan protests and some of the most decisive actions against the government and its riot police have been taken by Russian speakers, affiliated with the Right Sector or fans of various soccer teams that have provided protection for many protesters. The civic protests have demonstrated that language does not divide Ukraine.

A second and long contested issue has been the imprisonment of Yulia Tymoshenko, the charismatic leader of the Batkivshchyna party, and a political prisoner serving a seven-year sentence for her actions taken while Prime Minister under the presidency of Viktor Yushchenko. Her photograph was quite prominent in the peaceful protests of late November and early December, but while her case is still a factor, it seems to have receded into the background during the protests. There have been no serious attempts to bring about her immediate release, nor has she been able to guide or direct the movement in any way during her confinement.

Several analysts have observed the direction change of Euromaidan from one of demanding the government return to its pro-Western direction to one of focus on removal of the president and his closest associates, such as Prime Minister Mykola Azarov, who has now stepped down. Indeed, it has been the hapless and ill-considered responses of Yanukovych to the mass gatherings, such as beatings, shootings, and the laws of 16 January that have catalysed the anger and motivations of those at the barricades.

Another issue that has slowly risen to the surface is the power of the oligarchs over contemporary society. It embraces the personal wealth and property of the president and his chief backers, who include Rinat Akhmetov and Dmytro Firtash. But it also encompasses some supporters of the opposition. The vast gulf between these figures and the general population in terms of wealth is self-evident. For some protesters, the barricades are a better alternative than a low paying job with few prospects. The key problem of today's Ukraine is corruption and inequality of living standards, one that has been endemic since independence.

Many commentators believed that when the opposition leaders met with Yanukovych earlier this week and declined his offer to join his Cabinet, it demonstrated the weakness of the president. Perhaps it did. But it also highlighted the dilemma of the three main opposition leaders, namely that their own positions would also have been considerably weakened if they had suddenly departed from the Maidan to the other side of the barricades.

Clearly the international media has largely restricted its coverage of the opposition to the three main leaders, Arsenii Yatseniuk, Vitalii Klychko, and Oleh Tiahnybok. They are visible, hungry for a microphone, and anxious to publicise their own prominence in the protests. Of the three, only Klychko seems to have the makings of a national leader. But in many respects even he has found it difficult to lead what has at times appeared (misleadingly) like a headless monster trying to remove a discredited leadership.

Had the opposition leaders joined the Cabinet, the demonstrations would not have ended. They may have taken a different direction; one leading the country into a series of changes outside the parliamentary system that has been in place since the 1990s. These leaders were not behind the seizure of government buildings in the various cities. Euromaidan's regional support has grown impressively outside the capital, even in centres that traditionally might have voted for the Regions Party in past elections, but this has been a grassroots movement rather than one centrally directed.

Revolutions without leaders are like cars descending a hill without brakes.

One can never be quite sure where the descent will end, and whether the car will survive the impact of the crash. In Ukraine at each crisis point, the violence of the regime has been met with equal response by the demonstrators, but not always by the same activists. Initially one saw the flag of Svoboda prominently on the square; in the clashes on the streets, the Right Sector was in evidence. But neither is leading the protests. Many observers have noted correctly that the number of peaceful protesters, ordinary folk, have far outnumbered militants.

In other words, Euromaidan has united a key sector of Ukraine, perhaps more than at any time during its independence. Opinion polls that show the east or south opposed to the protests become irrelevant when a focused and determined minority decides to choose its own fate and not wait for the elected government – or opposition – to act. But now surely is the time for the latter to take the initiative, to outline its demands, and decide on a single leader to face Yanukovych or his Regions Party successor in early presidential elections. If it does not manage to lead and control the civic movement over the coming days then the result could be chaos and further bloodshed in the streets.

Certain demands seem obvious, starting with the resignation of a president who has used violence, kidnapping, and ordered gunfire on his own people. It is no longer enough that Yanukovych should resign, his Cabinet of Ministers should go along with him, and he must be brought to justice for his actions. It will then be critical that the new leadership pays attention to the demands of the protesters, but also focuses on a number of immediate questions that will need to be resolved.

First is the question of reviving talks with the EU, as well as the issue of a new IMF loan. Whether or not the Russian loan can be revoked or repaid, an alternative path must be mapped out.

Second is the need for new elections and the formation of a democratic coalition that can revive the ailing economy and revamp the structure of the government, most likely by reducing the power of the president and boosting that of parliament. The new leaders would also need to address the failings and inequities of the legal system.

Third, the new government of Ukraine will need to convince the public that it is committed to the task of rebuilding the country and can be trusted. The Ukrainian people have shown impressive self-organisation and commitment over the past nine weeks. In many ways, they have usurped the position of the political opposition and expressed their own will and determination. In so doing, they have created a vacuum of power that a new coalition could fill.

The protests are not evidence of the division of a nation or the start of a civil war; rather, they demonstrate above all its health and desire to construct a better world for future generations. And Ukraine has done this alone while Europe watched from the sidelines and Russia tried and failed to offer an alternative path. The opposition leaders, Klychko and Yatseniuk specifically, need to take heed of popular demands and show they have the capacity to lead the country. The road ahead for the moment looks clear, but the opportunity will be a fleeting one.

6

Analysing Euromaidan from the West

14 February 2014

Following the failure of the Ukrainian government to sign the Association Agreement with the European Union at the Vilnius summit last November, the world witnessed the protests termed the Euromaidan or Revolution of Dignity, to give it its later title. Reminiscent of the Orange Revolution, the crowds soon swelled to hundreds of thousands at their peak. The western media described it as a quest by Ukraine's young people for democracy and a European path. Today, however, young people no longer comprise the majority.

As an observer from afar, I found myself watching a live video stream of the confrontation between Berkut riot police and demonstrators in the square on 30 November 2013, and silently cheering when the former failed to break through the barricades. Nonetheless, I find several factors related to more recent Western reporting of the Euromaidan phenomenon disturbing.

The first is the overt and uncritical support for the civic uprising in the Western media and social networks. On Facebook and Twitter, reports from sources such as *Ukrainska Pravda* simply abandoned any pretence of objectivity from the outset. I have received various email and social media requests to sign petitions or in other ways express solidarity with the protesters. In short, many Western reporters and academic analysts have become supporters and advocates rather than critical observers.

A second concern is the intrusion into the protests of extremist elements, as symbolised by the huge portrait of Stepan Bandera outside Kyiv city hall, alongside the slogan 'headquarters of the revolution'. It coincided with a parade on 1 January 2014, the birth date of Bandera, the former leader of the radical branch of the Organization of Ukrainian Nationalists (OUN) after 1940, the views of which are a far cry from the sort of principles embraced by Eurocrats in Brussels. The red-black flag of OUN is displayed prominently whenever the demonstrators re-congregate en masse. The Pravyi Sektor (Right Sector) and soccer fan 'ultras' have been responsible for the most violent responses to the Berkut.

Some scholars, and they include friends of mine, maintain that the influence of these extremists is exaggerated and that the majority of the protesters are ordinary folks who sincerely seek an end to corruption and toward Europe. Yet, it is the members of the far right who are maintaining the barricades at night, and who have taken over government buildings. Dmytro Yarosh, who operates from the fifth floor of the seized Trade Union building, is the leader of Pravyi Sektor, and describes his forces as 'soldiers of the national revolution'. He has little or no interest in preserving democracy. His forces have occupied government buildings in at least ten cities of Ukraine. It need hardly be added that no one voted for Yarosh, nor would he likely win a seat in a free election.

The second issue is the goals of the protesters. From the West, it has never been clear exactly what these are, other than a desire to be part of 'Europe', and, latterly, a wish to remove the current government. The swelling of the crowds has coincided precisely with the irrational and clueless responses of the leadership – shootings, kidnappings, etc. In other words, the issues arise instantaneously in response to events or perceived events. We do not see a premeditated and clearly thought out programme of action with clear goals from the majority of those who have been in the square.

It is linked to the first question because it raises the issue of the makeup of a replacement regime if it includes substantial representation from political parties like Svoboda, which could not hope to be part of the leadership through the ballot box. Ukraine's more moderate parties and their leaders have never distanced themselves from the radical extremists. The government has already tried to exploit such ambivalence with its (abortive) introduction (16 January) of changes to the Criminal Code, imposing penalties for the public denial of the crimes of fascism. That it failed does not negate the fact that it was presented with the opportunity.

Third, and conversely, it is plain that the Yanukovych regime is corrupt and brutal, and does not hesitate to use occasional force against peaceful protesters. It has demonstrated in recent years that it is willing to subvert law courts, beat enemies, enrich friends, and generally purloin the resources of the country it is supposed to rule. On those grounds, without doubt, the protests make sense and it is time for change.

But should we in the West support the removal of an elected president by force? Isn't this an admission that the current electoral system is unworkable? The most recent 2012 parliamentary elections in Ukraine reflected very closely the results of opinion polls. Most polls also suggest that were there to be a presidential election today, Yanukovych would be leading in the first round, but would lose to most opposition leaders in a second-round run-off. The elections are scheduled to be held early next year. So why not wait and remove him by popular vote? Have those who are frustrated by what they perceive as the lack of positive support from Brussels for the Maidan protests (highlighted by Victoria Nuland's comment 'F...k Europe!') forgotten what happened in Egypt, or Libya, and, perhaps especially, Iraq when unsavoury leaders were removed by force?

Fourth, throughout the protests, opinion polls have been circulated, which suggest that support for and opposition to Euromaidan is distributed fairly evenly (40-50% in favour; and about 40% opposed), Russian intervention and Vladimir Putin notwithstanding, Ukraine itself is bitterly divided, but few in Western media are speaking with those on the other side of the divide. It is facile to suggest that most or all of them are supporters of Regions or Communists. It is even more simplistic to suggest that Donetsk-based Regionnaires would rather be part of the Russian Customs Union – for many of them that would mean the curtailment of a lucrative and freebooting lifestyle based in part on trade with Europe.

Is there such a thing as an average Ukrainian resident and, if such a person exists, could he or she possibly comprehend the prism through which Western analysts observe Ukraine? It would be naïve, I think, to believe that this imaginary figure would necessarily stand firmly behind those at the barricades or the corrupt regime, and one could be fairly sure that he/she would wish to keep a healthy distance from either the Ukrainian oligarchs or the machinations of Moscow. The Bandera portrait would likely induce similar concerns.

Unfortunately, it seems, the era of objective reporting, insofar as it can exist or ever existed, is over. It has been replaced by simplistic evocations of the virtues of Western democracy versus the perils of Russian authoritarianism, illustrated by the evil president (Vladimir Putin) and the bloodied journalist (Tetiana Chornovol) or opposition leader (Yurii Lutsenko). In taking such stances, Western observers insert their own beliefs as the best for the people of Ukraine. Their cause is our cause. But we need to adopt a broader perspective, one that encompasses the views of all residents of Ukraine.

Revolutions are complicated affairs, and there is always more gray than black and white.

7

Inside the Head of V. V. Putin

14 March 2014

On 2 March, Russian troops invaded Crimea, an autonomous republic of Ukraine in which 15,000 sailors of the Russian Black Sea Fleet are stationed. What was the Russian president's thinking in escalating a world crisis over the past week? Why has a politician, whom many considered to be a rational actor, chosen to intervene in Ukraine?

Analysing the mind of the Russian president is not a simple task. His statements are often contradictory. He maintains, for example, that Ukraine's new leaders should have adhered to the deal brokered by the European foreign ministers on 21 February that would have entailed former president Viktor Yanukovych remaining in office until new presidential elections in December 2014. Yet Russia took no part in that discussion nor did it sign that agreement, and perhaps even more significant, it has not advocated the return of Yanukovych, despite the fact that the latter has fled to Russian territory.

President Putin also maintains that because of the collapse of the EU-brokered deal, Russia is no longer bound by the terms of the 1994 Budapest Memorandum, by which Russia, the United States, and the UK committed themselves to guaranteeing the security of Ukraine after the latter gave up its nuclear weapons to Russia.

In essence, according to this line of reasoning, the Euromaidan leaders carried out a coup. Yet it was precisely as this deal was being debated that the ex-president reportedly ordered his troops to use live ammunition on the protesters, carrying out a massacre on the square. Consequently, Yanukovych lost his majority support in the parliament as many of the Regions Party MPs deserted to the opposition. He then fled the scene.

Putting these illogicalities aside, what else do we know about Putin's thinking on the situation in Ukraine? What could have prompted him to flout the Budapest Memorandum and perpetuate and give new credibility to the old canard of Russian aggression against Ukraine? If we assume for the moment that we are inside Putin's head, then it might run something like the following:

> *The Western powers refused to accept Yanukovych's decision not to sign the Association Agreement with the European Union last November in Vilnius. That decision came after my meeting with the Ukrainian president in Moscow on 9 November. Thus, they financed and openly supported a mass protest in the streets of Kyiv during which violent protesters, organised by Western Ukrainian nationalist extremists, set afire their own police with Molotov cocktails. As evidence of US involvement one can cite the following: John Kerry and Victoria Nuland[13] were overheard in a phone conversation choosing the next government of Ukraine; and Senator John McCain appeared in the Maidan, standing, outrageously, alongside the Svoboda leader Oleh Tiahnybok, a man whom even Yushchenko had thrown out of Our Ukraine over a decade ago for his racist views on Russians and Jews.*
>
> *Once the 'mobocracy' had attained the removal of Yanukovych, it elected its own government composed mainly of supporters of Euromaidan, and one devoid of any members of the Regions or Communist Parties, the parties traditionally supported by Russian-speaking Eastern Ukrainians. Moreover, the interim Cabinet promptly banned the controversial language law that had permitted Russian-speaking parts of Ukraine to conduct business in their own language. The Fascist leaders in Kiev had declared war on Russian and Russian-speaking residents of Ukraine.*

But to understand fully Putin's perspective, one would need to delve deeper. Here is a politician that would fit neatly into what Lenin perceived as the Russian chauvinist of 1922 when the Soviet Union was first forming: an adherent of the view that Kyiv – or more correctly Kiev – is the ancestral and founding city of the Rus', the East Slavic nation that accepted Christianity in 988 and eventually divided into three component parts of the same family: Russians, Ukrainians, and Belarusians, united by the Russian Orthodox Church.

---

[13] US Secretary of State and US Assistant Secretary of State respectively.

On several visits to Ukraine over the past years, Putin has made it plain that in his view, Ukraine is not a foreign country. One can take that further. In his view, it is not even a country, but rather, to cite what Metternich said about Italy in 1847, a 'geographical expression'. It is an anomaly that derived from what the Russian leader perceives as the greatest tragedy of the twentieth century: the collapse of the Soviet Union in 1991.

During one visit to Kyiv he made reference to the Treaty of Pereiaslav in 1654, when Russia and the Ukrainian Cossacks under Bohdan Khmelnytskyi signed a treaty in a war against the Poles. Ironically, it was on the 300th anniversary of that treaty that Nikita Khrushchev, in what some sources have described as a drunken moment, chose to give Crimea to Ukraine as a 'gift' from Russia.

It is of course quite reasonable to give a prized possession to one's brother. But if that brother subsequently leaves home and then renounces all family ties (Ukraine in 1991), the gift becomes a theft.

For Putin, Crimea, and especially its port of Sevastopol, is sacred Russian soil. The port suffered two great sieges after its conquest in 1783: one in the Crimean War of 1854-56; and another during the Great Patriotic War of 1941-45 against Hitler. Sevastopol is one of the original Hero Cities designated by Stalin in May 1945, alongside Leningrad, Stalingrad, and Odesa. Equally important Crimea is the one place in Ukraine that he can recognise as ethnically Russian – though that recognition is offset by a striking lack of recognition for the rights of the Crimean Tatars, deported by Stalin at the end of the war and still struggling for their rights today.

It is still unclear though what the Russian leader really hopes to gain from intervention. His statements do little to clarify the issue. Having secured all the main Crimean military bases, he declared on 4 March that there had been no invasion and no order to attack. Yet the actions of the mysterious forces who took over the parliament in Simferopol, the airport, and military bases followed his own request to the Russian Duma to deploy troops across the Ukrainian border.

What is clear is that nothing in Vladimir Putin's world will ever be the same. Already the freed Yulia Tymoshenko, a presidential candidate, has declared that she would remove the Russian Black Sea Fleet from Sevastopol at the earliest opportunity. The Americans are talking of asset freezes and trade embargos. The EU will discuss the crisis on 6 March, and even the Germans, who are most reluctant to sever ties with an important trading partner, may be wavering. The man who was nominated for a Nobel Peace Prize for brokering peace in Syria will surely never been seen in the same light again by his G8 or EU partners.

Moreover, he has managed to convince sceptics of what some Moscow detractors have tried to claim for years: that Russia in essence has retained its imperialist outlook, and is a predatory state that seeks to swallow its neighbours: that it operates less like Russia and more like Rossiya, seeking to regain its lost empire. Such comments until recently sounded far-fetched. Putin single-handedly has succeeded in giving weight to even the most outlandish of such claims.

Perhaps such policies worked in Chechnya in 2000 and Georgia in 2008; they seem doomed to fail in Ukraine because for once, the Russian president followed his heart rather than his head. Ukraine's residents may or may not be disturbed by the events of November-February in Kyiv; but there is no evidence whatever that anyone sought or welcomed a Russian invasion.

Whatever the outcome of the Crimean crisis, it is difficult to see where the lengthy political career of Vladimir Putin, one of the most self-obsessed and egotistical leaders of the contemporary world, goes from here.

8

Crimea: Recapping Five Months of Change in Ukraine

12 April 2014

From November 2013 to the end of February 2014, protesters gathered on Kyiv's central square, in a series of demonstrations known as the Euromaidan. These protests have involved several distinct stages, culminating in what some analysts have called a national revolution that removed the government and presidency of Viktor Yanukovych.

What follows is an attempt at a synopsis of events that encompass this extraordinary period that has turned into a conflict between Ukraine and Russia, and seen the latter country annex Crimea and support pro-separatist movements in various parts of the neighbouring country.

As a historian who has followed Ukraine since Soviet times, I recall two earlier civic protests of importance. The first was the occupation of the Maidan by Kyiv's university students in 1990, demanding the resignation of then Prime Minister Vitalii Masol. Though widely condemned by Communist officials, they ended with the removal of the unpopular figure.

The second was known as the Orange Revolution, and arose as a protest against the doctored results of the 2004 presidential elections. Ironically, this event served to prevent the same Yanukovych from winning the presidency. He did, however return as Prime Minister under the Yushchenko presidency, and then won the 2010 elections, narrowly defeating Yulia Tymoshenko.

In late November 2013, Yanukovych had signalled his willingness to commit Ukraine to signing an Association Agreement with the European Union at the EU summit in Vilnius. The Europeans had demanded in return that he release

Tymoshenko from captivity (she had served two and a half years of a seven-year jail sentence for signing an agreement with Russia on energy prices in 2009, when she was Prime Minister), and initiate constitutional and legal reforms.

After a visit to Moscow, where he spoke with President Vladimir Putin, Yanukovych made the decision not to sign the agreement. It seemed once again that Ukraine would remain within the Russian orbit, and would most likely commit itself to future membership of the Russian Customs Union, which is to come into force on 1 January 2015, and currently involves Russia, Kazakhstan, and Belarus, with Armenia a likely additional member.

Within hours, protesters came to the streets, motivated by anger at the change of direction. They were mainly youthful, alerted by social networks and text messages. What occurred was essentially a civic protest on the future of Ukraine and it took the authorities completely by surprise. Though the daily numbers would dwindle, every Sunday saw masses come out on the streets. At its peak, the numbers were so vast that it was impossible to count them. On the whole, the authorities reacted cautiously, deploying the Berkut riot police but without any serious confrontations. But on the night of 30 November and morning of 1 December, the order was given for the Berkut to clear the square by force. The Berkut descended on the Maidan, clubbing and beating demonstrators.

The protests were re-energised by this clumsy and thoughtless assault. The numbers rose again. On 16 December, Putin offered Ukraine $15 billion in loans and reduced gas prices to offset Ukraine's financial crisis, sparked by the near depletion of its hard currency reserves. More than anything the offer seemed to demonstrate that without Russia, Ukraine could not survive. Moreover, the sum was far more than the EU or the IMF was prepared to consider. In truth, it was probably more than Russia could afford.

The situation was exacerbated further by the quasi-legal rushing through parliament of draconian laws – the so-called 'anti-protest laws' on 16 January. Their goal appeared to be to curb freedom of speech and assembly, the outlawing of NGOs and the establishment of a dictatorship under Yanukovych. The laws were the brainchild of two MPs from the Party of Regions, Vadym Kolesnychenko and Volodymyr Oliinyk. Though repealed only twelve days later, these laws heralded the culmination of the Euromaidan protests.

The protests were now less about the EU and more about the future of Ukraine. More attention was paid to the innate and grotesque corruption of the ruling regime, of the prevalence of oligarchs who had enriched themselves at the expense of the state, of the lack of legal reforms. These protests had two immediate results. One was the agreement of Yanukovych to sacrifice his Prime Minister, Mykola Azarov (who promptly fled to Vienna on an Austrian passport) and try to make a compromise with opposition leaders.

The Prime Minister's position was offered to Arsenii Yatseniuk, the former Economy and Foreign Minister of Ukraine and leader of the Batkivshchnyna party following the incarceration of Tymoshenko. That of Deputy Prime Minister was offered to Vitalii Klychko, the former world champion boxer and leader of the party Udar, which ran third in the 2012 parliamentary elections. Both refused to take up these posts, possibly because they could detect the growing weakness of the government, but more likely because to have done so would have cost them influence on the square.

In reality, these leaders, and to some extent the third opposition leader Oleh Tiahnybok of Svoboda, had never led the protests. Rather they reacted to the moves on the Maidan. As the situation polarised, both sides changed character and personnel. On the government side, gangs of thugs were bussed into Kyiv from other cities, principally Kharkiv and Donetsk, simply to cause mayhem. They set fire to cars, beat up protesters, kidnapped people, and targeted prominent journalists. On the opposition side, several local militias formed, based partly on rightist groups like Pravyi Sektor. Batkivshchyna formed its own self-defence group.

The average protester, if one can deduce such a thing, was no longer the 20-something student, but more hardened 30 and 40-year olds, not only ready for a fight but unprepared to compromise. Many were from Western Ukraine. In their local regions, the government of Yanukovych no longer existed. They had established their own rulers.

The EU finally returned to active involvement. On 21 February, while it agreed to introduce sanctions against Ukrainian leaders, the foreign ministers of Poland, France, and Germany arrived in Kyiv. Working into the night, they brokered a deal between the government and the three parliamentary opposition leaders. It would have seen a temporary administration, constitutional reforms to reduce the powers of the presidency – returning to the situation as it was in 2004 – and new presidential and parliamentary elections by the end of the year. The stipulation, which was supported by the United States, was that in the interim, Yanukovych would remain as president. That provision proved unacceptable to those on the Maidan.

In the centre of Kyiv, the situation began to resemble the final scene of *Les*

Misérables, with barricades piled high, burning tyres that set off thick black smoke, and the accumulation of a variety of weapons – mostly Molotov cocktails, but some guns and clubs. The struggle was now for control of Ukraine. It ended as we know with carnage and bloodshed, as the government – Yanukovych and Interior Minister Vitalii Zakharenko bear the main responsibility – ordered troops to fire on protesters using live ammunition, situating snipers on rooftops who picked off targets at will. The government had begun to slaughter its own people. It was the moment of no return. The numbers of dead approached 100; hundreds more were wounded, many severely. But the assault, remarkably, failed and the protesters remained in place.

The immediate outcome has been the flight of the president and most of his Cabinet. The government of Ukraine fell on 22 February 2014. Yanukovych fled to Russia, where he has remained, used alternatively as a symbol of Russia's position that the government in Ukraine is illegal, and as a pawn in Vladimir Putin's strategy for the neighbouring country, but not one that is considered a likely catalyst of anything decisive. Putin has never had much time for Yanukovych.

Ukraine has a temporary president, appointed by a parliament in which many deputies of the Regions Party have abandoned their affiliation with the former president. The acting president is the new parliamentary speaker, Oleksandr Turchynov, a 49-year old economist from Batkivshchyna. Yulia Tymoshenko is free and is running for president. New elections have been brought forward from December – as agreed to in the deal between the old government, the opposition, and EU leaders – to 25 May. The frontrunner is an oligarch who according to Taras Kuzio is a political chameleon, chocolate manufacturer Petro Poroshenko.

In contrast to the Orange Revolution, the government has been overthrown. Ukraine has entered a new phase in its development. Russia, initially, was left on the sidelines, seemingly preoccupied with the Sochi Olympic Games. The EU and the United States also failed to influence the course of events in the later stages. The provisional government is making up rules as it proceeds. Some of the militants from the protests, for example, took over the Ministry of Internal Affairs. Threats from anti-Maidan elements to split the country initially proved futile. The Right Sector, an integral part of the more violent aspects of the Euromaidan, has been removed from central Kyiv by the Ukrainian police.

Revolutions are complex phenomena. This one is no exception. The innocence of the first days of Euromaidan was very different from 20 and 21 February, the most violent days in the history of independent Ukraine. The country removed some of the legacies of 1991 – a Donetsk-based regime of apparatchiks and gangsters, with their own private mansions and assets abroad – but it was by no means clear that the interim government could offer unity and compromise. The financial crisis in mid-April is much worse than was the case in late November. Ukraine badly needs help today as it mourns its victims.

Euromaidan entered a second phase on 27 February, when armed units in uniforms without markings took over the Crimean parliament and government buildings in Simferopol. They installed a new prime minister, Sergey Aksionov, whose party had received only about 4% in the most recent Crimean elections. Troops, who were supplemented by the 25,000 sailors of the Russian Black Sea Fleet, took over government buildings and military installations, forcing the surprised Ukrainian units to surrender.

The Ukrainians did not respond with force, and the attackers (now clearly identified as Russians) did not suffer any losses during the takeover. The annexation of Crimea was solidified by a referendum on 16 March, during which it was reported that over 95% supported the peninsula joining the Russian Federation. The alternative on the ballot, confusingly, would have led to the re-adoption of the Constitution adhered to briefly in 1992 (asserting Crimea's autonomy).

Russia and Ukraine then engaged in a war of propaganda about what was happening. The Ukrainians, backed by most of the democratic world and the UN, maintained that Russia had invaded their territory, violating international treaties signed in Budapest in 1994 and Kyiv in 1997, the latter a treaty of friendship and cooperation between the two states that agreed to existing boundaries. This treaty had been revised by the 2010 Kharkiv Accords, which extended Russia's lease on the Sevastopol base for the fleet for a further twenty-five years (i.e. from 2017 to 2042). Russian president Putin has officially revoked the 2010 treaty. The Russian version of events is that an illegal pro-Nazi junta has taken over Ukraine and is persecuting Russians and Russian speakers.

Aside from sanctions and travel bans, however, the Western response to events has been somewhat subdued. US president Barack Obama ruled out any form of military response to Russian intrusions into Ukraine. Russia has amassed a large military force on Ukraine's borders and is believed to be behind mass disturbances in several Ukrainian cities.

At the time of writing, small groups of around 200 people had taken over administrative buildings in Donetsk and Luhansk and erected barricades around them. They have declared the formation of autonomous republics. A similar attempt in Kharkiv failed. Russian political leaders have expressed their support for a 'federal system' in Ukraine, including in talks with the United States. Ukraine's richest oligarch Rinat Akhmetov has supported this position, with the proviso that Donbas remains in Ukraine. It might be termed a form of 'Finlandisation'.

Thus, Ukraine at present is in a critically unstable position and the threat of a Russian invasion is quite serious. Its interim leadership has acted cautiously and timidly, albeit insisting that Russia has no right to make demands on Ukraine as to its form of government. Though in the long term, international sanctions may imperil Russia's energy-centred economy, in the short term, there is no doubt that Putin's position is the more powerful. Already Russian prices for gas sold to Ukraine have risen to $485 per thousand cubic metres, from the earlier $268, and Ukrainian authorities have stopped payments for Russian gas pending talks.

The West is simply unable to predict Vladimir Putin's next move and NATO is belatedly bolstering its position in the eastern borderland member states. But there is no doubt that the Russian president has the initiative and the West is responding to his manoeuvres awkwardly. The third stage of Euromaidan approaches and may well be the most critical one in the history of Ukraine.

9

Odesa and the Escalating War

3 May 2014

The tragic events in Odesa[14] indicate the escalating war in Ukraine: from separatists, to ultras, football fans, or the Right Sector, the groups involved are fanatical and determined, though it is not always clear what their respective desired outcomes would be. Nor is it clear what the goals of Vladimir Putin are or when they will be revealed.

If we analyse the complaints and grievances of the separatists and their Russian patrons, the following spring most readily to mind:

1. The takeover of power in Kyiv through a coup allegedly conducted by a right-wing paramilitary group that brought about the ouster of the elected president, Viktor Yanukovych.
2. The establishment of an interim government that largely excludes representatives from Donbas and the south.
3. Threats to the rights of Russian-speakers throughout Ukraine and their right to use their native language.
4. Intrusions into Ukrainian politics both financially and personally by leaders of the United States and the European Union.
5. Fear that Ukraine will join not only European structures, but also, importantly, the NATO alliance. A subtext here is the post-2004 eastward expansion of NATO and its threat to the interests and territory of the Russian Federation.

All five of these points have been cited at various junctures as reasons why separatists have taken over East Ukrainian towns, established their own local leaderships, fought battles against Ukrainian government forces, and now

---

[14] https://nsnbc.me/2014/05/10/odessa-massacre-detail-investigation/

plan referenda on their future; and why Russia opted to annex Crimea, following a contentious referendum.

Taking the points in turn, none can be described as obviously valid. No doubt Euromaidan, at its peak a peaceful and sincere demonstration against the government and presidency of Yanukovych, the most corrupt leader in Europe, ultimately turned violent with clashes against Berkut riot police. But, while not condoning the violence and the policies of leaders of some rightwing forces (Dmytro Yarosh, Oleh Tiahnybok, etc.), simply to allege that the whole civic protest constituted a right-wing coup, led by neo-Nazis, is outright propaganda.

Moreover, as the British analyst J.V. Koshiw has convincingly argued,[15] former president Yanukovych was not overthrown; rather he abandoned his office, and ironically at a time when according to an agreement brokered with EU leaders and observed by Russia, he could have remained in power until the end of his legal term.

The interim government was elected from within the parliament. With the departure of Yanukovych, the assembly naturally assumed leadership of the country pending new presidential elections. Though some parties chose not to take part, most obviously Regions Party and the Communists – but also the opposition party UDAR, led by Vitalii Klychko – it is hardly surprising that they lack representatives in the interim Cabinet.

In fact, Batkivshchyna Party, whose members hold the positions both of Acting President and Prime Minister, has gained most. Prior to the Euromaidan, it was the second-largest political party in Ukraine. Yet even with the release of its leader Yulia Tymoshenko, there are few indications that in the event of a free and fair election, its representative will be the next president. It is, somewhat ironically given that Euromaidan was in part a protest against corruption and oligarchs, the chocolate manufacturer Petro Poroshenko who leads convincingly in opinion polls.[16]

Turning to the third question, namely the interim government established to conduct new presidential elections, it quickly rescinded an initial decision to abrogate the controversial language law guaranteeing citizens' right to use their language if they constituted more than 10% of the population. Aside from

---

[15] The blog site is no longer available. Koshiw provided the citation on his Twitter page on 29 April 2014.
[16] http://www.upi.com/Top_News/World-News/2014/05/02/Billionaire-Poroshenko-leads-field-in-Ukraines-May-25-presidential-election/3451399054225 /

that instance, there have been no threats to Russian-language speakers anywhere in Ukraine. On the contrary, they made up a substantial number of those who took part in the Euromaidan.

The fourth question is not so easily dismissed, at least in terms of perception. The taped conversations of Geoffrey Pyatt and Victoria Nuland,[17] and the public appearances in central Kyiv by John McCain did indeed signal that the United States supported the civic protests. Similarly, in my own country of Canada, Prime Minister Stephen Harper, who visited Kyiv on 22 March, supported the Ukrainian position unequivocally – even before the invasion of Crimea.[18]

Western leaders perceived the situation last November as one in which Ukrainians were deprived of their keen desire to sign the Association Agreement with the EU. And that may well be true, though there was also significant opposition. But their open involvement without doubt incited in part the Russian response.

It is also true (question 5), that the prospect of Ukraine joining NATO incensed Russia. Yet the idea was virtually inconceivable in Ukraine too, prior to the annexation of Crimea. And nothing Western leaders did merited the violent confrontations that have ensued. They are a result, it seems, of two factors: first, the innate fears of Russian president Vladimir Putin that once again, his country seemed to be in full-scale retreat before the onslaught of the liberal West; and second, the alienation of many parts of eastern and southern Ukraine from the changes in Kyiv.

The Putin issue has been analysed ad nauseam for several weeks in the Western media. He has his supporters,[19] and more frequently his detractors.[20] Both sides in turn have accused the other of being pro-Nazi,[21] causing University of Toronto political scientist Lucan Way to respond on Facebook to one such analogy: 'I think there should be a BAN on all Nazi analogies for the next 10 years. We will all be the better for it.'

But the situation in Crimea and East Ukrainian cities merits a thorough

---

[17] http://www.bbc.com/news/world-europe-26079957
[18] http://www.cbc.ca/news/world/stephen-harper-pledges-continued-support-for-ukraine-1.2582669
[19] See, for example, https://www.thenation.com/article/chance-putin-has-given-obama-diplomacy/
[20] http://www.faz.net/aktuell/politik/ausland/timothy-snyder-about-europe-and-ukraine-putin-s-project-12898389-p11.html
[21] http://lb.ua/news/2014/05/03/265204_ostanovite_fashizm.html

analysis. Their disaffection was noted by then Chair of Parliament Leonid Kravchuk following Ukraine's declaration of independence in 1991. He visited Simferopol in the latter part of that year (*Pravda Ukrainy*, 12 October 1991, p. 1); heading off calls for a referendum on independence. In Donbas there were calls for the introduction of a federative system and a secessionist initiative (*Pravda Ukrainy*, 3 October 1991, p. 3). Both regions ultimately supported the referendum for an independent Ukraine and to postpone their grievances.

A crisis nonetheless quickly emerged in Crimea in the early 1990s, when Republican Party of Crimea leader Yuriy Meshkov became president of the Crimean Autonomous Republic. It was 'resolved' only by Kyiv's firmness and the abolition of the position of Crimean president.[22] On the other hand, subsequently, there had been no major calls for independence on the peninsula or for joining Russia, other than from members of the Russian Duma and the then mayor of Moscow, Yuriy Luzhkov.

Donbas is a complex case. As Patricia Herlihy remarked in *The Los Angeles Times* with regard to Putin's New Russia ('Novorossiya') conception, its major towns,[23] Donetsk and Luhansk, owed their founding to a Welshman and Englishman respectively. Putin's historical understanding exhibits a peculiar, if not completely ignorant knowledge of the past. Donbas, however, was an important industrial region of both the Russian Empire and the Soviet Union. And perhaps most significantly, worker protests there have continued intermittently since the late 1980s, largely due to the economic downturn and dire situation in the Ukrainian coalmines.

It is critical that the Ukrainian government address the needs of industrial centres in the east of the country. These towns are run down and decrepit. Horlivka, which I visited a decade ago, is among the starkest examples. Coal miners and steelworkers are only too aware that in Russia, including in that part of the Donbas coalfield that runs into Rostov Oblast, their salaries could be up to six times higher overnight. They resent most bitterly the avarice, greed, and selfishness of regional self-made billionaire businessmen who have exploited their labour.

Still, taken overall, the claims of separatists and their supporters over the border regarding Euromaidan are largely specious. Though Western leaders may have encouraged the association with the EU, full membership for Ukraine was never on the table. In fact, most EU members are wary of further expansion. The violence that has ensued since March is the result of the

---

[22] http://gazeta.zn.ua/POLITICS/zvezda_i_politicheskaya_smert_yuriya_meshkova.html
[23] This citation is no longer available on line.

actions of a militant minority that has conducted kidnappings, carried out assaults on locals, and resisted government forces with the sort of weaponry of which most terrorists could only dream. Its actions have the covert and formidable backing of a substantial Russian army parked around borders of Ukraine in three directions and the open support of a belligerent Russian president.

Again, none of the above is to suggest that the temporary leaders of Ukraine have always acted wisely, but that reflects their predicament. They face a situation that changes daily, as they encounter yet another government takeover in eastern towns, led by self-appointed mayors and military leaders who act like local satraps in the manner of Chechnya president Ramzan Kadyrov (lacking only their pet tigers). Ukrainians see their country disintegrating about them, one that has struggled economically for twenty-three years, but has never questioned its own existence or territorial integrity. And nothing Ukraine has done merits such destruction.

A solution amenable to Putin would be to elect as president another Aliaksandr Lukashenka (Belarus), i.e. a hardline leader who may stabilise the country, offer some token national rhetoric, but ultimately be loyal and subservient to Moscow.

A second option, which seems inconceivable, is the division of the country, entailing the loss of its industrial heartland and Black Sea ports.

The third option is the one that has been chosen: new presidential elections, which should be followed closely by new parliamentary elections. All parts of Ukraine would then be represented in the new government. The separatists and their patron seem determined to prevent such an outcome, decrying neo-Nazis and juntas that supposedly threaten them from Kyiv. Eliminating the separatists carries the threat of a full-scale Russian invasion. Doing nothing results in the proliferation of city takeovers. And the longer the conflict continues, the more polarised the sides become.

10

King Coal and the Future of the Ukrainian Donbas

9 June 2014

The separatist insurgence in Donetsk and Luhansk has raised questions about the future of this region as part of Ukraine. Opinion polls suggest that the supporters of separatism constitute only a small minority.[24] On the other hand, much of the population was disaffected by the events of the Euromaidan and alienated by the interim government that was formed after the departure of former president Viktor Yanukovych. In late May, about 1,000 miners took part in a pro-separatist rally against the Ukrainian government's 'anti-terrorist operation' in the region, led by a miners' union with close ties to the former president.[25]

Clearly many miners are disaffected and discontented. The question that should be at the forefront of attention perhaps is the future of the coal industry; a sector that has been struggling since the 1980s, but retains the potential to play an important role in Ukraine's economic recovery. At the same time this area and industry were central to the authority of the ex-president, as well as his chief financial supporter Rinat Akhmetov, the major owner of privatised coal mines today.

What is the current state of the Ukrainian coal industry and what role can it play in Ukraine following the election of its new president, Petro Poroshenko?

---

[24] http://uacrisis.org/2237-kiis-survey-ukraines-southeast. For an alternative view, see the study by Elise Giuliano of Columbia University: http://www.ponarseurasia.org/memo/origins-separatism-popular-grievances-donetsk-and-luhansk . She notes that between one-quarter and one-third of the population of Donetsk and Luhansk support separatist goals.
[25] http://www.reuters.com/article/us-ukraine-crisis-miners-idUSKBN0E80VX20140528

The importance of this region to Ukraine was highlighted during the recent election campaign by the most popular campaigner in eastern Ukraine, former Deputy Prime Minister Serhii Tihipko, who stated that the Ukrainian government should create conditions for the population of the 'South-East' that would prevent them from even considering separation. He suggested that it was important to struggle for Donetsk and Luhansk to remain in Ukraine, and that the hypothetical loss of Donbas would have enormous negative consequences for the country: seven million people and in economic terms 30% of its GDP, and 25% of its exports. Essential in Tihipko's view is decentralisation of power, raising the influence of the regions, electing local governors, and expanding the use of the Russian language.[26]

Granted the theoretical imposition of such policies, would they be enough to ensure the revival of the region? The response here is limited to the coal industry, which is the most important industry in the two major regions.

In the Soviet period, prior to the large-scale development of nuclear power, Donbas coal (by which is denoted here the Donetsk and Luhansk, but not the Russian Rostov part of the coalfield) fuelled thermal power stations that accounted for up to 75% of Ukrainian electricity production. By 2011, however, that proportion had declined to one-third, despite the fact that coal reserves, at 54 billion tons, are practically infinite, equivalent to a further 390 years at the present rates of production.[27]

In that same year 149 coalmines were operating in Ukraine, 120 of which were state-owned, employing 271,000 people. Since 2010, a programme to privatise coalmines has been under way. Today the biggest private energy company, DTEK (Donbas fuel-energy company, the energy sector of Rinat Akhmetov's company System Capital Management), is the largest coal producer in Ukraine, owning 31 coalmines and 13 coal enrichment plants.[28] Prior to the present troubles, the privatisation of about half the coalmines saw a rise in production peaking in 2012 that resulted in a coal surplus and concomitant lower coal prices.

The government thus asked some state companies to lower production and shut down 17% of mines on a short-term basis.[29]

---

[26] http://www.segodnya.ua/politics/pnews/za-doneck-i-lugansk-nuzhno-borotsya-tigipko-521632.html
[27] https://www.mbendi.com/indy/ming/coal/eu/ua/p0005.htm
[28] http://www.platts.com/latest-news/coal/kiev/ukraines-dtek-plans-to-boost-2014-coal-exports-21831374
[29] http://www.coalage.com/features/3235-ukraine-faces-oversupply-crisis.html#.WKty-hIrLAx

Ukrainian Coal Output, 2010-14 (in tons)

2010: 75.2
2011: 81.8
2012: 85.9
2013: 83.7
2014: 83.0 (projected)

Approximately 62% of coal produced is steam coal used for energy generation and the remainder is coking coal.[30] Unsurprisingly, the violent encounters between government and separatist forces in eastern Ukraine in the spring of 2014 have had a negative impact on coal production. From January through April 2014, coal output declined by 0.4%, at 27.87 million tons, signifying a potential annual output of around 83 million tons.[31]

Paradoxically, however, a small drop in production may benefit the coal industry because of the likely rise in prices, as long as it does not have a significant impact on those industries dependent on coal: thermal power stations, coke, and metallurgical plants. In the case of the latter two sectors, Ukraine cannot provide all their needs because they require coking coal with low sulphur content, which, as Ilona V. Kochura points out (Kochura, 2012), is only found regionally in the coalfields of the Russian Federation. But the main critiques of coal mining in contemporary Ukraine are less about production per se, than about organisation, planning, and renovation, all areas in which the country appears to be lacking.

An analysis published in a Kyiv-based newspaper (no author was cited) offered a forthright criticism of the current leaders of independent Ukraine for the decline of the industry. It noted that in spring 2014, most coal enterprises had continued to work despite the blockade of Slaviansk and Kramatorsk. Yet miners were afraid of the forthcoming removal of subsidies to unprofitable mines, which would force Ukraine to raise imports of gas, the cost price of which exceeds coal more than 1.8 times, even taking into account state subsidies.

The impact on those industries that depend on Donbas coal would also be catastrophic, it continued. Yet the newly elected president (Poroshenko) appeared ready immediately to sign an Agreement on economic integration with the EU, meaning that Kyiv would have to completely abandon subsidies

---

[30] http://sadovayagroup.com/operations/ukrainian-coal-market/

[31] https://steelguru.com/coal/ukrainian-coal-mining-output-down-by-0-4pct-in-jan-apr-2014/390510

in all sectors of the economy, including the coal industry. In the independent period, moreover, many industrial research institutes had been closed and their financing practically ended. The branch has long needed a full 'technical retooling' to make it cost effective, but instead the region has been sucked into war and is being dragged into the European Union.[32]

In truth, the problems of the region are somewhat deeper than the above article suggests. For many years, and especially during the Yanukovych presidency, the coal industry has been mired in corruption. In an important investigative article, Denys Kazansky and Serhiy Harmash reveal the findings of the East-European-based Organised Crime and Corruption Reporting Project.[33] They show how companies connected to former government officials and businesses owned by the former president's son – and almost all linked in some way to the former president – regularly sold coal on the black market.

About 11% of Ukraine's annual coal output is derived from illegal mines that operate outside both the state and private system, and can be found wherever coal seams exist, including in fields and around private homes. Miners work for abysmal pay and in very dangerous conditions in so-called *kopanki* (illegal coal mines), mainly around Donetsk. MP Oleh Medunytsya (For Ukraine faction) requested an investigation after it was noted that the amount of coal transported on railways exceeded official annual production by almost 6 million tons. The coal mined at *kopanki* is sold at about 20% of the official price to managers and 'businessmen', who in turn resell it at 'normal' prices to buyers.

Another critique of this practice was offered by First Deputy Minister of Energy and the Coal Industry Yurii Zyukov (he took up the post only in April), who noted the high rates of corruption and that state mines were selling coal to private companies at cheap prices, with numerous intermediaries taking a slice of the profits, before it was resold to the ultimate buyers for higher prices.[34] Most coalmines in Ukraine are unprofitable. Eighty percent have been operating for more than two decades without being modernised or upgraded, coal seams are very deep, and methane gas explosions are common.

In late 2003, the Ukrainian government established a state company, putting

---

[32] http://rg.kiev.ua/page5/article30891/
[33] https://www.occrp.org/en/investigations/2461-ukraines-illegal-coal-mines-dirty-dangerous-deadly
[34] https://steelguru.com/coal/ukrainian-cabinet-to-sell-off-coal-mines-and-reduce-subsidies-report/390563

an end temporarily to privatisation – *Vyhillya Ukrainy* (Ukrainian coal).[35] In 2008, nonetheless, during Yulia Tymoshenko's second term as Prime Minister under President Viktor Yushchenko, some $22 million worth of illegal coal was sold to electric power stations. The situation was no better after Mykola Azarov (Prime Minister under Yanukovych) cancelled Vyhillya Ukrainy's monopoly in the spring of 2010, because that decision allowed private entrepreneurs to profit from the underground sales of coal.[36]

Donbas miners justifiably have felt for some time that they are a forgotten factor in what was once considered a proud industry. Indeed, coal mining could in theory be revived, especially as a means to avoid future reliance on Russian oil and gas. Much depends on the major oligarch Akhmetov, assuming that he can retain his large holdings in the industry both from separatists and demands for the closure of losing mines by the IMF, in return for its now-essential loan to Ukraine.[37] In the past Ukrainian miners have demonstrated that once called into action they can be a formidable force, particularly during the coal miners' strike in the late Soviet period, which turned briefly into a powerful political movement. Today, however, they appear to be at a crossroads, not least because of the unstable political situation and the uncertainty of their position within independent Ukraine.

How can the financially struggling Kyiv government invest sufficient funds in the industry to modernise it and, if not, how many coal mines would survive 100% privatisation? Without doubt that would entail closures and job losses. As was the case with the recent presidential elections, the industry may have to rely on its oligarchs, regardless of their misdeeds or affiliations. In the past, these figures plundered Ukrainian industry and resources for their own benefits. Today the Donbas miners no doubt hope Akhmetov and others make some sacrifices for the good of the country.

Coal is no longer 'king' in Ukraine, but it is plentiful and a potential source of economic survival – it remains the most viable long-term resource the country possesses. And while few miners wish to see their regions separate or be answerable to separatists, they oppose just as vehemently the corrupt practices in the coalfields and the current inclination of Kyiv leaders to orient Ukraine toward Europe.

---

[35] See http://www.dpvu.com.ua/
[36] http://hetq.am/eng/print/54829
[37] http://uk.reuters.com/article/uk-ukraine-crisis-idUKBREA2J1E820140327

11

Igor Strelkov: Moscow Agent or Military Romantic?

13 June 2014

On 11 June, the self-proclaimed mayor of Slaviansk, Vyacheslav Ponomarev, was placed under arrest for actions inconsistent with his duties, most notably unwarranted spending of money.[38] The order to remove him was given by the military commander of the separatist forces of the so-called Donetsk People's Republic, Igor Strelkov (Girkin), and highlighted his consolidation of authority over various rivals. The Ukrainian Security Service (Sluzhba Bezpeky Ukrainy, or SBU) insists that Strelkov takes his orders directly from Moscow. But how true is this? Who is Strelkov and what is his background and outlook?

Man of Mystery

The question has intrigued many observers and analysts of the crisis in Ukraine, which has shown little sign of abating since the presidential election of 25 May and the installation of businessman Petro Poroshenko as the new president of Ukraine on 7 June. It sparked the interest, inter alia, of the investigative journalism blog site *Investigate This!* which has provided several helpful articles and transcripts of interviews in recent days. Not surprisingly there has also been some interest in the Russian media, particularly that of the far right, where Strelkov, generally, is regarded as a hero figure, one prepared to sacrifice his life to the cause of the Russian state and its future. And certainly, the Ukrainian media, the Ukrainian authorities, and the European Union have all taken an interest in this enigmatic figure, regarding him as an enemy, a terrorist, and a criminal responsible for several high-

---

[38] https://sputniknews.com/voiceofrussia/news/2014_06_13/Vladimir-Pavlenko-appointment-new-mayor-of-Slavyansk-3417/

profile killings.

On 29 April, the EU expanded its list of sanctioned Russians who were posing threats to Ukraine's independence, and it included Strelkov in their number. At this time, separatist forces in Slaviansk were holding captive seven representatives of the OSCE, and it was proving difficult to negotiate their release. Strelkov was described as an active officer of the Russian Main Intelligence Directorate (GRU).[39] Writing for the *Moscow Times*, in a withering article on separatist leaders in Ukraine, Ivan Nechepurenko described Strelkov as 'a Russian civil war romantic' and based on materials found on the Anonymous International hacker group, claimed that he served for the Federal Security Service (FSB) of Russia in Chechnya between 1999 and 2005.[40] Thus the conclusion could be derived that Strelkov works or has worked for both the FSB and GRU, a somewhat unusual distinction.

The (Almost) Complete Picture

It should be added that few such allegations can be definitively authenticated and much is based on speculation. But it is possible to piece together fragments that provide some suggestion of the complete picture. Writers for the Russian ultra-rightist military newspaper *Voennoe obozrenie* have also delved into Strelkov's past, making no secret of their admiration for the military leader of separatist Donbas. Writing on 20 May, Roman Skoromokhov begins with a depiction of 'The man who emerged out of nowhere and for some time has attracted everyone's attention' and notes the various allegations about his affiliation. First of all, the author comments, is his name, or more precisely two names: Ivan Vsevolodovich Girkin and Ivan Ivanovich Strelkov, the first the birth name and the second obviously a pseudonym.

Ivan Girkin, continues the author, was born in Moscow – some sources say he was born on 17 December 1970[41] and graduated from the Moscow State Historical Archives as an historian before entering the armed forces for his military service from June 1993 to July 1994. Prior to that, however, he had evidently served in Transnistria in June-July 1992 and Bosnia, from November 1992 to March 1993,[42] which raises questions about the duration of his academic training.

---

[39] https://www.washingtonpost.com/world/national-security/eu-issues-new-round-of-sanctions-on-russia/2014/04/29/3b766ebe-cf80-11e3-a6b1-45c4dffb85a6_story.html?utm_term=.6f580d3848ea
[40] https://themoscowtimes.com/news/santa-for-hire-soapmaker-run-insurgency-in-ukraines-east-35496
[41] See, for example, https://vk.com/slavstrelok
[42] https://topwar.ru/48026-portrety-veka-igor-strelkov.html

Skoromokhov reveals that the soldier was also a diarist and published a 'Bosnian Diary' in another far-right Russian newspaper *Zavtra* under the name 'Igor G'. In Bosnia Strelkov became acquainted with another figure prominent in the events in Donbas, Aleksandr Boroday.[43] Girkin/Strelkov served in both Chechen campaigns, though there is some contention about his military rank, i.e. whether he is a captain or a colonel.

Skoromokhov has some doubts about both rankings, observing that sixteen years of service is rather long for a captain, but may not be enough to achieve the position of colonel. He notes that some sources suggest Girkin/Strelkov visited the Middle East, which is confirmed indirectly by his frequent writings and comments on the Arab Spring and deep knowledge of Libya and Egypt (and also, it transpires, especially of Syria). By August 1999 he was writing – now as Strelkov – along with Boroday as a special correspondent for *Zavtra* from the Kadar zone in Daghestan, where Ministry of Internal Affairs troops were conducting a 'cleansing' of several villages inhabited by Wahhabi Muslims.[44]

In addition to writing for *Zavtra*, Strelkov also worked as a correspondent for the separatist Abkhazia Network News Agency (ANNA). One can thus see a clearly discernible pattern of Strelkov's presence in areas of the world of geostrategic and military interest to Russia, contrasting between states in which the incumbent government was threatened (Middle East) or those in which Russia had a clearly defined position of supporting a breakaway region (Transnistria and Abkhazia).

His writing for ANNA makes no secret of the links between the various events, which Strelkov perceived as of deep concern to the future of Russia. Writing with the by-line 'colonel in the reserves', he expressed his fear that in Russia there could be developing a situation similar to that in Syria, where Sunni Muslims, representing the vast majority of the population wage a war against a leadership that represents only 10% of inhabitants. In Russia, ethnic Russians are likewise declining in numbers and this it may be necessary to take radical action to preserve the state against 'radical Islam', resorting if necessary to methods that infringe on human rights.[45]

Skoromokhov's article reveals another side of Strelkov, namely his love for military role-playing and re-enactment of battles. Following the article there are a number of photographs of the separatists' leader in uniforms of civil war

---

[43] See also Catherine Fitzpatrick's analysis at: http://www.interpretermag.com/is-separatist-colonel-strelkov-the-kremlins-wag-the-dog-gone-out-of-bounds/
[44] https://topwar.ru/48026-portrety-veka-igor-strelkov.html
[45] http://old.anna-news.info/node/11634

generals (generals of the White Army, it should be noted), as a Cossack, and in a suit of armour.[46]

Other facets of his personality are worth noting. He has an ex-wife and children still living in Moscow.[47] His appearance and demeanour are very different from the Ukrainian separatist leaders that have emerged since the spring. He is the antithesis of a gangster or revolver-touting thug. He looks and has probably cultivated the image of a military officer of an earlier generation, with short hair and clipped moustache, complementing his 'little green man' military fatigues; he is quiet-spoken, calm, and – his extreme political views notwithstanding – highly intelligent. His writing is lucid and arguments clear. And what may make him unusually dangerous is a clear belief in his mission, which currently is to consolidate his authority in Donetsk and Luhansk, but in the longer term, to remove the Kyiv government from power.

A Fanatical Romantic

A second article about Strelkov in *Voennoe obozrenie* appeared on 12 June, authored by Kolya Taraskin, essentially in the form of lament concerning his *non-recognition* by some of the remaining liberal sectors of the Russian media. Taraskin maintains that there are many lies circulating about Strelkov, including his membership in the GRU and KGB. Behind the polite 'romance re-enacter', he declares, 'are rigorous years of service' and direct participation in at least four armed conflicts in recent years. His feat, he adds, holding off the 'entire Ukrainian army' for a month with several hundred volunteers is comparable to the defence of the Brest Fortress in 1941, 'but no one cares'.

Just as Soviet history removed from textbooks details of major victories by the tsarist armies, so today Strelkov's feats in Slaviansk are underrated. The author takes issue with the 'red-headed broadcaster' for *Ekho Moskvy* (presumably Yulia Latynina) for praising the successes of the 'gallant Mujahideen' in the North Caucasus and the depictions of vodka-swilling Russian mercenaries in Syria. These same 'drunken mercenaries', he claims, 'are protecting Slaviansk' under the leadership of 'Uncle Igor'. His depiction of how Strelkov's troops contrast with the images of Russian mercenaries circulating borders on racism but is worth quoting if only to demonstrate the writer's emotions:

---

[46] http://www.kp.ru/daily/26225/3108701/
[47] http://www.businessinsider.com/r-elusive-muscovite-with-three-names-takes-control-of-ukraine-rebels-2014-15

> They are not posing with rubber dolls and bottles, they do not squander dollars in bars with hot negresses. They calmly, without the hysterical hatred of their enemies, and trusting in God, look death in the eye without blinking.[48]

Returning to Strelkov's biography, his earlier sojourns in war zones were followed by his arrival in Crimea, where he reportedly played a key role in capturing the parliament building, installing his friend Sergey Aksyonov as Prime Minister, and eliminating SBU agents, officers of the Ukrainian General Staff, and 'spies from the OSCE', as Skoromokhov describes them.[49] He then took the bulk of his forces from Crimea directly into eastern Ukraine to fight against the interim Ukrainian government established in Kyiv after the flight of former president Viktor Yanukovych.

The inference is evident: a Russian officer, whether in the reserves or active, took an active role in the annexation of Crimea and ostensibly has tried to do the same thing, with less success, in eastern Ukraine. Is this proof of the direct involvement of Russia in Strelkov's operations? That certainly seems to be the case. In addition, he has now demonstrated his growing authority by removing Ponomarev. The answer, however, remains somewhat ambivalent because at present he lacks the support of the Russian president and appears to be operating as a lone wolf.

By Whose Authority?

In an interview with the newspaper *Komsomolskaya Pravda* on 26 April,[50] Strelkov stated that to date Russia had not supplied any weapons for his forces and that he was thus reliant on weapons seized from the locality. His forces were hardened veterans, mostly from Ukraine, who had fought in the Russian army in Chechnya and Central Asia, as well as in Iraq and Yugoslavia with the Ukrainian army. Until the recent crossing of the eastern border of Ukraine by Russian tanks,[51] there had been little evidence of any firm commitment of the Russian authorities to the forces of Strelkov.

The question, in any case, is somewhat redundant in that Strelkov has no tolerance whatsoever for the existence of an independent Ukraine, let alone respect for its elected leaders. He represents rather the forces of imperial Russia, with or without the backing of Vladimir Putin. The latter figure

---

[48] https://topwar.ru/51580-voyska-dyadi-igorya.html
[49] https://topwar.ru/48026-portrety-veka-igor-strelkov.html
[50] http://www.kp.ru/daily/26225.7/3107725/
[51] http://uainfo.org/blognews/339354-rossiyskie-tanki-v-ukraine-aktualizirovali-vopros-vvedeniya-novyh-sankciy-protiv-rf.html

understandably says little about Strelkov, but much about the assault of the Ukrainian Anti-Terrorist forces on 'peaceful citizens' in the Ukrainian East.

Nevertheless, it is difficult to dismiss all the evidence provided by the SBU and other sources of Strelkov taking orders from superiors. He does not operate with complete independence, and it would be far-fetched to anticipate that an officer with such long military service in world trouble spots would dispense with military hierarchy. He may be part of the Greater Russian vision that permeates some sections of the Russian establishment, from political scientist Aleksandr Dugin to Vasily Yakemenko and harkens back to earlier luminaries such as Aleksandr Solzhenitsyn.

Strelkov appears to live in a different era, but his play roles have become confused with reality. Eventually, this quiet and eccentric fanatic may represent little more than a pawn in a much broader power game, but for the Ukrainian government he represents a difficult opponent who is unlikely to surrender, with or without support from the Russian military and its commander-in-chief.

12

Putin's Dwindling Options in Ukraine

25 June 2014

Vladimir Putin's options in Ukraine appear to be diminishing as the war in Donbas continues, despite an official ceasefire initiated on 20 June by Ukraine's new president, Petro Poroshenko. After almost four months of conflict, which began on 1 March 2014, when Russian forces occupied Crimea, the impetus for further dramatic changes in revising territorial boundaries in Ukraine has slowed notably.

A survey conducted by the fund Public Opinion,[52] reveals that today over 50% of Russians want Putin to run for president of Russia after 2018, when his current term expires. The survey points out that the increase in the president's popularity stems directly from the annexation of Crimea. The direct costs to date have been serious without being dangerous. Ukraine refers to the situation as one of 'temporary occupation'. The UN General Assembly Resolution 68/262 of 27 March 2014, which stated that the Crimean Referendum 'cannot be the basis for any changes of status' of the peninsula, received the support of 100 member countries out of 193, with 11 opposed, and 58 abstentions.

The costs of the occupation will likely prove severe in future (up to 1 trillion roubles over four years), and building the bridge over the Kerch Straits alone will amount to R283-349 billion – around $8.3-10.3 billion. These future impositions will eventually take a toll on the Russian economy, but may not affect Putin's popularity for the immediate future.

---

[52] http://www.golos-ameriki.ru/a/russia-crimea/1945085.html

But if Crimea has necessitated acceptable sacrifices, the situation in eastern Ukraine has been more problematic from Moscow's perspective. Despite intensive propaganda directed at local residents, there is little to suggest that a majority of the local population supports the Donetsk People's Republic (DNR) or the Luhansk People's Republic (LNR). Moreover, while nebulous concerning details, Poroshenko's peace plan has acknowledged the need for decentralisation of authority to the benefit of these regions. On the basis of a new Constitution, he declared, new local councils will be elected and form executive committees, which elect their own leaders.

The proposed amendments would allow regions wide rights in the spheres of historical memory, cultural traditions, and language policy, and local communities in Donbas would enjoy the right to use Russian, along with the state language (Ukrainian). The president also added that the programme would create new jobs in the region with the assistance of the EU, but no investments would be forthcoming until warfare ended. Poroshenko is willing to talk to those who joined the separatists, but not those involved in acts of terrorism, murder, or torture.[53]

Putin showed some signs of willingness to support the ceasefire, requesting the Federation Council to withdraw the resolution permitting military intervention in Ukraine. Valeriy Bolotov, head of separatist military forces in Luhansk and Aleksandr Khodakovskiy, commander of the Vostok battalion, both took part in the press conference in support of the ceasefire, which was to expire on 27 June.[54]

Three former presidents of Ukraine, Leonid Kuchma (he has been Poroshenko's designated mediator in discussions with Russia), Leonid Kravchuk, and Viktor Yushchenko had earlier sent an open letter to Putin, demanding that he ends aggression against Ukraine and starts negotiations. Kravchuk remarked that without Putin, no peace proposals suggested by the Ukrainian side could be implemented.[55]

On 22 June, Putin made a conciliatory statement on the need for a compromise acceptable to all sides, including the people of southeast Ukraine 'who should feel they are an integral part of this country',[56] which taken

---

[53] http://www.segodnya.ua/politics/pnews/poroshenko-obnarodoval-detali-svoego-mirnogo-plana-po-vostoku-530685.html
[54] https://www.theguardian.com/world/2014/jun/24/ukraine-crisis-putin-russia-military-intervention-ceasefire
[55] http://zn.ua/POLITICS/kravchuk-kuchma-i-yuschenko-prizyvali-putina-prekratit-agressiyu-protiv-ukrainy-147613_.html
[56] http://expert.ru/2014/06/22/putin-vazhno-chtobyi-na-baze-peremiriya-na-ukraine-voznik-dialog/

literally would imply that the Russian president no longer recognises the authority of the separatist regimes.

The difficulties, however, lie at the heart of these quasi-regimes and their self-appointed leaders. The 'people's governor' of Donetsk Oblast, Pavel Gubarev, proposed his own plan to resolve the conflict in south-eastern Ukraine, which he posted on his Facebook page. It demanded that all Ukrainian troops be removed from the two breakaway republics and Kyiv should recognise their legitimacy, as well as the creation of conditions for a referendum in other regions of 'Novorossiya'. He also stated that Ihor Kolomoiskyi (governor of Dnipropetrovsk), Arsen Avakov (Ukraine's Minister of Internal Affairs), and Oleh Lyashko (leader of the Ukrainian Radical Party) must voluntarily give themselves up to the militia, while oligarch Rinat Akhmetov must return everything he has 'stolen from the people', gather his belongings, and leave the country.

On 21 June, at Lenin Square in Donetsk (i.e. the day after the ceasefire was introduced), the armed forces of the breakaway regions took an oath of loyalty, attended by 'Prime Minister' Aleksandr Boroday, former MP Oleh Tsarev, and the head of the Novorossiya party, Gubarev.[57] These are hardly the actions of people in a mood for compromise.

The same can be said of the head of the armed forces of the DNR, Igor Strelkov (Girkin), who stated in an interview with *LifeNews* on 25 June that he was prepared to observe a ceasefire only on three conditions. First, that the Ukrainian army should move 10 kilometres from the main army garrisons of the DNR and LNR; second, flights of Ukrainian military planes over zones controlled by rebels must stop; and third, artillery fire on settlements and separatist bases must end.[58]

While Strelkov has declared his gratitude to Russia for the provision of weapons, which have undoubtedly been used at his base in Slaviansk (resulting in the deaths of 49 military personnel after the shooting down of a Ukrainian plane in mid-June),[59] his frustration with his ostensible masters in Moscow has been evident for some time. Further, the demands of both Strelkov and Gubarev are far-fetched in a situation where the Ukrainian president would prefer not to deal directly with those who wish to break up or challenge the territorial integrity of his country.

---

[57] http://zn.ua/UKRAINE/narodnyy-gubernator-doneckoy-oblasti-gubarev-predlozhil-sobstvennyy-plan-mirnogo-uregulirovaniya-147592_.html
[58] http://www.novayagazeta.ru/news/1683868.html
[59] http://zn.ua/POLITICS/poroshenko-obyavil-o-kontrnastuplenii-protiv-terroristov-na-donbasse-147118_.html

Russian opposition politician Boris Nemtsov[60] maintains that Putin has betrayed the Russian mercenaries, who went to Ukraine brainwashed by propaganda.[61] He points out that 'Putin's channels' (on Russian television) talk constantly about the heroic fight against 'Fascists and Banderites' but they do not show Strelkov. The latter had been among the first to be obsessed with the anti-Ukrainian propaganda and had taken up guns and travelled to Slaviansk. His example was followed by hundreds of fighters from Russia, who became the backbone of resistance to the Ukrainian army.

But whereas all television propaganda focused on Strelkov's armed detachments, the leader himself was kept in the shadows. Nemtsov's theory is that after the war, Strelkov and his companions will return to Russia incensed at Putin for his betrayal of them, and their next actions will not be in Slaviansk, but in Moscow.[62] The implication is that they would want Putin removed from power for inciting them to action and then withdrawing support.

Nemtsov's analysis, while perhaps overblown, nonetheless delves into the heart of the dilemmas facing Vladimir Putin. He gained a surge of popularity for the successful annexation of Crimea, but the intervention in eastern Ukraine – the concept of the so-called 'Novorossiya' – has run into serious difficulties and cannot be sustained without a full-scale Russian military invasion. In one operation alone, Ukraine's anti-terrorist forces killed over 250 separatists,[63] and while costly in terms of casualties and impact on the local population, the sustained, if error-strewn drive in place since Poroshenko's inauguration has effectively ended prospects of separatist victory assuming the current array of forces is maintained. In that respect, the ceasefire may have been somewhat premature.

For Putin, however, a desperate situation is masked behind what seem to be 'peace manoeuvres'. In reality, without further escalation, the Russian leader will lose control over the forces he has created.

In this respect, Putin's fatal mistake was less his encouragement of the likes of Strelkov, and rather his intervention into Crimea on 1 March (2014), which at one stroke changed a border in place for sixty years. At present, none of these events seems to pose an immediate danger to the Russian president,

---

[60] Eight months later, Nemtsov was assassinated close to the Kremlin on 27 February 2015. See http://www.newyorker.com/news/news-desk/the-unaccountable-death-of-boris-nemtsov
[61] http://www.ostro.org/general/politics/news/447463/
[62] Ibid.
[63] http://www.segodnya.ua/regions/donetsk/za-sutki-v-zone-ato-unichtozheno-bolee-250-terroristov-528662.html

but he is wise enough to recognise that his position is deteriorating. His actions have incurred human losses, great expenses, the alienation of much of the international community, and the lasting enmity of the vast majority of Ukrainians, all of which he might have been prepared to sustain if the result had been the end of Ukraine's move toward the West or the self-rule or independence of its eastern territories.

But none of this has happened, and separatists in Slaviansk, Kramatorsk, and other Donbas towns are now in peril. They cannot agree to a ceasefire because it will signify the end of their mission and the Russian leader seems to have abandoned them. In turn, Putin has no wish to initiate full-scale war and face the quagmire of another Afghanistan. If he deluded himself into the view that he would receive widespread support in eastern Ukraine, he recognises today that any major conflict would be protracted and costly. His actions on 1 March are now coming back to haunt him.

13

Long Live the Donetsk People's Republic!

8 July 2014

The loss of Slaviansk to Ukrainian government forces has placed the so-called people's republics of Donetsk and Luhansk (DNR and LNR) in a quandary. Can the war be continued from the main oblast centres and, if so, for how long? And is there realistic hope of substantial military aid from Russia? Has the balance of power changed irrevocably for the separatist forces? And how should the Ukrainian leaders proceed?

Though the separatist forces, until recently, were far from united, perhaps the clearest enunciation of the priorities of the DNR – the most prominent of the two republics – was provided on 12 June by the press centre of the 'Southeast' movement coordinated by Oleg Tsarev. It listed several main objectives, the first of which was the creation of a union state with Russia, which would provide a common security system, contractual relations with Ukraine, and a state with full language rights for all citizens.[64]

The action plan envisaged compensation payments by the end of August for families and victims who suffered 'from the aggression of the Kiev junta', and material assistance for those with destroyed property. It also 'guaranteed' the prompt payment of wages, pensions, and social benefits, and proposed to cancel a 200% rise in tariffs for gas, electricity, and public utilities, announced by the government in Kyiv. Wages were to rise in factories owned by oligarchs (most notably those of Rinat Akhmetov) and there would be a transitional period during which Ukrainian institutions would fall under DNR control. The acquisition of Russian citizenship was also to have been permitted.[65]

---

[64] http://www.ostro.org/general/society/news/446903/
[65] Ibid.

These policies fall under the heading of federalism as defined by the Russian leadership of Vladimir Putin. Notably they do not include foreign or security policy, in which respect they are not dissimilar to the sort of vision for Donbas that Mikhail Gorbachev had devised for the former Soviet Union through his abortive Union agreement in 1991. Like Gorbachev's Union Agreement they appear to be unworkable.

According to a pro-Russian source, the leaders of the DNR based in Donetsk, in the face of the sustained attacks from the Ukrainian army, were inclined to reach a compromise that would have signalled the end of the republic. In the view of this same author, negotiations between Akhmetov, the renegade leader of the Vostok battalion Aleksandr Khodakovskiy, the pro-Putin Ukrainian oligarch Viktor Medvedchuk, and officials such as Vladislav Surkov, the former First Deputy Chairman of the Presidential Administration in Moscow were intended to sacrifice Igor Strelkov, the 'defense minister' of the DNR and remove from regional decision-making Aleksey Mozgovoy (leader of the 'people's militia' in Luhansk) and Pavel Gubarev ('people's governor' of the DNR). The conciliatory position reflects in part the 'substantial influence' of Akhmetov over the Donetsk-based leadership of the DNR.[66]

Strelkov scuttled all these plans, when he arrived in Donetsk over the past weekend, declaring that he wished to put an end to the contradictions – what the first author called 'grave digging' because of its defeatist attitude – and unite all forces under a single command.[67] Prior to that, many assumed that Strelkov would die a hero's death in in the defence of Slaviansk. Instead, according to one source, he departed 'like Kutuzov',[68] a reference to the calculated retreat of the Russian general in the face of Napoleon's Grande Armee in the war of 1812. His arrival in Donetsk and assumption of command appears akin to a coup d'etat, replacing the hitherto uncoordinated leadership of the DNR.

In an interview with *Lifenews.ru*, Strelkov stated that he left Slaviansk to protect the lives of peaceful residents and his militia. In order to cover his retreat, a diversionary attack was organised, but the group commander bungled it and most of the troops involved perished. Nonetheless, it allowed Strelkov to depart with 90% of his troops and most of his weapons intact. On 7 July, he established the Central Military Council, which included all the main field commanders, with himself in the key position as commander of the Donetsk garrison.[69] Shortly afterward, Strelkov appeared in Luhansk for a

---

[66] http://cassad.net/category/war/117-o-politicheskoy-podopleke-travli-strelkova.html
[67] http://www.argument.ru/world/2014/07/350848
[68] http://www.rus-obr.ru/opinions/32315
[69] http://www.Lifenews.ru/news/136068

meeting with Valeriy Bolotov, the leader of the LNR, to coordinate activities.[70]

The loss of Slaviansk to the DNR forces can hardly be underestimated. It was, as DNR supporters acknowledge, the key point of the breakaway republic's defensive structure, with over 60 heavy guns in place. By 7 July, however, the city had no electricity or water supply, and the Ukrainian government's 'Anti-Terrorist Operation' (ATO) had disabled the nearby power station at Mykolaivka with a shell.[71] The retreat appears to have been much less orderly than described. But it raises the question of where the DNR goes from here, and how it will be affected by the change of leadership.

Strelkov's arrival will likely escalate the conflict. He has never made any secret of his commitment to the war, which he perceives as one for the 'liberation' of Ukraine, not merely the southeast. Under his command, whatever his difficulties, compromise with Kyiv is highly unlikely. That leaves a major decision to be made by Ukrainian president Petro Poroshenko, namely whether to continue the attack, raising civilian casualties even further, in order to bring about a united Ukraine. What would be Putin's response to the destruction and 'occupation' – from the Russian perspective – of the DNR and LNR?

In an interview with Bloomberg on 7 July, Ian Bremmer, president of the Eurasia Foundation, maintained that Putin would not be 'the loser in Ukraine'. He (Putin) wants 'at the very least a federal Ukraine' with its own foreign policy – as we have noted this was not on the DNR agenda – and trade policy. For Bremmer this 'federalism' constitutes a 'red line' beyond which Putin will not move. It includes 'Russian retention of the cities of Donetsk and Luhansk. Nevertheless, in his view, the Russian president need not rush to attain his goals in southeast Ukraine because the latter is facing an economic crisis that will only get worse as winter approaches and which has been exacerbated by the high number of migrants from the conflict regions of Donbas.[72]

Yet the division of forces in the southeast is increasingly complex and many players remain in place, not least Akhmetov, who are looking for a way out. The size of the 'Novorossiya' faction is dwindling. Other than Strelkov's small band of forces, virtually no one now believes that Ukraine will disintegrate or that the concept of Novorossiya is viable. On the other hand, it is clear that for large swathes of the Donbas population, full control by the present Ukrainian

---

[70] http://www.dialog.ua/news/8427_1404745771
[71] http://www.rus-obr.ru/opinions/32315
[72] http://www.bloomberg.com/video/ukraine-makes-gains-against-rebels-Rw7k2jCEQWSTtNIZimMeIw.html

administration is as undesirable as a Russian invasion and, Ukrainian media reports aside, the general sentiment after the arrival of the Kyiv army is likely to have been one of relief at the end to fighting rather than triumphalism and liberation.

In other words, there is significant scope for compromise, though any agreement would need to distinguish between regional autonomy and Putin-style federalism or 'power sharing'. An autonomous or semi-autonomous Donbas within Ukraine is a logical alternative and moreover, it might appeal to the population at large, even to some of the pro-separatist elements that voted in the contentious referendum last May. But Ukraine could not tolerate a new Transnistria or Abkhazia in its eastern territories, which would continue to destabilise the country. The removal of Strelkov and his forces is the key prerequisite to any progress, and they are increasingly isolated.

In Western Ukraine during Euromaidan, regional governments were virtually autonomous.[73] A federal system has worked successfully in countries such as Germany and Canada – in the latter case with the retention of priority for the French language in Quebec.[74] In Ukraine, it is imperative that the Donbas region be adequately represented in the Cabinet and in parliament generally when Ukrainians go to the polls in the fall. Full language rights must be retained for Russian speakers.

This proposal makes one assumption, namely that Vladimir Putin is also looking for an exit plan, having run out of options and fallen foul of more militant hawks in Moscow. Already, the Russian president was prepared to sacrifice Strelkov, indicating limits to the expansion of 'the Russian world'. Admittedly this scenario offers a very different interpretation of where Putin stands from that of Ian Bremmer. But, in reality, it seems that the Russian president has lost control of his chess game. He has gambled foolhardily and now must try to extricate himself as best he can.

---

[73] http://ukrainianpolicy.com/did-lviv-just-declare-independence/
[74] http://www.theglobeandmail.com/globe-debate/editorials/choose-federalism-to-keep-ukraine-together/article18706295/

14

The Aftermath of MH-17

22 July 2014

The massive outpouring of media commentary and analysis following the tragic loss of lives on the downed Malaysian airliner has given much pause for thought. Three items in particular attracted my attention: one from the perspective of misreading the situation, and the second and third offering informed but questionable statements by experts on Ukraine. They provide an introduction for an analysis of the reaction from the Russian side, which seeks to deflect responsibility for the catastrophe from the Kremlin and even from the anti-Ukrainian forces that currently occupy the cities of Donetsk and Luhansk, which, most sources concur, were responsible for the missile that brought down Flight MH-17 from Amsterdam to Kuala Lumpur last Thursday.

Writing in the London *Daily Mail*, a tabloid better known for its gossip columns than reasoned and informative analysis, Peter Hitchens blames the European Union for the current conflict in Ukraine, maintaining that it was the EU's expansionism that sparked the insurgence:

> [The] aggressor was the European Union, which rivals China as the world's most expansionist power, swallowing countries the way performing seals swallow fish (16 gulped down since 1995) ... Ignoring repeated and increasingly urgent warnings from Moscow, the EU – backed by the USA – sought to bring Ukraine into its orbit. It did so through violence and illegality, an armed mob and the overthrow of an elected president.[75]

Hitchens presumably suffers from a short memory. Had he contemplated the events of six years ago, namely the Russian war with Georgia that resulted in

---

[75] http://www.dailymail.co.uk/debate/article-2698652/PETER-HITCHENS-Mourn-victims-dont-turn-one-tragedy-global-catastrophe.html#ixzz389p23pYM

the defection from that country of two states recognised today by less than five countries – Abkhazia and South Ossetia – he might have recalled why the Eastern Partnership Project (initiated by Poland and Sweden) came into being, and why the EU opted to give states in the neighbourhood of Russia some political and economic alternatives.

It should be added that the EU has offered membership to none of them. Even if it had, most EU states retain considerable independence, as demonstrated by the recent examples of France selling two Mistral-class warships to Russia and German reluctance to impose more severe sanctions on Moscow. Blaming the EU for the war given its demonstrable lack of participation and restrained sanctions makes no sense.

A more serious analysis of the current troubles is offered by Ivan Katchanovski, writing for *The Washington Post* blog, who concludes that: 'The second-largest country in Europe is now formally in a state of civil war, since the battle-related casualties exceed 1,000, a mark that political scientists and conflict studies scholars often use to formally classify an armed conflict as a civil war'.[76]

This statement, however, is also questionable. It requires an explanation of how one defines civil war, other than numerically. Which residents of Ukraine are fighting each other? The war began last March with the Russian invasion of Crimea, the most significant alteration of European boundaries since the Second World War (not 1954, since both Ukraine and Russia were part of a single state). Moreover, there was a clear continuation of that war into eastern Ukraine, even including the leaders of the Crimean invasion forces lead by Igor Girkin (Strelkov), a resident of Moscow. Notably when the Ukrainian army recaptured the former terrorist stronghold of Slaviansk on 5 July, the fighting stopped and people returned to the streets.

What the polls cited by Katchanovski demonstrate is disaffection with Euromaidan and the government installed in Kyiv earlier this year. No doubt that alienation remains in parts of Donetsk and Luhansk – though less so in any other region other than Crimea. But that is not civil war.[77]

Yaroslav Tynchenko, deputy director of the National Military-History Museum of Ukraine, points out that these three regions, in addition to Kharkiv and

---

[76] http://www.washingtonpost.com/blogs/monkey-cage/wp/2014/07/20/what-do-citizens-of-ukraine-actually-think-about-secession/
[77] See also Adrian Karatnycky's comment: http://www.newrepublic.com/article/118765/putins-lockerbie-why-russias-propaganda-machine-high-gear

Odesa took exception (during Euromaidan in Kyiv) especially to the appearance of the red-black 'Bandera' flag, Dmytro Yarosh, portraits of Stepan Bandera, and the party Svoboda and that they neither knew nor understood the 'western Ukrainian culture'. As Tynchenko recalled, this situation had prompted the late Viacheslav Chornovil in the early 1990s to advocate a system of federalisation for Ukraine.[78] Clearly Euromaidan always had as many opponents as supporters. But civil war requires more than disagreement. After all, the Ukrainian state is approaching its 23rd anniversary.

On the other hand, to state, as Chrystia Freeland did during her CNN debate with Stephen Cohen,[79] that Vladimir Putin could end the war 'tomorrow', also seems far-fetched, though in general her comments were much better informed and credible than those of her interlocutor, who took the Ukrainian government to task for liberating its own territory. In fact, Moscow tried to prevent (unsuccessfully) the Donetsk and Luhansk referendums, and it supported, belatedly, the holding of the Ukrainian presidential election, while the militants in these two cities generally obstructed people from voting. In short, while Russia has armed and trained the insurgents, it has not always controlled them. But the looseness of command can be perceived as one of understanding and trust. The occupants of Donetsk and Luhansk would not be there without the bidding and support of the Russian government.

Girkin and his troops – let us call them 'anti-Ukrainian forces', because it seems the most accurate phrase to use (he is not a separatist leader as he is not a resident of Ukraine) – had already shot down two military planes earlier in the week before the downing of the civilian airliner on 17 July. They then boasted about the latter event in recorded conversations, released by the Ukrainian Security Service (SBU), as well as in Girkin's own diary annotations, before realising what they had hit.

Girkin's diary seems quite a credible source. He has kept such records in the past, for example during the Bosnian conflict, and his earlier entries of the Ukrainian war were never retracted or amended. That may be because Girkin is a military adventurer who believes his mission is to implant his and Russia's preferred form of government not only in Ukraine, but worldwide, including places like Syria and the former Yugoslavia. US radar also detected the source of the missile as being close to the village of Hrabove (Donetsk Oblast).

So why cannot Russia and the anti-Ukrainian insurgents acknowledge what they did, explain that it was in error, and express their regrets and apologies

---

[78] http://novosti-n.org/analitic/read/1789.html

[79] http://www.cnn.com/videos/bestoftv/2014/07/20/exp-gps-panel-ukraine.cnn

to the families of those killed? That should be a simple task. Undoubtedly this is a chaotic scene with many armed groups not necessarily working in unison, as OSCE observer Michael Bociurkiw has pointed out.[80]

But a command structure remains in place and a completely disorganised group could not have fired such an advanced weapon. It required training and orders. Putin's statement that 'the state over whose territory it occurred is responsible for the terrible tragedy'[81] is absurd. By that same token, the United Kingdom was responsible for the Lockerbie plane destroyed by a terrorist bomb in 1988 or Ireland for the 1985 Air India flight, both of which had huge death tolls like MH-17. Similarly, irresponsible commentary came from RIA Novosti on 18 July, which reported that: 'there has been no evidence' that Russia has supplied arms to resistance forces in Ukraine, a statement that even the cautious Angela Merkel rejected.[82]

Such denials belittle the Russian president's expressions of regret at the losses. His general attitude of avoiding responsibility and living in a state of denial is reminiscent of that of another former KGB leader, the ailing Yuriy Andropov, after a Soviet jet shot down Korean Air 007 on 1 September 1983 west of Sakhalin Island. The order to do so was given by General Anatoliy Kornukhov, who paradoxically died, unrepentant, on 1 July 2014. Both Putin and his predecessor Boris Yeltsin had decorated him previously for his loyal service to his homeland.

While it would be facile to deny the one-sidedness of many Western reports on this war, they pale beside the propaganda on the Russian side, which goes well beyond distortion. According to analyst Viktor Ukolov, the campaign is intended to ensure that the Russian military do not have the slightest sympathy for their adversaries when the time comes to 'pull the trigger'. They include stories such as the crucifixion of a young child by the Right Sector in Slaviansk.[83] The campaign's impact has extended to more peaceful parts of Ukraine. Ukrainian Interior Minister Arsen Avakov has declared it a war for the minds of people that is having a pernicious effect on his country.[84]

As for Russian residents, as a Radio Liberty report by Robert Coalson noted, a June opinion poll conducted by the Levada Centre showed that 90% of

---

[80] http://zn.ua/POLITICS/yacenyuk-prizval-putina-prekratit-voynu-149116_.html

[81] http://expert.ru/2014/07/18/putin-vozlozhil-otvetstvennost-za-krushenie-malazijskogo-lajnera-na-ukrainu/]

[82] http://www.ostro.org/general/society/news/450675

[83] http://zn.ua/POLITICS/polittehnolog-cel-rossiyskoy-propagandy-degumanizaciya-obraza-vraga-149273_.html

[84] http://zn.ua/POLITICS/yacenyuk-prizval-putina-prekratit-voynu-149116_.html

Russian residents obtain their news directly from Russian Television, and over 50% rely on a single source. A further 60% considered the treatment of Ukraine to be objective.[85]

There is little question therefore that most Russians believe what they hear. But it is also a campaign that has entrapped the Russian leadership as well: once initiated it is difficult to stop, and it undermines any attempts at compromise once the enemy [Ukraine] is portrayed as a 'neo-Nazi Junta', a depiction incidentally that has found its way onto the Facebook and Twitter sites of many gullible Westerners, despite a presidential election in which rightist forces were heavily defeated and a forthcoming parliamentary election in the fall.

It is this sort of mindset that has brought about the callous and otherwise unfathomable reaction to the loss of MH-17 and its innocent passengers, accompanied by a plethora of conspiracy theories, aspersions on the Ukrainian government, and of course denial of complicity on the part of Russia and its allies.

Ultimately the first way out of this maze of fabrications and distortions is quite simple: an admission of guilt and open access to the crash scene. Very few observers believe that those who launched the missile deliberately fired on a civilian airliner – even including a Canadian analyst who describes the tragedy as a war crime and 'mass murder'.[86] On the other hand, the tragedy is a result of escalation of the war by Russia and its anti-Ukrainian insurgents inside Ukraine, most of whom are Russian-led and armed. Its impact is exacerbated and deepened by the continuing denials of guilt from the Russian president and his ministers.

---

[85] http://www.rferl.org/content/russia-media-mh17-airline-crash-coverage-malaysia/25462227.html
[86] http://www.ctvnews.ca/video?clipId=402226

15

The Ukrainian Army Is Unprepared for War

15 August 2014

Co-authored with Myroslava Uniat

The recent news in Ukraine, from the perspective of the government side, has been very positive. At least 60 settlements have been recaptured from the anti-Kyiv forces led by the Russian officers Igor Girkin/Strelkov and Vladimir Antyufeyev; they are now confined to two small pockets inside the two regional capitals of Donetsk and Luhansk. They are well provided with weaponry but desperate for a full-scale Russian invasion to begin.

Drawing Room Generals

This picture, however, masks fundamental problems at the upper levels of the Ukrainian army. Evidence is emerging of large-scale corruption among generals and lower-ranking officers, particularly in Ukraine's Ministry of Defence. It is undermining the war effort and lowering the morale of the rank-and-file. Many soldiers have come to the conclusion that it would be better to change the leadership in Kyiv before dealing with the separatists in Donbas.

Command over troops in the Anti-Terrorist Operation (ATO) is divided among several sectors, including the ministries of Defence and Internal Affairs, along with some volunteer formations. Arsen Avakov, Minister of Internal Affairs, announced on 29 July that at least 20,000 troops in Donbas were needed to replace deserters and traitors. Almost 600 troops had been found collaborating with officials of the self-styled Donetsk People's Republic (DNR). A further 242 people who had been on vacation 'for a long time' were also under investigation.

The Business of War

After months of fighting, the border with Russia still remains open. Anton Herashchenko, an adviser to Avakov, notes that daily, hundreds, and sometimes thousands of mercenaries cross from Russia to join the fighting in Ukraine. Some are influenced by Russian state propaganda, but others come as mercenaries. Some Ukrainian soldiers suspect that the border has remained open because some of their own leaders are making profits from the hiring of Russian troops and equipment.

One soldier (we have withheld his name) complained that ATO generals were ignorant of what is taking place on the war zone. They prefer to sit in hotels well away from the battlefront, 'eating lobster' and cavorting with prostitutes. They remain restricted to the 'Soviet mindset.' Oleh Lyashko, Leader of the Radical Party, had visited them and provided biscuits, chocolate, food, and sleeping bags, but the commanders had confiscated them and put such goods under lock and key. He quoted a border source that said Russia was prepared to pay $100,000 for a truck loaded with weapons to cross the frontier, and $10,000 for an individual mercenary. These funds fall into the hands of Ukrainian military leaders. The war, in his view, could be ended in a month using two battalions with twenty snipers in each, but people at the top are more interested in prolonging it.

Parents of soldiers from Uzhhorod region complain of corrupt and irresponsible military commanders. About 280 soldiers were picked up at Luhansk airport and informed that their destination would be the Moscow-Luhansk highway, a virtual death sentence, since the road is the only remaining link between eastern Ukraine and Russia and controlled by separatists and Chechens. The troops abandoned their mission; only 25 paratroopers from Zhytomyr were willing to take it on and suffered heavily. The Uzhhorod parents believe their Ukrainian commanders betrayed their whereabouts to the Chechens for cash, and took vacations on the proceeds. Captured Chechens have also been suddenly released. The soldiers do not complain about shortages of food and water, and are willing to defend Ukraine. But they believe also that the war is being prolonged for profits.

ATO Headquarters

According to Dmitryi Tymchuk, coordinator of the group 'Information Resistance', the main problem lies with army generals at ATO Headquarters. They are, he reports, pathologically inclined to lies, are afraid to take on the slightest responsibility, unable to make simple decisions, and utterly incompetent. Military commanders of all units are psychologically unprepared for combat. Starting with the war in Crimea (March 2014), examples abound of middle and junior commanders refusing to obey orders or sabotaging them.

Treachery and corruption at the top is rampant. Both Oleh Tiahnybok, leader of Svoboda party, and Serhii Melnychuk, commander of the Aidar battalion, maintain there are traitors in the central office of the ATO. Tiahnybok has proposed a lie detector test to prevent the delivery of secret information to Moscow, end corruption, and facilitate the delivery of necessary military equipment. A volunteer from the 'Wings of the Phoenix' from Mykolaiv region complained that, 'The generals have saunas and fitness centres in the rear of ATO Staff. They have no idea what's going on here, where our guys are dying'.

Kyiv is the Problem

One soldier bemoaned the fact that in Kyiv the oligarchs have returned to power and 'nothing has changed.' The generals do not care about soldiers; they remain in hotels, secure comfortable positions, and are content to replace dead troops with.[87] Even Ukrainian Minister of Defence, Valerii Heletei, acknowledged the depths of the problems of the high command, noting that the Ukrainian army has 20-30 generals who are quite adept at preparing battle plans on tablets and on paper, but they have no idea what is happening at the Front. In order to understand the situation, he commented, 'one should at least go there'.

Igor Strelkov, the DNR's defence leader, recently imposed martial law in Donetsk. Such options are not open to the Ukrainian side, complained Ihor Lutsenko, Deputy of the Kyiv Council. Yet, he believes, its imposition would allow the military to detain suspected separatists. The Front abounds in enemy agents and traitors, yet local police forces leave the separatists in peace. Lutsenko maintained that: 'The main problems with fighting the terrorists are located in the capital; and to overcome them will automatically ensure victory – at least over those enemies who are in our country right now. The ATO must start in Kyiv!'

In the 2014 state budget, the government of Ukraine proposes to allot about $1 billion for the ATO, the costs of refugees, and restoring the cities of Donetsk and Luhansk. It has also raised financial assistance to the families of dead servicemen in the ATO zone to around $50,000 per soldier. In reality,

---

[87] https://www.youtube.com/watch?v=9DVsAElpdNc

however, families do not receive such compensation since the soldiers are blamed for their own deaths – failure to follow instructions, misuse of weapons, improper behaviour, etc., as the testimonies of their widows reveals.

Conclusion

The failure to deal with fundamental problems of the army is undermining the war effort and alienating the troops conducting the main fighting. Not only does it endanger the future of Ukraine, but also it contributes to volunteer extremist paramilitary groups like the Azov battalion, taking over the war effort.[88] The victims of high-level corruption in the current Ukrainian army are the rank-and-file troops who are neglected, betrayed, and often abandoned to their fate as cannon fodder. This fact is largely concealed in the Ukrainian and Western media amid reports of ATO successes and the liberation of eastern towns and villages. But it will affect the future of Ukraine long after the demise of Igor Strelkov and the so-called People's Republics of Donetsk and Luhansk.

---

[88] See, for example, http://www.bbc.com/news/world-europe-28329329

16

@FuckYouPutin

22 August 2014

Slowly, the Ukrainian government's Anti-Terrorist Operation (ATO) is succeeding, as the anti-Kyiv insurgents are reduced to small areas within the cities of Donetsk and Luhansk. The future is far from clear since there is no guarantee that all the rebels will be captured and they appear to have ample weaponry at their disposal. Russia may or may not launch a full-scale attack, though it seems increasingly unlikely. Its leaders will clearly not be happy at the outcome and the failure of the Novorossiya vision embraced by some Russians and separatists.

Those of us who study Ukraine, in my case for over three decades now, the events of the past nine months seem in many ways bewildering: for their violence, the polarisation of parts of society, the severing of ties with once friendly neighbours, the loss of Crimea, and not least for the rhetoric of hatred, which has permeated media. Somewhat lost in the overwhelming haze of propaganda disseminated over social networks, is the human tragedy that has taken place in Donbas, which is not always evident in analyses, though it permeates dispatches from troops on the ground. Several cities that form the heartland of industrial Ukraine are in ruins, their economies shattered.

Yet we read mainly about the triumphs of the ATO or, earlier, the rebels, not about the civilian population that is facing destitution. No doubt most would leave if they could, but one suspects those who were financially able to leave have already departed. Reportedly about 175,000 refugees had left the two oblasts of Donetsk and Luhansk by 20 August.[89]

---

[89] http://tsn.ua/politika/ponad-190-tisyach-bizhenciv-zalishili-svoyi-domivki-v-zoni-ato-ta-v-krimu-oon-364073.html

What has struck me most – and I am writing from the distant city of Sapporo, Japan, and thus cannot speak as a direct observer – is the polarised and often bitter nature of the reporting from outside Ukraine, and not just in Russia. The combination of academic and public interest in events has brought about an inflamed discussion in which there seems to be no middle ground. Its focus is largely limited to the person of the Russian president.

Even a glance at the names of Facebook and Twitter sites provides ample evidence of the degeneration of the debate into platitudes and crude insults: Facebook has Blow-up Putinism, Putin khuylo worldwide, Khuylo Putin, and Fuck U Putin; the ubiquitous Twitter carries @FuckingPutin, @FuckPutin123, @PutinPrick, @DarthPutinKGB, @BOYCOTTRUSSIANS, and @Putinis-Faggot.

The level of discussion at such sites can easily be imagined. That is not to say, however, that one cannot disagree (as I do) with scholars like Stephen F. Cohen, who has taken a strong stance in support of the position of Putin. But there is no call to refer to him, as American journalist Julia Ioffe has done, in terms such as 'Putin's toady'.[90] Reasoned and civil discussion has been lacking for some time in public discussions of this conflict.

Western political leaders have been quick to resort to similar sloganeering, headed by my own Prime Minister Stephen Harper, who not only compared Putin with Hitler – as did some other leaders – but then claimed he was a Communist as well, and thus responsible for all the evils of the Soviet past.[91] Harper has led the charge against Russian imperialism despite the fact that Canada only spends 1% of its annual budget on its military, the same level as Papua New Guinea.

The Hitler analogy has come up quite often in comments from Western statespersons, from Hillary Clinton to Prince Charles (whose great uncle, the former Edward VIII, was a Hitler admirer) and, less surprisingly, Senator John McCain.[92] No doubt Western leaders are right to be preoccupied with the machinations of Putin, but to compare him with the perpetrator of the Holocaust is taking things too far.

Alexander J. Motyl, who by his own admission has been comparing Putin to

---

[90] http://www.newrepublic.com/article/117606/stephen-cohen-wrong-russia-ukraine-america

[91] http://www.huffingtonpost.ca/2014/05/30/stephen-harper-communism_n_5421360.html

[92] http://www.businessinsider.co.id/people-who-compared-putin-to-hitler-2014-5/#.U_a1WLySxss

Hitler since the late 1990s, goes even further:

> Both Germany and Russia lost empires and desired to rebuild them. Both Germany and Russia suffered economic collapse. Both Germany and Russia experienced national humiliation and retained imperial political cultures. Both Germany and Russia blamed their ills on the democrats. Both Germany and Russia elected strong men who promised to make them grand and glorious again. Both strong men employed imperialist arguments about 'abandoned brethren' in neighboring states, remilitarized their countries, developed cults of the personality, centralized power, gave pride of place in the power structure to the forces of coercion, constructed regimes that may justifiably be called fascist, and proceeded to engage in re-annexing bits and pieces of lost territory before embarking on major land grabs. Both strong men demonized friendly nations.[93]

It is a weak analogy. How can one compare Germany, dismembered by the Treaty of Versailles, prohibited from having an army of more than 100,000, with French troops occupying the Saar, an enormous reparations bill for allegedly starting the First World War, as well as suffering – perhaps more than any other country – the impact of the Great Depression bringing rampant inflation, with post-Soviet Russia? Russia has enjoyed overall a relative economic boom in Putin's time, thanks to high world prices for oil and gas.

And if Russia's government is Fascist, and the term is not defined by Motyl, it is a form of fascism that has little in common with National Socialism, which focused attention on the disaffected and disillusioned lower middle class and former war combatants. Putinism caters to entrepreneurs, cronies, and security services. Whereas Weimar Germany in late 1932 was destitute, contemporary Russia is, at least by this comparison, relatively prosperous. And Putin improvises policy; one would be hard pressed to discern a programme, let alone an expressed policy, calling for the elimination of entire races from Europe as the ostensible cause of all the world's problems. He did not cause the frozen conflict in Transnistria and even in Georgia in the 2008 war, the operation was limited and inconclusive. Hitler moved decisively, swallowing entire countries at a gulp.

The situation in Ukraine today appears more similar to the Spanish Civil War in the 1930s, which prompted many to join the proud, if doomed, cause of the Republicans against the Falangists, one of good versus evil. But the reality on

---

[93] http://www.worldaffairsjournal.org/blog/alexander-j-motyl/hitler-and-putin-tale-two-authoritarians

the ground, as George Orwell and others showed, was very different from that envisaged by the crusading writers and poets. Ultimately, the major Fascist powers helped Franco to win that war and Stalin's USSR did not do enough to assist the Republicans. The Western democracies did nothing at all.

In Ukraine, Western powers, while embracing the Ukrainian cause, have acted rather like Britain and France in the 1930s, perhaps, but they are not facing a similar adversary. Putin already appears to have failed in eastern Ukraine, and his protégés such as Pavel Gubarev, who governed the 'Donetsk {People's Republic' for most of 2014 (he was the director of a company that supplied Santa Clauses in the region) and misfit right-wing ideologists have already largely departed the scene.

Let us be clear: the vitriol and outright distortions of Russian propaganda have exceeded that of the Soviet era. The Soviets were adept at rewriting history, doctoring photographs, mythologising key events like the October Revolution and the Great Patriotic War, covering up mass atrocities, and idolising leaders. But they lacked the technology to broadcast fabricated information as Russian networks did when they showed people – allegedly from eastern Ukraine – crossing the Russian border, which was actually the Polish one, or photographs of crucified children and other atrocities that were blamed on right-wing neo-Nazi extremists and the 'junta' in Kyiv.

The entire depiction of the war in Russia is based on fantasy. It has failed entirely to acknowledge any responsibility, even indirectly (providing BUK missile systems to the insurgents), for the shooting down of the Malaysian airliner last month. Likewise, Russia has depicted the United States (and to some extent, the European Union), falsely, as the architect of the uprising that removed former president Viktor Yanukovych from office last February. In reality, while Washington was supportive of Euromaidan (perhaps noisily so), it never directed or controlled it. The EU's Association Agreement, in turn, never entailed the loss of Ukrainian ties with Russia.

Perhaps Euromaidan itself was the catalyst that prompted many Westerners to leap on to a bandwagon in similar fashion to 2004, during the Orange Revolution. But Euromaidan was violent and, as participants inform, was many things to many people. It is simplistic to portray it as a straightforward movement toward Europe, away from Russia and authoritarianism. Yet both politicians and even reputable analysts often use such phrases. Chrystia Freeland wrote recently, for example, that 'in the historic fight over the future of democracy in Ukraine, Kyiv is winning and the Kremlin is losing'.[94] It is all

---

[94] http://www.politico.com/magazine/story/2014/08/kiev-is-winning-the-war-109935.html#.U_biKrySxss

too easy to overlook the deeper societal problems of Ukraine that existed before and after Euromaidan, which was about power rather than democracy.

Petro Poroshenko, the newly elected president of Ukraine, for example, is an oligarch, who has appointed another oligarch, Borys Lozhkin, as his chief of staff. His closest associates are 'businessmen' with shady pasts. Lozhkin declared his income last year to be just over $102,000, which seemed questionable considering his sale of his media holdings in this same period for $450 million to a company linked to Yanukovych.[95]

Poroshenko was also one of the founders of the Regions Party, now largely defunct, that carried Yanukovych to power. He was perhaps the popular compromise candidate, but he does not represent fundamental change. Ukraine's most pervasive and crippling problem is corruption, and it is as deeply embedded as ever. There are many key problems yet to be addressed.[96] But there is no indication so far that the new president intends to uproot corruption, as Yulia Tymoshenko promised to do in the 2010 presidential elections. Indeed, to do so might endanger his business empire and connections.

It is illogical therefore, to place all Ukraine's problems today at the door of Vladimir V. Putin. If separatism or federalism has gained a foothold in Donbas towns, there are reasons why. It will remain long after the ATO mission is over, when rebuilding of destroyed towns and villages begins. Even in a free and fair vote Crimea might (just) have voted for union with Russia. Certainly, the city of Sevastopol would have done so, and even a decade ago, Crimean leaders tried to hold a referendum on independence. The problems and disaffection of these regions were not created by Putin. He has behaved abominably, but he has exploited and exacerbated a situation rather than initiated one.

Yet, thanks to Putin, Ukraine is united as never before. Even those who detest the Kyiv government do not support a Russian invasion. So how should he be viewed? Like Yanukovych and Belarus' Lukashenka Putin is essentially a gangster who perceives politics as a conflict and life-and-death struggle.[97] In this respect, his actions are quite rational. One should keep in mind that he leads a country with a GDP less than that of California and *seven* times less than the EU. Its population, which until recently was

---

[95] http://www.rferl.org/content/poroshenkos-right-hand-man-emerges/25426487.html
[96] See Taras Kuzio, http://www.kyivpost.com/opinion/op-ed/taras-kuzio-20-question-for-poroshenko-parliament-and-government-353902.html
[97] See my comment at http://www.themoscowtimes.com/opinion/article/what-putin-lukashenko-and-yanukovych-share/488684.html

declining at an alarming rate, is 45% that of the United States.

Russia is not a Great Power even though it may pretend to be; it is a fading middle power with nuclear weapons. If the West is resolute, Russia cannot win. But the point to be made is that Ukraine has problems that are not derived from Russia or the Putin presidency.

Perhaps it is unreasonable to expect that the Ukrainian Diaspora will ever look at Russia differently, given the Soviet legacy. But most would also prefer to see Ukraine as a unitary state, which means that they need to take into consideration the views of all residents, probably of which at least 40% (without Crimea) are opposed to both Euromaidan and the current government in Kyiv. They need to consider the future of Donbas, the industrial heartland, as well as other regions, like Dnipropetrovsk, which is ruled like a medieval fiefdom by governor Ihor Kolomoiskyi, who has his own private army, controlled, along with at least three airline companies, by his company Privatbank.[98]

Analysts of Ukraine in the West likewise need to examine the situation more rationally. Soviet texts always used to cite the devastation caused by the German army to towns and villages in European USSR, as if the powerful Red Army that moved westward in 1943-45 carefully avoided causing any damage. The same applies today to the Ukrainian reports that are designed to exculpate the ATO from the deaths of civilians and the destruction of property. That was the choice of Poroshenko: it may bring victory but it will be at a terrible cost. The president clearly had his reasons for this choice. But few analysts, the American-based Ukrainian scholar Serhy Kudelia is a notable exception, dwell on the human losses brought about by the Ukrainian president's decision.

On 19 August, Mark 'Franko' Paslawsky, an American fighting as a private in the Ukrainian army even though he was a graduate of West Point, died at the age of 55. As Simon Ostrovsky indicates, Paslawsky was motivated in part by hatred of Russians. But he was also disarmingly honest and his tweets about the war are far more revealing than most official media reports. Paslawsky was deeply troubled by the corruption at the head of the Ukrainian army and predicted also that 'volunteer battalions' would turn on Kyiv when the war in the east was over.[99]

---

[98] http://www.foreignpolicy.com/articles/2014/08/14/ukraines_oligarchs_are_still_calling_the_shots_0
[99] https://news.vice.com/article/the-only-american-fighting-for-ukraine-dies-in-battle

Thus, it is time to dwell less on a 'struggle for democracy' or West versus East in a new Cold War to quell the mad Putin – barring of course a full-scale Russian invasion – and more on the future of Ukraine, which is facing not only a social and economic crisis and plummeting currency, but hard decisions about its future destiny. As Ukraine commemorates 23 years of independence these questions are far from resolved. It must address the problems of Donbas and ensure the region has appropriate representation in parliament and other bodies, and it must deal with corruption.

In the ranking of corrupt nations by Transparency International last December, 'Ukraine tied for 144th place in the ranking with Cameroon, the Central African Republic, Iran, Nigeria, and Papua New Guinea'.[100] Corruption ultimately is a more serious problem than ideology or language, or whether Ukraine can be part of the EU in the future. It is why radical dilettantes who promise to address it, like Oleh Lyashko, have gained instant popularity and it will be a critical issue on the October parliamentary elections.

It is also one reason why Yanukovych was ousted from office. It will outlast the separatists and Russian convoys, will persist after this war is won, and could be the source of a new Euromaidan. But all too often Western analysts perceive only one problem: the ogre in the Kremlin.

---

[100] http://www.kyivpost.com/content/ukraine/transparency-international-slams-ukraine-as-most-corrupt-in-europe-332965.html

17

Assessing Ukraine's Options

29 August 2014

We have entered a new stage in the lengthy conflict in eastern Ukraine, one in which regular Russian army units have provided direct manpower and materiel to the so-called People's Republics of Donetsk and Luhansk. The latter were on the verge of total collapse following a successful advance of the Anti-Terrorist Operation by the Ukrainian army and volunteer battalions.

The direct invasion by Russia, its second in Ukraine in a period of six months, has changed the balance of forces dramatically. It follows the 26 August meeting in Minsk between Russian president Vladimir Putin and Ukrainian president Petro Poroshenko, mediated by Belarusian leader Aliaksandr Lukashenka. According to Russian analyst Stanislav Belkovskiy, Putin did not consider that he was dealing with equal partners and sought mainly to belittle Poroshenko.[101] The talks achieved little.

The occupation of Novoazovsk by Russian troops and the potential battle for Mariupol trapped a large contingent of Anti-Terrorist Operation (ATO) forces (around 700 troops) in the Donetsk corridor and there are now options for the 'Novorossiya' forces to attack Mariupol, open up a pathway to Crimea, and even beyond. On the other hand, Russia's forces remain quite small, between 1,000 and 15,000, according to different accounts,[102] but which Russia refers to as 'volunteers'.

These figures, even at the upper limit, suggest that the Russian leadership has not yet committed to a full-scale assault on Ukraine, but is rather seeking to push the Ukrainians out of Donbas and create a stalemate. First and

---

[101] http://www.radiosvoboda.org/content/article/26549687.html
[102] See, e.g. http://www.ft.com/intl/cms/s/0/8275bec4-2ea2-11e4-afe4-00144feabdc0.html#slide0

foremost, it wishes to protect the two proxy governments and ensure that Ukraine does not take possession of its far-eastern provinces.

For Ukraine, the situation poses new and serious problems. One option is to order a martial law in Donbas, and try to relieve the Luhansk airport and other areas captured by separatist forces[103] That choice might lead to a full confrontation with troops that are clearly from Russia. It could be costly and deadly and bring about far more civilian casualties. It might free the region, but a complete victory would likely provoke a much broader Russian assault. Vladimir Putin would be unlikely to accept complete defeat, which is why he ordered the invasion in the first place.

A second option would be to withdraw ATO troops unilaterally from Donbas. That option would leave the region under separatist and Russian control for the immediate future. It would be a humiliating climb-down for the commander-in-chief of the army, i.e. President Poroshenko. It would prevent Ukraine from holding nationwide parliamentary elections in October, the main means to stabilise the political situation in the country. It would also create yet another 'frozen conflict' in this part of Europe to add to Transnistria, Abkhazia, and South Ossetia, all of which resulted from Russian intrusions.

A third option would be to try to bring about immediate peace through negotiations. Russia would insist that the 'people's republics' must be included at the table. It might also demand recognition of the much-criticised referendums that took place in Donetsk and Luhansk last May on separation from Ukraine.[104] On the other hand it would bring the EU and the United States into the equation, and allow Ukraine to weigh its options. If the country has little support from its Western friends, then there is little point of engaging in a military conflict with Russia. The poor state of its army is well known and soldiers have little respect for their high-level officers, many of whom are holdovers from Soviet days.

None of these options is particularly attractive. They all purport that outside aid to Ukraine will continue to be limited. At present, the EU seems badly divided on the war in Ukraine. Hungary, the Czech Republic, and Slovakia are very concerned about the economic losses to be incurred through sanctions against Russia.[105] Germany has taken a firmer stance, but advocates a federalist solution.[106] The United States has ruled out direct military

---

[103] See, e.g., http://www.newsru.ua/ukraine/28aug2014/stavkuprezident.html
[104] http://maidan24.eu/ua/news/referendum-w-donecku
[105] http://www.bbc.com/news/world-europe-28801353
[106] http://www.ft.com/intl/cms/s/0/2b0b440c-2ac8-11e4-811d00144feabdc0.html#axzz3Bqh26pSv

involvement and restricted its responses to sanctions and verbal condemnations. On the other hand, it has extended non-lethal military aid to Ukraine.

But Kyiv must act resolutely. As Pavel Felgenhauer has pointed out, Russia must demobilise its current contingent of troops in the fall, the days are becoming shorter, and the difficulties of direct air support for Russian troops mount.[107] Thus Putin requires a quick solution to the impasse, namely the withdrawal of the ATO from Donbas. Is a fourth option available for Ukraine?

One possibility that will not appeal to the more nationalistically minded is to cut losses and solidify what remains. Ukraine might agree to Donbas' full autonomy or even independence – but not its joining Russia – provided that the latter (as well as the ATO) withdraws its troops and all aid to separatist forces, if the rest of the country were allowed by the West to take certain irrevocable steps.

The first of these would be direct, fast-track entry into the EU for the remainder of Ukraine, reducing the timeline for the usual bureaucratic processes and bringing about a quick vote in Brussels.

The second would be for Ukraine to join NATO, which would then offer full protection for the country minus Donbas and Crimea. It is to be hoped that in doing so the West would continue to refuse recognition for Russia's military conquests and heighten sanctions. NATO would also need to help in transforming and reequipping the Ukrainian army, as well as by establishing military bases inside Ukraine. Although in the past, many Ukrainians have been reticent about joining NATO, the vote today would be much closer, and without Donbas and Crimea, it would likely be positive.

The caveats to this notion are that Ukraine would be severely affected by the loss of direct control over Donbas, far more so than the Crimea and that entry into NATO would likely take some time. But Donbas will already take many years to recover from the war, and even under the best of circumstances it is unlikely to attain its former hegemony as an industrial power house. It would seem to signal that Putin has won a partial victory through subterfuge, barbarity, and direct aggression but he would have failed to undermine the current government in Kyiv.

The idea would also require a degree of commitment from the EU and the United States to preserving Ukraine that hitherto has not been evident. US

---

[107] Cited in http://20committee.com/2014/08/29/the-russo-ukrainian-war/

president Barack Obama hesitates even to use the word 'invasion' in describing Russian actions in Ukraine.[108] But the Western countries need to weigh the importance of preserving a post-Cold War state versus the 19th century 'spheres of interest' vision of the Russian president. The latter concept is based neither on an accurate reading of history, nor any form of liberal worldview. Rather, it seeks to change the status quo at the first opportunity.

And if Ukraine cannot be preserved in full, then by now it should be recognised what is needed to maintain what is left. It can no longer be attained, it seems, by means of peaceful diplomacy because its enemies do not acknowledge its right to exist. But if the West is unwilling to protect Ukraine, then the government in Kyiv's options are very limited as long as the current Russian leadership remains in place.

Ultimately, under this scenario, it would remain in the Russian orbit, and be integrated into Russian-led structures like the Customs Union and Collective-Security Treaty Organisation. Few Ukrainians seek that option, which they would see as a step backward; many are bitterly against it. One can posit that rebellions and discontent would be manifest for many years. It is not an option that would benefit Russia, but it is one that may satisfy hawks around the Russian president.

The EU, in particular, needs to recognise the consequences of its actions, initiated with the Eastern Partnership Project five years ago, headed by Poland and Sweden. Are these countries really partners or just friends visiting from a house owned by Russia? Does the EU foresee in the future full membership for Georgia, Moldova, Azerbaijan, or even Belarus? Because Russia's responses demonstrate above all that there cannot be two options: these countries will not be permitted to keep open both the front and back doors, as former president Viktor Yanukovych wanted to do.

The EU and NATO are the best options for Ukraine, but only if these two organisations demonstrate in turn their full commitment to maintaining that country's independence and supporting it economically and militarily. That statement is not an advocacy of war, but of complete protection for the part of Ukraine that can still be secured. The time for debate is very limited; decisive and clear responses are needed. Otherwise Ukraine will be lost.

---

[108] http://www.rferl.org/content/ukraine-russia-lying-invasion-us-samantha-power/26555401.html

18

Preparing for New Parliamentary Elections in Ukraine

14 September 2014

Two years after the previous elections for the Ukrainian Parliament, a new election campaign is underway. The vote will take place on 26 October under the most difficult conditions the independent state has ever faced. What is the likely outcome and what impact might the newly endorsed Parliament have on Ukraine, the continuing conflict with Russia and the war zones of Donbas?

It is worth recalling that the previous parliament, elected in 2012, will bear little resemblance to the future one. Three of the five parties that crossed the 5% barrier to attain seats in the assembly are now either defunct, not running, or banned (Regions, with 185 seats; the Ukrainian Democratic Alliance with 40; and the Communist Party of Ukraine, with 32). Another – Svoboda – is no longer the chief representative of the radical right, while Fatherland (Batkivshchyna, 101 seats) has been undermined by deep internal divisions. In this sense, therefore, the parliament will represent something quite new. But some seven million potential voters in the east are unlikely or unwilling to take part, meaning that the election is essentially about the views of those who live in central, western, and southern Ukraine.

One of the most recent polls on parties and blocs was conducted by the Kyiv Institute of Sociology on 21-28 August 2014.[109] The survey encompassed 2,040 respondents from 110 settlements of all Ukrainian oblasts, with the exception of the Republic of Crimea and Luhansk. Presumably, though it is

---

[109] http://www.kiis.com.ua/?lang=ukr&cat=reports&id=393&page=1

not stated expressly, it also included some respondents from the city of Donetsk, which is currently in the hands of separatist rebels. Perhaps the most pertinent category of questions concerned the likely voting habits of those committed to participation in the elections. The results were as follows:

- Solidarity Party (Petro Poroshenko): 28.5%
- Radical Party (Oleh Liashko): 16.5%
- Fatherland Party (Yulia Tymoshenko, Arsenii Yatseniuk): 10.0%
- Civic Position (Anatolii Hrytsenko, former Minister of Defense): 9.2%
- UDAR (Vitalii Klychko): 7.2%
- Svoboda (Oleh Tiahnybok): 6.9%
- A Strong Ukraine (Serhii Tihipko): 4.7%
- Communist Party of Ukraine (Petro Symonenko): 3.9%

In terms of the regions of Ukraine, more than one-third of those polled in the east and 22.9% of those in the south responded that they did not intend to take part in the elections. Likely participation rates in the west and centre were very high. In the west support was almost evenly divided between Solidarity and the Radicals, whereas in the centre, support for the former was double that of the latter.

Several recent developments have occurred since President Poroshenko dissolved Parliament on 25 August after the fall of the coalition 'European Choice'. In late August, Solidarity, which had failed to achieve much influence in past elections, became known as the Petro Poroshenko Bloc.[110] In this way it identified itself with a popular president who had achieved a resounding victory in the May 2014 presidential elections. The name change was announced by the former Minister of Interior Yurii Lutsenko, who served a prison sentence under the Yanukovych presidency, and has taken on the role of party chairman.[111]

On 13 September, Prime Minister Arsenii Yatseniuk's newly created Popular Front declared that it would oppose the Poroshenko Bloc, following its withdrawal from the Fatherland (Batkivshchyna Party), reportedly because of disagreements with Yulia Tymoshenko. Alongside Yatseniuk will stand the Speaker of the Parliament Oleksandr Turchynov, who took over as Acting President of Ukraine following the departure of former president Viktor Yanukovych last February. Also included in the party's ranks are Interior Minister Arsen Avakov and journalist Tetiana Chornovol, his current Advisor.

---

[110] http://www.kyivpost.com/content/politics/solidarity-party-to-be-renamed-bloc-of-petro-poroshenko-362218.html

[111] http://vsim.ua/Pres-sluzhby/tochka-zoru-blok-petra-poroshenka-ob%E2%80%99yednaye-usih-tih-hto-ghotovij-zmi-10414780.html

Chornovol is second on the party list, with Turchynov in third place.[112]

On the following day, the Secretary of the Presidium of the Party of Regions, Borys Kolesnikov, announced that the party would not participate in the elections, but would form an 'opposition government' in the new Parliament.[113] Finally, the Ukrainian Democratic Alliance (UDAR), headed by the new Kyiv Mayor Vitalii Klychko, announced that it would take part in the elections jointly with the Poroshenko Bloc,[114] thus repeating a practice followed in the earlier presidential elections when Klychko opted not to oppose Poroshenko and to settle for the mayoral role in the capital city.

On 14 September, the Poroshenko Bloc announced that it already had a full slate of candidates on a list that seemed to include both competent and unlikely personalities. It included the three Baloha brothers in Zakarpatska (Viktor, Ivan, and Pavlo – Viktor was formerly the head of the Secretariat of the President of Ukraine during Viktor Yushchenko's administration). Ihor Palytsya, the governor of Odesa region; the controversial former Minister of Justice Roman Zvarych who in 2005 lied about his qualifications);[115] the former Chairman of the National Bank Stepan Kubiv; the executive-director of the conference 'Yalta European Strategy (YES)' platform associated with the Viktor Pinchuk Foundation, Ivanna Klympush-Tsintsadze, and finally the president's son Oleksii, who is running in a riding in Vynnytsia Oblast.[116]

Clearly the president is financially well-backed for the campaign and running high in the standings. But his path appears far from smooth. As noted on 14 September by analyst Timothy Ash, who provides regular briefings on Ukraine for Standard Bank of South Africa, the leaders of Ukraine have essentially formed two fronts: a Party of Peace, headed by the president; and a Party of War, under the leadership of Yatseniuk, who is already adding to his party list the leaders of volunteer battalions that are fighting in Donbas. Ostensibly this move may be calculated to undermine the influence of the Radical Party, whose leader Liashko recently advised Parliament to shoot all deputies who collaborated with Russia.[117] It may also serve to create a new divide between the 'Euromaidan' parties.

---

[112] http://en.ria.ru/politics/20140913/192905569/Ukraines-Yatseniuk-Says-His-Party-to-Compete-With-Presidents-One.html

[113] http://www.presstv.ir/detail/2014/09/14/378723/ukraine-regions-party-to-boycott-vote/

[114] http://un.ua/eng/article/532266.html

[115] (http://www.kyivpost.com/opinion/editorial/an-utter-disgrace.html?flavour=mobile

[116] http://un.ua/eng/article/532266.html)

[117] http://www.dialog.ua/news/16193_1409655203

What that rift signifies is that a likely comprehensive victory of the presidential forces may be followed by a more serious power struggle in which the Radicals and the Popular Front may find common cause. The struggle will be affected by three key factors.

First, it may depend on the long-term results of the 5 September battle of Ilovaisk, which marked the intrusion of regular Russian army units into the Ukrainian conflict, as well a decisive turn in the war. Will Poroshenko continue the conflict and try to retain Donetsk and Luhansk – as well as regain Crimea – at some future point, or will he seek a compromise solution with Russian president Vladimir Putin?

Second, and related to the first question, will the Ukrainian president permit either the loss of the eastern territories or the federalisation of Ukraine? Clearly Yatseniuk will not entertain either option, and at the recent YES conference, he took a much more uncompromising position when he declared that the goal of Putin was the 'elimination' of Ukraine.[118]

Third, can Ukraine, with or without the eastern regions and Crimea, recover from the devastating economic crisis that now embraces it? Valeria Hontareva, Chairperson of the National Bank of Ukraine, estimates that over this year, the GDP will decline by as much as 10%, much higher than original forecasts, and that the ratio of debt to GDP may rise to 73% by next year, compared to 43% in 2013).[119] Added to the costs of war, thousands of refugees, and the direct impact of the conflict on East Ukrainian industry, one can anticipate acrimonious and bitter debates in the new Parliament. And clearly, the new Parliament must deal decisively with corruption and introduce new and substantial reforms, and not simply to satisfy the demands of the IMF.

Nevertheless, a new Parliament is badly needed. In the short term, at least it will bolster the position of Poroshenko and increase the credibility of the new Ukrainian leadership among the public. Yet with the division of the Euromaidan forces, it will face before long two serious dilemmas. First, if too many concessions are made to the Russians, there will be potential for the formation of a more radical bloc of deputies, including both Yatseniuk's forces and those of the Radical right (Lyashko, Tiahnybok, Dmytro Yarosh, and leaders of the volunteer military formations), raising the possibility of a new Euromaidan. And second, there is the question of accommodating the

---

[118] http://www.dw.de/Yatseniuk-accuses-putin-of-aiming-to-eliminate-ukraine/a-17919606

[119] http://online.wsj.com/articles/ukraine-economy-battered-as-fighting-resumes-despite-cease-fire-1410627836; and Ash, 14 September 2014

southern and eastern regions that were unhappy with Euromaidan and feel unrepresented in the current leadership.

Much of this electorate opposes a Russian invasion or separation; but it needs to be convinced why it should show allegiance to Kyiv. Lastly there is the sinister presence of Vladimir Putin and his obdurate and Gromyko-like Foreign Minister Sergey Lavrov (ironically, he is of Georgian-Armenian background), who have at times seemed to favour Poroshenko over other opponents during the conflict (especially during the presidential elections) and who seek to expand Russia's influence over Ukraine by any means.

At the minimum, for any kind of rapprochement with a government run by Poroshenko's forces, they will demand a neutral Ukraine that commits itself neither to NATO nor the European Union, meaning in effect a Ukraine that falls firmly within the Russian sphere of influence. No Ukrainian leader is likely to survive such concessions; but likewise, none can avoid the question of how to counter Russia or deal with its president. In this respect, the 'defection' of Yatseniuk, one of the ablest politicians in the Rada, is a serious blow, though not one that will have a serious impact on the Poroshenko Bloc's chances of victory.

19

The Snipers' Massacre in Kyiv

23 October 2014

On 17 October, at a symposium on 'Negotiating Borders' organised by the Canadian Institute of Ukrainian Studies at the University of Alberta, Ivan Katchanovski, an Ottawa-based scholar, presented a paper on 'The "Snipers' Massacre" on the Maidan in Ukraine'. He argued that leaders of the Maidan gained power as a result of a massacre organised by their own supporters, using as evidence video footage, TV and Internet broadcasting, and radio intercepts, as well as bullet holes, in trees and other places.[120]

The paper was received rather coldly. Indeed, Bohdan Harasymiw, one of the organisers of the conference, ignoring the usual politeness one might expect would be accorded to a guest speaker, derided the paper as having neither theory nor analysis, while another participant from the host institution, Taras Kuzio, dismissed Katchanovski personally as an anti-Ukrainian, noting that his opinions mirrored those of Vladimir Putin and Russian propaganda organs.

On the other hand, after the appearance of this paper on a Facebook site, Volodymyr Ishchenko, who offers analysis on Ukrainian politics from a leftist perspective, described it as an important study, commenting: 'This is the most documented and coherent interpretation of Feb 20 events I've seen so far…. And, of course, if it was proven that the incumbent government came to power in [sic!] the result of a huge bloody provocation, it must have political consequences'.

A reading of this 29-page paper would therefore seem warranted. As preliminary comments, one notes some oddities about this paper. On three

---

[120] http://www.academia.edu/8776021/The_Snipers_Massacre_on_the_Maidan_in_Ukraine

occasions the author refers to it as an 'academic' study. It is not. It is an unpublished research paper that has not yet been peer reviewed. That is evident from its layout, which is a chaotic listing of facts, one after the other, often in a very confusing manner. An editor would have asked the author to highlight the important facts and say why they are significant.

An editor would also have suggested the removal of passages that are completely off topic, such as the author's allusion (p. 28) to crimes committed by Nazis, the Organisation of Ukrainian Nationalists (OUN), and the Ukrainian Insurgent Army (UPA) in the Second World War, which are compared directly, without the addition of a single date, to deaths in Odesa and Donbas in 2014.

Moreover, the paper appears politically driven, i.e. it sets out to prove that the change of regime in Kyiv last spring was illegitimate and that a democratically elected president (however corrupt) was forced out of power by a rightist-orchestrated coup. The conclusion is a veritable jumble of illogical reasoning and statements that do not seem warranted by the findings, which are themselves confusing, as will be noted below. Here is one example:

> *The seemingly irrational mass shooting and killing of protesters and the police on February 20 [2014] appear to be rational from the self-interest based perspectives of rational choice and Weberian theories of instrumentally rational action.*

What these Weberian theories are, the reader is left to ponder.

Katchanovski declares that the massacre of protesters and police 'represented a violent overthrow of the government in Ukraine and a major human rights crime' (p.29). After denouncing the 'violent overthrow' as the root cause of all that followed, he makes another remarkable statement. While the evidence shows that both the Maidan opposition and the 'far right' were clearly carrying out the killing of the 100-plus innocents in the square: 'the involvement of the special police units in killings of some of the protesters *cannot be entirely ruled out* based on publicly available evidence' (p. 29) [my italics]. So, were they involved or not?

The meat of the paper is a long chronicle of who was shooting from where and at whom. But it is very difficult to follow and the blurry photographs included do not help very much. At one point the author notes that the pro-Maidan snipers were holed up in Hotel Ukraina. On page 7, for example (lines 1-3) we read that, based on video evidence, two protesters were shot from this direction, one with 7.62mm bullet, and one wounded 'in his backside'. Further, on page 25 (lines 1-2), there is a firm statement that 'the types of guns and ammunition used and the direction and type of the entry wound among both protesters and policemen also confirm that the shooters came from the Maidan side' (p. 25).

Yet on page 26, the author cites a parliamentary commission report that the police on the Maidan were shot by firearms and ammunition that protesters stole from the police after raids on various arsenals in Western Ukraine. So how is it possible to determine the perpetrators if both had access to the same types of weapons? They could indeed have been members of the Right Sector. They could also have been police agents. We have no names or identities.

On page 19, one reads about gunfire from the Kozatskyi Hotel and from the Trade Union building, as well as from the Main Post Office (p. 20). On this same page, the author cites a statement by an 'unidentified intruder' to Internal Troops that people were 'aiming a rocket propelled grenade launcher into the Hotel Ukraina from the 6th floor of the Trade Union building'. Assuming one wants to accept this statement as evidence, were they shooting at their own snipers? And hotels are rather large places; it seems unlikely that either side would completely occupy or control a building as large as Hotel Ukraina. The author informs (p. 15) us that ABC News reporters were based here, for example. There are other apparent anomalies. If the massacre and subsequent events constituted a coup by the Right Sector, then why are its supporters not in power today? One recalls their unceremonious eviction from the Hotel Dnipro on 1 April 2014.[121] Can one have a successful coup that does not result in a takeover of power by the perpetrators?

If these events constituted simply a violent overthrow of a democratically elected regime, other things need explaining too: the subsequent holding of presidential and (forthcoming) parliamentary elections; and the explanation of why former President Yanukovych had been preparing for several days (if not weeks) to leave his residence, as evidenced by the fleets of vehicles moving his goods from Mezhyhirya. It was not a sudden departure forced by the threat of his capture. Central Kyiv after all is 12 miles away.

Not all of Dr. Katchanovski's findings should be dismissed. He has raised some compelling evidence that suggests new investigations into the sniper massacres are much needed. The official version of events is indeed deeply troublesome and his gathering of new material is commendable. His paper does provide evidence that there were several separate groups of snipers, including anti-government ones.

---

[121] http://www.foreignpolicy.com/articles/2014/04/01/ukraines_unfinished_revolution

The problem is that while the paper is not devoid of analysis, Bohdan Harasymiw's comments were unjustified in this respect, it appears to be based on preconceived conclusions, all heavily weighted against the supporters of Maidan and the current government of Ukraine. In short it reads less like an academic paper and more like a polemic that addresses its findings in an unsatisfactory and unconvincing manner.

Virtually anyone interested in Ukraine with access to the Internet watched live feeds of the unprovoked police violence of 30 November and 1 December 2013, which in the eyes of many Kyiv locals transformed the protests from 'Euromaidan' to a 'Revolution of Dignity'. As subsequent election results corroborated, peaceful supporters of Euromaidan heavily outnumbered the violent activists of Right Sector and other forces. The protests and the attempt to form a more democratic government based on popular support must be given their due before any analysis of why events turned so violent.

That statement in no way implies that the new government was universally popular, or that Euromaidan was welcomed in all parts of Ukraine. Nor does it suggest that right-wing forces were not growing and problematic.

The author's depiction of such groups seeking to benefit from the mass protests and use them as a means of taking power, even to the point of killing their own fellow demonstrators on the square, is an important issue. But the paper doesn't debate this question; it simply assumes it as a given fact, in a conclusion that seems somewhat divorced from the rest of the paper.

It would have been advisable for the author to focus on his findings and offer some preliminary assessments as to what they might mean. If the reader discerns that the apparent purpose of a paper is to discredit and malign the current government, then it ipso facto becomes a political tract (and moreover one that appears to fall closely into line with the RT version of events disseminated in the Russian Federation), which then leads to suspicions about its methodology. A more objective approach is needed. Without it, even the most startling revelations will not receive serious attention.

20

The People's Republics Cast Their Votes

2 November 2014

The 2nd of November was election day in Donbas, the second election in the history of the 'People's Republics' of Donetsk and Luhansk (henceforth the DNR and LNR). On 12 May 2014, following referendums the previous day, the republics declared their independence from Ukraine. Ukraine's acting president at that time, Oleksandr Turchynov, referred to these elections as a 'sham' and the Western governments maintained that they violated international law.

Much has happened over the past six months. Following the takeover of eastern cities by armed militias, a lengthy conflict developed in which the Ukrainian army fought against pro-Russian leaders in what was termed by Kyiv an 'anti-terrorist operation' More than 4,000 died before the two sides agreed to a ceasefire on 5 September that was brokered by Ukraine, Russia, and the OSCE, and held in Minsk, under the unlikely mediation of Belarusian president Aliaksandr Lukashenka.

The resulting document was known as the Minsk Protocol. It permitted 'special status' for Ukraine's two breakaway republics, the creation of a security zone on the Ukrainian-Russian border, the removal from the area of 'unlawful military formations', and the holding of pre-term local elections. It was signed on behalf of the OSCE by the Swiss diplomat Heidi Tagliavini, by former president Leonid Kuchma for Ukraine, and for Russia by its Ambassador to Ukraine, Mikhail Zurabov – who together formed what was called, somewhat clumsily, the Trilateral Contact Group. Below their signatures, with a slight spacing in between, were those of DNR leader

Aleksandr Zakharchenko and LNR leader Igor Plotnitskiy.[122]

At a follow-up meeting two weeks later, the parties agreed to a 30-kilometre (18.5 mile) buffer zone between the two sides, and bans on offensive operations and military flights over the area.[123] The ceasefire, however, barely held, and shortly afterward a new conflict arose for control of the Donetsk airport, which unlike the capital city of the region has remained in the hands of the Ukrainian forces. The DNR leader Zakharchenko expressed his wish to recapture cities and towns lost during the ATO advance (particularly Slaviansk and Kramatorsk), which preceded a direct Russian intrusion into the conflict – as opposed to earlier Russian support for the rebels, which has always been fiercely denied by Moscow. Zakharchenko also wished to capture the port of Mariupol, the second largest city in Donetsk Oblast.[124]

The Kyiv government under President Petro Poroshenko maintains that the DNR and LNR elections violate the Minsk Protocol.[125] The Ukrainians fear that Zakharchenko and Plotnitskiy plan to renew the conflict and remove their regions permanently from Ukraine. Following the Ukrainian parliamentary elections of 26 October, pro-EU parties dominate the assembly, and the opposition, which includes former members of the Donbas-based Regions Party, has been reduced to a bloc of 29 seats, shorn of its former heartland of Crimea and the two major Donbas cities. The result isolates the DNR and LNR, but also offers the disputed republics an opportunity to forge a new path toward independence or union with Russia.

Oddly the two breakaway enclaves do not work in unison. There were even differences in how the elections were conducted. In the DNR, those 16 or over were permitted to vote, whereas in the LNR the minimum age was 18. Moreover, there were other oddities that reflected the makeshift nature of the event. Since a large part of the two republics remains under Ukrainian control, residents were allowed to vote on the Internet. Five polling stations were opened for refugees from the area in three regions of Russia: Rostov, Voronezh, and Belgorod. There was no registration list of voters and in the LNR voting was extended until 10pm, allegedly because of lengthy line-ups at polling stations.[126] Armed militia present in the area were also allowed to vote.[127]

---

[122] http://www.osce.org/ru/home/123258?download=true
[123] http://www.bbc.com/news/world-europe-29290246
[124] http://news.rin.ru/eng/news///68375/)
[125] http://www.citynews.net.ua/news/37929-poroshenko-schitaet-chto-vybory-lnr-i-dnr-stavyat-pod-ugrozu-peremirie.html
[126] http://e.itar-tass.com/world/757386
[127] http://www.dw.de/separatist-controlled-regions-of-eastern-ukraine-go-to-the-

Over 3.1 million residents were declared eligible to vote for the 'People's Councils' and for their respective republican leaders. From exit polls, however, it was clear that Aleksandr Zakharchenko had a healthy lead over his two rivals in the DNR, Aleksandr Kofman (first deputy prime minister of the so-called parliament of Novorossiya), and Yurii Sivokonenko (a veteran of the Berkut special police forces). Zakharchenko's party, Movement of the Donetsk Republic, likewise was well ahead of its rival Free Donbass, led by Yevgenniy Orlov.[128] In Luhansk, Plotnitskiy was leading his 'rivals' Oleg Akimov, the leader of the Federation of Trade Unions, and Viktor Penner, a businessman who was born in the city.[129]

All factions declared their wish for peace and offered humanitarian aid to their lands and the restoration of 'normal life'. Voter turnout was declared to be very high – over 50% in the LNR.[130] The Russian Federation gave its backing to the elections even before the vote took place and declared that they did not violate the Minsk Protocol.[131] The Ukrainian side reported also that at the time of the elections, Russia was sending troops and heavy weapons into the rebel-held territories.[132] The ostensible goal was to ensure that the elections ran smoothly without provocations.

The DNR and LNR are essentially makeshift entities that are unlikely to achieve international recognition anytime in the near future. Most residents of Ukraine do not believe that they represent a majority of voters even in the territories under their control. According to a recent survey conducted by the International Foundation for Electoral Systems, on the other hand, only 15% of Ukrainians are satisfied with Poroshenko's handling of the conflict in the east, despite general confidence in the president (68%) and his coalition partner Arsenii Yatseniuk (60%). In Donbas itself, 94% 'believe the situation [has become] definitely or somewhat worse' over the past six months.[133] The dissatisfaction reflects mostly the economic decline of this old industrial centre.

The DNR and LNR leaders' real problem is their perceived (even self-perceived) lack of legitimacy. They are trying in painstaking fashion to carve

---

polls/a-18035057
[128] http://en.itar-tass.com/world/757892
[129] http://en.itar-tass.com/world/757913
[130] http://www.pravda.ru/news/world/formerussr/ukraine/02-11-2014/1233896-donbass-0/
[131] http://www.pravda.ru/news/world/formerussr/ukraine/30-10-2014/1233439-minsk-0/
[132] http://www.inquisitr.com/1580820/russia-sending-more-troops-heavy-weapons-into-ukraine-as-conflict-intensifies/
[133] http://www.ifes.org/Content/Publications/Press-Release/2014/IFES-2014-Ukraine-Survey-Press-Release.aspx

out the symbols of a separatist government, with a central bank and taxation office, and forcing locals to register their businesses and pay their taxes to the breakaway regimes rather than to Kyiv. The businesses in question are obliged to comply in order to avoid dissolution or bankruptcy.[134] Already Zakharchenko has declared his wish to sell coal to Ukraine and that his region would refuse to deliver coal to the cities of Kharkiv and Lviv without payment.[135] How much coal is actually being produced under the current circumstances is a moot point.

Yet Zakharchenko and Plotnitskiy are at best compromise figures who have taken over from the former Russian leaders who were in place during the summer. Their chief asset is that they are natives of their regions, unlike Igor Girkin (Strelkov) – an outsider who had played a role for the Russian Federation in several earlier conflicts, or the Russian-born Valery Bolotov, Plotnitskiy's predecessor in the LNR. The new leaders embrace the concept of Novorossiya, initially espoused by Russian president Vladimir Putin after the takeover of Crimea last March, but it is a symbolic and distant goal, given the economic collapse of Donbas following the severe battles and shelling.

Ultimately, the survival of the DNR and LNR depends on the degree of Russian support, not only military, but also material. The attitude of Moscow toward them has been somewhat ambivalent. During the summer, Girkin came very close to complete defeat, fleeing with his troops from Slaviansk in busses. In the last two weeks of August, however, Russian intervention changed the course of the war around Ilovaisk, forcing Poroshenko to seek terms after serious losses of troops.[136]

Yet the level of Russia's direct involvement has remained limited for a number of reasons. Moscow recognises the unpopularity of a full-scale invasion, and that outside Donbas, residents are loyal, even fiercely loyal, to Ukraine despite the economic hardships brought by the Yanukovych presidency and the war. Donbas itself is a complex case: it has long been suspicious of the nationalism in the western regions of Ukraine and of the Euromaidan and its consequences. It has seen the rule of clans and oligarchs, and the deep corruption of Yanukovych and leaders of the former Regions Party. It has also been at the heart of the decline of Ukraine's traditional industries: coal, steel, and chemicals. It has often expressed its differences from both Kyiv and

---

[134] http://www.reuters.com/article/2014/10/30/us-ukraine-crisis-east-idUSKBN0IJ22G20141030
[135] http://zarusskiy.org/novoross/2014/10/30/prodavat-ugol/print/
[136] See, for example, http://www.nybooks.com/blogs/nyrblog/2014/sep/05/ukraine-catastrophic-defeat/

Moscow, its uniqueness and multinationalism.[137]

Many voters have no doubt would prefer that order and stability should be attained at all costs, but the regimes of self-appointed gangster leaders in military uniforms are more likely to bring lawlessness, chaos, and potential starvation. On the other hand, while the Ukrainian government may not have lost these regions permanently, after the ATO-led attacks and tragic losses it may be some time before it can convince residents that it represents the ideal alternative. It has not in fact offered such a choice, preferring instead to embrace the European project to take Ukraine out of Moscow's orbit. In turn, the cynical policies of Vladimir Putin seem geared to promote further conflict to undermine the Kyiv government rather than seeking solutions.

The 6.5 million residents of Donbas now face a winter in dire conditions. Their homeland is a devastated war zone, mostly without water, power, or heating, and often without a ready supply of nutritious food. The victories of Zakharchenko and Plotnitskiy offer little respite and seem more likely to exacerbate their dilemma than to provide any viable solutions.

---

[137] See the poignant essay by Hanna Perekhoda at http://www.europe-solidaire.org/spip.php?article32923

21

Poroshenko's Choices after the Parliamentary Elections

11 November 2014

After almost six months in power, Ukraine's president Petro Poroshenko appears to have strengthened his position following the victory of pro-Western parties in the 25 October parliamentary elections. In theory, he can now turn to address, through a new parliamentary coalition, the two most pressing problems: the breakaway regions of Donbas; and radical economic reforms. Concerning the former, he has already responded firmly to the 'elections' one week ago: they were illegal and the Luhansk and Donetsk 'People's Republics' (LNR and DNR) violated the Minsk Protocol signed in September.[138]

Poroshenko's position, however, is weaker than it might appear.

In the first place, whether or not the 'elections' in the DNR and LNR broke the Minsk Protocol, the accords themselves represented a form of recognition for regimes that can at best be termed 'thugocracies', and which are unsustainable in the long term. Even if those regimes should manage to expand their territories to capture Mariupol, or towns that were once under their control like Slaviansk, they cannot survive without support from Ukraine for such basic commodities as food and water. Yet in order to reach an agreement that would halt the advance of Russian regular troops, the Ukrainian side recognised de facto the existence of the two Donbas regimes when they also signed the Protocol in Minsk on 5 September.[139]

---

[138] http://ukr.segodnya.ua/politics/pnews/psevdovybory-v-donbasse-resheniya-ukrainy-i-reakciya-zapada-566025.html
[139] http://www.osce.org/home/123257

Second, while the Ukrainian parliamentary elections of 25 October were hailed in Western media circles as a triumph for pro-European forces, they were probably not such an unqualified success in the eyes of Poroshenko. The turnout was woefully low by Ukrainian standards at 52%, even accounting for the difficulties in voting in some regions, signifying the weariness of the electorate. Moreover, the popular success of Prime Minister Arsenii Yatseniuk's People's Front, which received a higher percentage of electoral support than the president's Petro Poroshenko Bloc,[140] may have secured the coalition, but also represents a potential divergence of official goals. Yatseniuk took a more militant position in his election campaign than Poroshenko, and the People's Front became known as 'the party of war', with a more militant anti-separatist stance.

During the formation of the parliamentary coalition, the duties of the victorious parties have been carefully divided, with the Poroshenko Bloc reportedly occupied with constitutional, budget, and infrastructural reforms, and the People's Front concerned with national security and defence. Also involved is the new Self-Reliance Party headed by the former Lviv mayor Andrii Sadovyi, whose area of concern is energy independence and reforms of the agro-industrial complex. Still, there are prognoses that the coalition might be short-lived and even the most ardent reformers might struggle to implement their goals because of the economic situation in which the country now finds itself.

The national currency, the hryvnia, has fallen dramatically (it was trading at over 14Hr to $1 on 7 November)[141] and Ukraine has lost several important industrial bases since the spring of 2014. Currently, 40% of the national budget is devoted to debt repayments and servicing,[142] and the GDP has fallen by an estimated one-third over 2014.[143] The only solace is the achievement of an agreement on reduced prices for Russian gas, as a result of discussions between Ukraine, Russia, and the European Union,[144] but the country remains the third largest purchaser of Russian gas after Germany and Turkey.[145]

The third factor limiting the optimism after the elections is desire to end the period of corruption in Ukraine, which in the past was identified with former president Viktor Yanukovych and his Regions Party. But the new president,

---

[140] http://www.bbc.co.uk/ukrainian/politics/2014/10/141029_electoral_geography_sx
[141] http://economics.unian.ua/finance/1006462-grivnya-na-mijbanku-prodovjue-padati-1496-za-dolar.html
[142] http://www.day.kiev.ua/ru/article/podrobnosti/osobennosti-nacionalnoy-koaliciady-0.
[143] http://news.finance.ua/ua/news/~/336785
[144] http://news.finance.ua/ua/news/~/337577
[145] http://www.rferl.org/content/russian-gas-how-much-gazprom/25442003.html

unlike Yatseniuk, can hardly shed his status as an oligarch who was successful in exploiting the post-Soviet transition to develop highly profitable business interests. The avoidance of the perception of Poroshenko as 'part of the problem' rather than a solution may depend on his willingness to take on fellow oligarchs in cleansing the system of government and business that has plagued Ukraine since independence. *The Guardian* newspaper has already delineated Poroshenko as a 'reformist' oligarch,[146] but removing these powerful figures without bringing economic and social upheaval will be hard to achieve.

It is the east that surely occupies most of the president's waking hours. The parliamentary elections succeeded in eliminating the influence of Regions, Communists, and other parties that might be called pro-Russian or Soviet-nostalgic, representing that part of the electorate that seemed wedded to the Soviet legacy, as well as the most corrupt of Ukraine's business clans. The Parliament no longer includes the parties that dominated Donbas for the past two decades. The new situation appears to give the president a mandate to carry out substantial changes that can take Ukraine along a new path, yet Poroshenko in reality has minimal options as to the direction the Ukrainian state can take because of external factors that are largely beyond his control.

First of all, the Western powers seem, quietly, to have shelved the Ukrainian question. Their position was reflected on 9 November by the departing Ukrainian ambassador to Canada, Vadym Prystaiko, who commented bitterly that the West was no longer interested in Ukraine, and its fear of Russia precluded any real forthcoming aid. By contrast, he noted, the West was much swifter to take the fight to the Islamic State in Iraq: 'You're bombing, you're sending F-18s... Iraq's government is asking for help and you're sending everything. Then the Ukrainian government asks you the same... and you tell us what? No'.[147]

The United States seems resolved to perceive the Ukrainian crisis as a European issue, a priority of Brussels, rather than Washington. Yet the Europeans are also divided, with leaders of some states, most notably the Czech Republic, Slovakia, and Hungary, demanding that the sanctions on Russia be lifted. Other 'friends' of the West are joining the chorus, and even former Soviet president Mikhail Gorbachev felt obliged to comment during the 25th anniversary celebrations of the collapse of the Berlin Wall that the Western powers should take into account Vladimir Putin's comments at the recent Valdai Discussion Club. These remarks, stated Gorbachev, reflected a

---

[146] http://www.dialog.ua/news/25136_1414481321
[147] http://www.cbc.ca/news/politics/vadym-prystaiko-says-west-losing-interest-in-ukraine-1.2827717

desire for a reduction of tensions and eventually a new partnership with the West.[148]

Concerning relations with Russia, Poroshenko has made concessions that weaken his domestic standing. As noted by a team of Belarusian analysts, Ukraine has postponed the introduction of trade issues in Ukraine's Association Agreement (Title IV: Trade and Trade-Related Matters) with the EU and retained a Ukrainian presence in the Free Trading Area of the Commonwealth of Independent States (CIS). The postponement may allow Russia to interpret any changes in the provisions of Title IV as a violation of the agreements with Moscow, to be penalised through heightened import duties. The analysts note also that the prospects of Ukraine joining NATO, though more popular than in the past, has few prospects of success at present, and maintain that the most likely scenario for Ukraine is a delay of both moves toward the EU and radical reforms – they term it a 'mothballing' of the current socio-political system for several more years.[149]

As winter approaches, the prospects for a resolution of the conflict in the east seem dim. The rump states of the DNR and LNR remain, with their gangster-style leaders trying to form the semblance of state structures. Over the past week, convoys of tanks have entered these territories from Russia,[150] suggesting that the Russian Federation, while not committing itself to all-out war, intends to continue its protection of these quasi-regimes, which are too weak to stand alone. Poroshenko's halting of the ATO attacks followed the catastrophic defeat at Ilovaisk, which although not decisive – the Ukrainian army per se was not destroyed – proved to be a psychological setback that demonstrated the prospects of restoring Ukrainian rule in Donbas were slim. It has also provoked much soul-searching as to its causes.[151]

Moreover, despite the significant reduction of separatist territory over the summer, not all the Messianism of the so-called Novorossiya movement has dissipated. On 9 November, the 'newly elected' leader of the DNR, Aleksandr Zakharchenko decorated the notorious former Defence Minister of the DNR Igor Girkin (Strelkov) with the title 'Hero of the DNR'.[152] The ceremony suggested not only that the current leaders of the breakaway regions wish to create their own heroic legends, but also that their ambitions may go beyond the more cautious approach of the Russian leadership in Moscow, which has

---

[148] http://en.ria.ru/russia/20141108/195321770/Gorbachev-Urges-West-to-Lift-Sanctions-Consider-Putins-Valdai.html
[149] http://belinstitute.eu/en/print/2246
[150] http://galinfo.com.ua/news/176302.html
[151] http://tyzhden.ua/Society/122995
[152] http://vlasti.net/news/205908

studiously ignored Girkin since his departure from Ukraine.

The Donbas conflict has also raised a pressing problem of displaced persons. Some residents, as demonstrated in the DNR and LNR 'elections' when they were permitted to vote, moved to Russia, but many more dispersed throughout Ukraine. In Dnipropetrovsk, their numbers had reached 400,000 by late October, prompting governor Ihor Kolomoiskyi to declare that he would not permit a repeat of the tragedy in wartime Leningrad in the winter of 1941.[153] The lack of water, heating, and food supplies in several towns of Luhansk still under Ukraine's control is being exacerbated by constant attacks by forces of the LNR.[154]

But the question that faces Poroshenko most urgently is how to satisfy an electorate that has first voted him into power and now has endorsed a pro-European parliament. There is no gate to the West waiting for him to open, let alone prospects for Ukraine promptly joining the European Union or NATO.[155] The Western powers have rejected his request for weapons to continue fighting, and his forces are ill-equipped to recapture Donbas. The displaced persons factor adds to Ukraine's economic woes. It is unlikely that Poroshenko perceives the future with the same euphoria with which many Western governments greeted the sweeping victory of the pro-EU and reformist parties in Ukraine. The new coalition will require a delicate balancing act that may test even this most polished of political leaders.

---

[153] http://ua.korrespondent.net/ukraine/3436057-dnipropetrovska-oblast-chekaie-naplyvu-bizhentsiv-z-donbasu-cherez-kholody
[154] http://tvi.ua/new/2014/11/08/cherez_obstrily_terorystiv_chastyna_luhanschyny_zalyshylasya_bez_svitla_hazu_i_vody
[155] See, for example, the remarks of former US ambassador to Ukraine, Steven Pifer: http://nationalinterest.org/feature/compromise-over-ukraine-will-be-hard-11629

22

Minsk-2

13 February 2015

The peace agreement reached after sixteen hours of talks in Minsk between the French and German leaders, Vladimir Putin, and Petro Poroshenko represents the second attempt to stop the fighting in Donbas. Quickly, analysts assailed it or offered faint praise and even Angel Merkel, Chancellor of Germany, the leader of the initiative, would say only that it offers a 'glimmer of hope'.

The first point to be noted is that Minsk-2 does not supersede Minsk-1, which remains in effect though neither side has followed its mandates very closely. Before offering an assessment, one should examine briefly its contents.

Minsk-2 agreed to a ceasefire by midnight on 14 February and the removal of heavy weapons from the conflict zone within sixteen days, with an exchange of POWs over the following three weeks. There have been cynical comments in the Western media as to how an immediate ceasefire could take two days, but in fact the original text does not contain the word 'immediate', it states 'not slowly'.

Ukraine is to retain control over the separatist regions of Donetsk and Luhansk, but must grant them more autonomy, and by the end of 2015, the country is to restore its control over the border with Russia.

Concerning the first point, the time lag is dangerous, because it allows both sides to consolidate their positions and in the separatists' case to try to capture the strategic town of Debaltseve, which constitutes a Ukrainian salient in rebel-held territory. Debaltseve is on the main highway M-04 between Donetsk and Luhansk, but more importantly it is a rail junction. Its capture would allow the rebels to transport coal from the mines to consumers.

The logistics of monitoring the agreement have been left to the Organisation for Security and Co-operation in Europe (OSCE), which lacks the numbers to do so efficiently at present. Moreover, over the past year the OSCE has had considerable difficulty in accessing areas held by the rebels. Since Minsk-1 was so flagrantly ignored, one cannot assume that the same fate will not befall Minsk-2, particularly if the separatists believe that they can strengthen their position.

Neither Ukraine nor the Donetsk People's Republic (DNR) and Luhansk People's Republic (LNR) emerge as winners from the agreement. Ukraine has effectively conceded some sovereignty over the eastern regions, and the subject of Crimea is excluded. Ukraine has also agreed to lift restrictions imposed on these areas, which on paper at least can now receive goods from Ukraine and restore regular trading practices.

For President Poroshenko, the difficult task now arises of getting the constitutional changes through a parliament that is much more radical in the absence of its former Regions and Communist delegates. The deal moreover implicitly recognises the DNR and LNR, habitually referred to by the Ukrainian government as 'terrorist' regimes. The Ukrainian president increasingly cuts an isolated figure, forced to take a moderate line in order that an agreement could be reached, traveling frequently to European capitals in search of support, and distancing himself from what might be termed the Euromaidan factions in Kyiv that would prefer a more confrontational approach.

The conflict, which has taken thousands of lives over the past months, and has escalated sharply over the winter, has never been confined to Kyiv and Donbas. Many Western analysts believe that Vladimir Putin is entirely to blame for its longevity and intensification, both by providing advanced lethal weaponry to the separatists and for encouraging 'volunteers' (his term) to join in the fight against the Ukrainian ATO.

Putin in turn claims heavy US involvement both in Euromaidan and the ATO operation. Western analysts in contrast often chide Barack Obama for his reluctance to confirm the US Congress' decision to send lethal defensive weapons to the Ukrainians. And US Senator John McCain constitutes his own personal war cabinet, threatening to send weapons, with or without the consent of his president.

The arguments in favour of providing lethal weapons to Ukraine seem dubious. What weapons and how many? Will advisors and technicians also be sent to assist Ukrainian forces in using them? What response would there be to further Russian buildup and escalation to what will be perceived as

NATO's move into Ukraine? Logically there would be little to dissuade Moscow from endorsing much heavier troop movements over the border.

The Ukrainian Army has not elicited confidence among the citizens it purports to defend, particularly not from those in Donbas subject to regular shelling from both sides in the shambles that used to be their hometowns. The coal-mining areas were grim places at the best of times, but now they have become a devastated war zone. The officers are still transplants of the former Soviet army, many are corrupt, and perceive the war as a way to make profits.

Poroshenko thus relies heavily on volunteer battalions whose loyalty to the government is shaky at best. Some speak of another Euromaidan to deal with the government once the conflict in the east is over.

Both Ukraine and Russia need some breathing room, mainly to restore their economies. In this respect, Minsk-2 constitutes a respite. And Ukraine's position was improved by a $17.5 billion loan from the IMF, which covers approximately half of its current debts, but tranches of that loan will be forthcoming only under certain conditions, namely stability, reforms, and stringent economic policies, and above all a reduction (only the most naïve would demand 'the end of') corruption.

None of this is to say that the deal should be belittled or ridiculed. Merkel and Hollande did their best. Several months ago, I suggested that Ukraine might cut its losses, abandoning Donbas and Crimea, providing that the rump state remaining could apply to join NATO and be slowly integrated into European structures. That remains, I still believe, one alternative, but it would be small consolation to those seeking to retain the integrity of the 1991 state and its borders, which Russia recognised not once, but at least three times in various treaties (1990, 1994, and 1997).

It would moreover leave Donbas in the hands of the DNR and LNR, both of which are led by Russian security officials and freebooters, gangsters and militant locals. Some of the first group took part in earlier separatist movements, including in Transnistria in the early 1990s. They have few moral scruples and no recognition for an independent Ukrainian state. There is no benefit to Ukraine, short or long term, in dealing with the DNR and LNR, but Poroshenko was obliged to agree to their inclusion in the agreement.

Putin's Russia has consistently violated Ukrainian borders, just as it has done with borders of other states of the former Soviet Union. In this respect, we should lay blame on the Kremlin. On the other hand, the problems of Donbas precede Putin, and they have been exacerbated by the war. Its residents oppose a full-scale Russian invasion; but they are equally angry with the government in Kyiv – a very different issue from whether they would wish to leave Ukraine given the choice.

Ukraine above all needs a backup plan if Minsk-2 fails. It must use the armistice wisely and above all consider some serious questions. Can it retake Donbas without foreign assistance? Can it afford to live without Donbas and Crimea? Would its membership of NATO be guaranteed if it is forced to lose these regions for the immediate future?

If the answers to these questions are no, yes, and yes, then a fourth question, EU membership, might also be placed on the table once extensive and deep reforms are clearly under way. Ukraine, lamentably, needs to resolve not one problem but three: the conflict in the east, relations with Russia, and its failing economy. It is highly doubtful that it can address all three simultaneously.

23

One Year after Euromaidan

23 February 2015

Commemorations of the first anniversary of Euromaidan and the fall of the Yanukovych presidency have been taking place in Ukraine. Conversely, the Russian government and media have indulged in denunciations of the same, including a march through Moscow on 21 February.[156]

It is worthwhile to reflect on the current status of the country and offer an analysis of the conflict, which has taken thousands of lives among both military and the civilian population.

Vladimir Putin, President of Russia, declared on 23 February that Minsk-2 had become a legal document, and that if put into practice, one could envisage stability in eastern Ukraine. He also believes that war between Russia and Ukraine is 'unlikely' and continues to maintain that the Russian army has not taken part in the Donbas conflict.[157] It was his first public statement since the agreement reached in Minsk some ten days ago, which was followed by the rebels' capture of Debaltseve.

Likely both sides need a period of peace at this point. It is a good option for Russia as well as Ukraine. Russia needs to keep communication lines open to Germany, its most important ally in Europe and cannot simply ride roughshod over this agreement. Though it has options elsewhere, its European links remain valuable and are a critical connection to its former republics and satellite states as well as prime purchasers of Russian oil and gas. Putin has never made a secret of his plans for influence over the 'Near Abroad' or the fact that he considers Ukraine part of Russia's past, present, and future.

---

[156] https://meduza.io/feature/2015/02/21/rasserzhennye-patrioty
[157] http://www.bbc.com/news/world-europe-31596634

His comments today appear a fairly accurate reflection of where he stands. Putin postures and derides the government in Kyiv. He is especially dismissive of Euromaidan and the changes that resulted from it and his main goal is to facilitate the fall of the new government of Ukraine or ensure that it is so weak as to be incapable of taking any decisive actions. Both goals do not include a full-scale military invasion, which Russia can neither afford nor accomplish without major losses.

The rebels are in a weaker position than in the summer of 2014 when they held most of the Donetsk and Luhansk oblasts, but stronger than at any time since that time. They have gained control over the two major cities, and defeated Ukrainian forces with the aid of Russian arms and so-called volunteers in two major battles at Donetsk airport and Debaltseve. The latter one gives them control over an important rail link connecting the two towns. It also provides them with a firmer base for future expansion when the possibility arises.

But the rebel governments are dependent on outside help for basic necessities. In no sense do they constitute stable regimes that could prepare, for example for statehood, or even full autonomy. The area they control is a devastated warzone, a situation they as well as the Ukrainian government have brought about, from which it will take years to recover. Neither the DNR nor the LNR has taken the shape of a full-fledged government or indicated any desire to rule rather than fight.

Nevertheless, the rebel leaders, Aleksandr Zakharchenko and Igor Plotnitskiy, have achieved at least partial recognition from Ukraine through Minsk-1 and Minsk-2 and signed both agreements. They have received a promise of special status for their territories that will require Kyiv to amend the Ukrainian Constitution and ratify it through Parliament. Therefore, they can claim a modicum of success. They have come a long way from the time when Ukraine's president Petro Poroshenko announced his refusal to deal with terrorist leaders and initiated the Anti-Terrorist Operation.

By contrast, Poroshenko's position has weakened since his election last June and he is being forced to make unpopular adjustments that seem to contravene the spirit of Euromaidan. And Putin is right in one respect, Ukraine does need to focus on the economy and corruption. Though it has Western support generally, especially from North America, thus far (the IMF loan aside) such aid is largely confined to rhetoric rather than the requested commitment of lethal weapons. At the time Minsk-2 was signed, the United States did seem close such a move, but the question is shelved for as long as the amended peace agreement endures.

The performance of the Ukrainian army is a source of concern not only to the more moderate elements but also to some leaders of the more radical volunteer formations, which believe the country was deceived about the situation in Debaltseve, and that the High Command is in need of overhaul.[158] One can anticipate more demands in the future to strengthen the army and change its leadership. Talk of another Euromaidan is not entirely idle; it could take place without much warning.

The question for Poroshenko as well as for Prime Minister Arsenii Yatseniuk is one of timing. Which should be the first priorities: the return of lost territories, reviving the economy, or dealing with corruption? And how can an overhaul of the leadership of the army take place without addressing first the latter two issues? The first in any case is not on the table unless there is a significant strengthening and arming of the military, thus again a breathing space is vital.

Another question is what exactly is happening in the eastern regions? The Ukrainian leadership has constantly spoken of terrorism but not of civil war. It asserts that Russia has invaded Ukraine, but the reality is that Russia has intervened in support of the two rebel republics, the troops of which have become more professional, ruthless, and brutal with the aid of hardened regular Russian units and some advanced Russian weapons. But even if one takes the much bandied figure of 9,000 Russian soldiers in Ukraine,[159] that figure does not represent an invasion force. Putin's role is critical but the rebel armies have gained in status over the past six months.

Putin has achieved his current goal – to weaken and divide Ukraine, ensure it does not join EU structures and to ensure that there is no chance of it joining NATO. The anti-Euromaidan forces have benefited from a number of factors other than Russian aid, however: divisions within the EU, more manifest now than a year ago; the EU's lack of any kind of military power outside NATO; and Ukraine's weakness as a military power, facilitated ironically by treaties signed after the end of the Soviet Union and guaranteed by the major powers, including Russia but also because of longstanding deficiencies in the higher officer caste.

While the OSCE is the body monitoring the ceasefire and its provisions, to the extent that this is possible, it is the UN that is critical. The UN remains the only organisation recognised worldwide as a legal voice in resolving international conflicts, and Russia, like the United States, has always been a

---

[158] http://www.bbc.co.uk/ukrainian/politics/2015/02/150220_genshtab_criric_criticism_vs

[159] http://il24.ru/ussr/328-poroshenko-2000-rossiyskih-soldat-voshli-v-ukrainu.html

permanent member of its Security Council. Only once did Russia relinquish that right, when its delegates walked out in protest at the lack of recognition of Communist China and were powerless to prevent the decision to go to war against North Korea in 1950. It is unlikely to make that mistake again. The UN is in this respect an important tool and ally for Russia.

For the Ukrainian government, the consolation is that its statehood has been consolidated by the events of the past year. As Yaroslav Hrytsak remarked, the consensus on and faith in an independent Ukraine has moved further to the east,[160] rendering Donbas the last, and possibly only irreconcilable, outpost of separatism. Without doubt it has been mistreated, neglected, and ultimately attacked by the Ukrainian government that purports to control it. Just as many Ukrainians now believe that Russia is a hostile state, similarly many of those who remain in Donbas have lost hope of sympathy and aid from Kyiv.

And while the rest of Ukraine remains firmly in the government camp, loyal residents will demand improvements of living standards, working conditions, and the reduction of corruption in all walks of life. Euromaidan removed a corrupt regime and attained a 'revolution of dignity', but it has engendered new dilemmas and a dangerous and crippling war that constitute much greater problems than faced hitherto in its 24th year of existence.

---

[160] https://ukr.media/politics/225671/

24

Comparing Maidan 2004 with Euromaidan 2014

10 March 2015

Several analysts have examined the links between the so-called Orange Revolution in Ukraine of 2004 and Euromaidan in 2013-14. There were also other earlier mass protests in the Maidan, including one by students in 1990 that played a role in the removal of the then Prime Minister Vitalii Masol. Thus there was something of a tradition of using the Maidan for a mass protest. Both 2004 and 2013-14 focused to some extent on corruption, particularly in the office of the president, though it had reached a much higher scale under Viktor Yanukovych than under Leonid D. Kuchma.

There are, however, more differences than similarities, indicating a lack of continuity rather than a revival of past animosities, and I would single out in brief the following twelve:

First of all, the Orange Revolution was not really a revolution at all. It was an uprising that brought about a change of president through a more accurate counting of votes but not a change of government. That Viktor Yushchenko was such a failure as president derives from several reasons, not least his own incompetence, but there was also a second factor that emphasises the contrast.

In 2004, the European option was a distant hope rather than anything tangible for Ukraine, whereas in November 2013 it appeared to offer a serious alternative to the Russian Customs Union and a common economic space with Russia, Belarus, and Kazakhstan. European unity on Ukraine after Euromaidan did not last and whether the Association Agreement offered a viable alternative is a moot point. Nonetheless, that option was at least on the table.

In 2004, the protests focused on many things but there was always an elite alternative to the government of Kuchma in the persons of Viktor Yushchenko and Yulia Tymoshenko. In 2014, there were no discernible leaders and patently the parliamentary opposition leaders remained marginal figures. Rather there were factions that came to the fore at different times. Essentially there was a total rejection of the leaders within the existing government, as well as significant antagonism to parliamentary parties such as the Regions and Communists.

In 2013-14, the protests were marked by outbursts of extreme violence on the part of both the government and the demonstrators, culminating in the massacre of 21 February 2014. Though there have been exhaustive studies of the influence or non-influence of militant rightist forces in Euromaidan, and clearly these groups were negligible in terms of electability, there seems no doubt that at crucial times they were prepared to force the issue during the periods of confrontation. In this respect, the lessons of 2004 may well have been a factor behind the militancy, i.e. the failure of the Orange events to change fundamentally the power structure of the country.

In Euromaidan, in contrast to the Orange Revolution, the protests outside Kyiv outpaced those in the centre. In various parts of Ukraine pro-Yanukovych local governments and leaders were removed from office.

Russia was a factor in both 2004 and 2013-14. In the earlier events, Vladimir Putin had attempted to influence the outcome of the presidential election and had fully endorsed Yanukovych's campaign beforehand. In 2013, Russia offered an alternative to the Association Agreement and advanced the offer of a substantial loan to Ukraine. The direct intervention of Russia in Crimea followed the removal of Yanukovych from office and Putin insisted that he was protecting Russian language speakers in Ukraine. The question why Russia was prepared to intervene in 2014 but not in 2004 is easily answered: in 2004, while Russia disapproved of the uprising, it did not necessarily signal a complete change of direction in Kyiv and the potential 'loss' of Ukraine to 'Russkiy Mir'.

There was no obvious oligarchic involvement in 2004, perhaps because these personalities were less entrenched in society than a decade later. In 2014, however, several oligarchs supported the cause of Euromaidan and subsequently. The Donbas magnate Rinat Akhmetov ultimately did so as well, and the allegiance of Ihor Kolomoiskyi in Dnipropetrovsk was vital in ensuring that that city remained on the Ukrainian government side when rebels began to take over administrations in the east. And an oligarch politician (hardly a rarity in the parliament), Petro Poroshenko, became the fifth president of Ukraine.

On both occasions, Western powers supported the protests in Ukraine as a progressive and pro-democratic manifestation of the popular will. The extent of US involvement in both uprisings is debatable, but it was manifested much more overtly in 2014 than in 2004 through the appearance in Kyiv of government officials and maverick individuals such as Senator John McCain.

In 2013-14, unlike 2004, social media played a vital role at various times: summoning people to the square, communication – locally, nationally, and internationally – and not least the organisation of factions, sections, military 'hundreds', and relaying information about government responses.

In 2013-14, representation on the square was wider and subject to changes. Analysts detected a youthful pro-European element initially, but after the end of November, and even more so after the short-lived so called dictatorship laws of 16 January 2014, the makeup of the protesters was older, more varied, with significant representation from the centre and east, as well as western Ukraine.

The scale of the 2014 protests was broader and the numbers in the streets significantly higher than in 2004 though they varied between weekdays and weekends.

The Orange Revolution lasted for roughly five weeks. Euromaidan continued after the departure of Yanukovych, though it reached its climax on 21 February 2014, which was thirteen weeks after it began. Regarding contemporary analogous events, it was far longer than the 2011 Revolution in Egypt but shorter in duration than the Libyan civil war of 2011, with which it has sometimes been compared. On the other hand one could make the argument that Euromaidan has not yet ended and may see further revivals as a result of military shortcomings in the war in the east, the failing economy, and not least the sluggishness of the Poroshenko-Yatseniuk leadership in unraveling corruption in society. Clearly the outcome has not yet been determined.

25

Ethnic and Social Composition of Ukraine's Regions and Voting Patterns

11 March 2015

This paper looks at the ethnic and social makeup of Ukrainian regions and its impact on voting patterns over the past two decades. While sceptical of a simplistic division of the country through spoken language and ethnic affiliation, it maintains that there are particular patterns of voting that have been repeated in each presidential and parliamentary election, and that regional voting is the most characteristic feature of Ukrainian elections. At the same time, there are a number of other factors that may affect voting that are not dealt with here, such as the social and economic initiatives of the candidate or party, the social position of the voter, fluctuations in the standard of living, and incentives to vote a particular way.[161]

Upon gaining its independence in 1991, Ukraine had several distinct regions and a number of significant ethnic minorities, most prominent of which were Russians. The only part of Ukraine with a Russian majority was the Autonomous Republic of Crimea, but Russians comprised significant communities in the far eastern oblasts of Donetsk and Luhansk, as well as in Dnipropetrovsk, Odesa, Kharkiv, and others. The far western region of Transcarpathia has a significant Hungarian population, and there are numerous smaller nationalities that have had homes in Ukraine for many generations, such as Poles, Belarusians, and Jews, as well as Bulgarians in the Odesa Oblast in the south.

---

[161] Two of the best studies to appear to date on or related to this topic appeared four years ago: Kulyk (2011) and Colton (2011).

One difficulty about making any sweeping assertions about the composition of the population is the lack of censuses in the independence period. To date there has been a single census in 2001 (the first since 1989), and an anticipated new census in 2010 has been postponed until 2016. That census may also be in doubt given enforced territorial changes in Ukraine, with the Russian annexation of Crimea, and separatist movements in Donetsk and Luhansk, with the establishment here of so-called People's Republics supported by the Russian Federation. The 2001 census indicated mainly the consolidation and growth of the Ukrainian population (77.8%, up from 72.7% in 1989), partly through assimilation and changes in self-identity, and partly through migration, of Russians in particular. The Russian population, correspondingly, declined from 22.1 to 17.3%).[162]

There is a marked difference, however, between ethnic Russians and Russian-speakers, and the latter predominate in the East and South, and maintain a significant presence in all parts of Ukraine other than the far western regions. In 2006-07, research conducted by the Razumkov Centre revealed that the percentage of Ukrainians who considered Russian to be their first language was 25.7% and that 52% of the population considered Ukrainian to be their native language.[163] A more recent study suggests that about 27.5 million 'actively' use Russian language at work and about 37 million (or 80% of the population) has fluency in it. Ten years earlier the figure had been 42 million.[164]

Keith Darden has noted a tendency in Ukrainian elections to continue habits that were familiar in pre-Soviet times. Thus, the former Austrian-Polish territories of Ukraine behave quite differently: supporting pro-Western candidates, adopting strong pro-European Union positions, and fearing Russian influence above all else.[165] These regions are Ukrainian speaking, and have consistently supported pro-Western candidates in presidential elections: Leonid Kravchuk rather than Leonid Kuchma in 1994; but Kuchma rather than the Communist candidate Petro Symonenko in 1999; Yushchenko in 2004; and Tymoshenko in 2010.

The main difference between the pre-Soviet period and today is that ethnic Ukrainians now comprise a majority in urban centres, whereas in the past

---

[162] State Statistics Committee of Ukraine (2001). Incidentally, the former Prime Minister, Mykola Azarov, claimed in 2012 that there were over 20 million Russians in Ukraine! See http://lb.ua/news/2012/06/26/158078_azarov_naschital_ukraine_20_mln.html
[163] http://lenta.ru/news/2007/12/17/language/
[164] Arefev (2013).
[165] Darden (2013).

they were rural, marginalised, and at times disaffected. Many Western Ukrainian cities have adopted a strong nationalistic position and Western Ukrainians played a prominent role in the 2013-14 protests known as the 'Euromaidan'.[166]

Western Ukraine remains the most rural region of Ukraine. Yet its history is the most turbulent and controversial. The integral nationalism of the 1930s, which saw the rise of the Organisation of Ukrainian Nationalists (OUN) with its dictum of 'Ukraine for Ukrainians' and the formation of the Ukrainian Insurgent Army (UPA) during the war (traditionally declared to have taken place in October 1942, but in reality in the spring of 1943) has created many of the legends of current historical memory: a quest for independence and freedom from the Russian-led Soviet Union, and from the incursive Russian Federation today.

The legacy of these formations is controversial. They are accused not only of being anti-Soviet, but pro-Nazi, and anti-Semitic.[167] Though right-wing nationalism has been notably unsuccessful in terms of winning seats in Parliament, many observers perceive significant influence of right extremism during Euromaidan, and in the current war in the eastern regions.[168]

Western Ukraine forms one part of an electoral magnet that has pulled the country in two different directions simultaneously. The other is eastern Ukraine, but more specifically the two far eastern oblasts of Donetsk and Luhansk. Before discussing the characteristics of this region, it should be noted that the term 'eastern Ukraine' was formerly much broader than it appears today. The area was the heartland of industrial development in the Russian Empire, and its traditions were transferred to the Soviet Union during the crucial phase of its industrial development.

It was eastern Ukraine that embraced Stakhanovism in its coalmines in the mid-1930s – a work ethic largely based on 'shock troops' and over-fulfilment of state plans by artificial means. It was also the very centre of the Soviet Communist Party. Former leader Nikita Khrushchev (1964-71) made his career in Donbas, nurtured by his mentor, the Stalinist henchman Lazar Kaganovich. Leonid Brezhnev (Soviet leader 1964-82) was born in Dniprodzherzhinsk, a city named after the first leader of the Soviet secret police (the Cheka), Feliks Dzerzhinsky.

---

[166] One study suggests that about one-third of participants in 2013 came from Western Ukraine. See Nuzhdin et al (2013).

[167] See, for example, Katchanovski (2010).

[168] See, for example, the comments of Cohen (2014).

Not surprisingly, therefore, between 1991 and 1999, the Communist Party of Ukraine remained the most powerful force in the region. But after independence, there was a growing entrepreneurial class that arose from the ashes of Communism, using links to the former Communist leadership to establish private businesses. Bitter competition took place between elites of the cities of Donetsk and Dnipropetrovsk. In the mid-1990s, the latter city was in the ascendancy: Kuchma, the president, had been manager of the rocket-manufacturing plant at Yuzhmash in the region; Pavlo Lazarenko, Prime Minister in 1996-97, had headed the 'agro-industrial complex' of Dnipropetrovsk in the early 1990s, and his Deputy Prime Minister, Yulia Tymoshenko, was born in the city.

The current governor of Dnipropetrovsk, the billionaire Ihor Kolomoiskyi, was originally a supporter of Tymoshenko and her Tymoshenko Bloc in parliament. Today, however, Dnipropetrovsk under Kolomoiskyi's leadership has taken a strong pro-Ukrainian and pro-Western stance, separating it firmly from the staunchly pro-Russian cities of Donetsk and Luhansk.[169]

Donetsk and its region, on the other hand, have been the centre of the rise of the Regions Party, financed by the oligarch Rinat Akhmetov, and personalised by the figure of Viktor Yanukovych, the central figure in the disputed election that brought about the Orange Revolution, and the eventual victory of Viktor Yushchenko. The party's tentacles extended well beyond Donetsk, but the city remained its central location, and the Yanukovych Cabinet formed in 2010 was dominated by Donetsk politicians.

The Party of Regions expanded through financial support of businessmen who exploited the country's assets, manipulated the legal system, controlled banks and businesses, and used parliament as a forum to control the rest of the country.[170] The year 2010 represented the peak of the Regions' power. The party's rise appeared mercurial, but it was facilitated by disillusionment with the Yushchenko's presidency that appeared initially to be about to launch Ukraine on a bold new Western-oriented journey.

Between these two magnets of the West and 'Far East', the rest of Ukraine has not exhibited particularly strong political directions. In 1999, most voters perceived Kuchma as the most viable alternative, although the Communist Symonenko won a respectable 37.8% of the votes. In 2004, in the initial election runoff of the two leading candidates on 21 November, Ukraine was

---

[169] On the other hand, Kolomoiskyi remains a controversial figure, and there are reports that a confrontation between he and Poroshenko is distinctly possible in the near future. See http://rian.com.ua/analytics/20141129/360126913.html

[170] See, for example, Kuzio (2015); and Riabchuk (2012).

divided almost equally between supporters of Yushchenko and Yanukovych (voting manipulations aside). The latter had been endorsed by Vladimir Putin and his election posters appeared in Moscow, as well as Ukraine. The Orange Revolution represented a protest against electoral manipulations and a movement toward Europe. Yet the most notable feature of the second runoff on 26 December 2004 was the lack of districts in which voting was relatively even, despite the fact that Yushchenko won overall with 52%, compared to his rival's 44%.[171] The points are worth elaborating.

In the twenty-seven regions of Ukraine (the cities of Sevastopol and Kyiv each constituted one region), in only one – Kherson – was the voting close (43.4% for Yushchenko and 51.3 for Yanukovych). Elsewhere voters opted for one candidate or the other by large margins, and particularly in the two polarised regions noted above: Western Ukrainians (Galicia and Volhynia) voted over 90% for Yushchenko; the far east over 90% for Yanukovych; Crimea 81.4% for Yanukovych, and Sevastopol 88.8%.

The election demonstrated a fatal divide in Ukrainian society, a lack of middle ground, and heralded the uncertain developments of the future. One cannot examine the 2010 election in the same way because of the deep divisions within the pro-Western, pro-European camp: former president Yushchenko thus campaigned against his former Prime Minister Tymoshenko.

In 2014, on the other hand, electoral politics were simplified and altered fundamentally by the events of the Euromaidan. Two elections were held in this year: the 25 May presidential elections and the 26 October parliamentary elections. Both were affected by protests and the continuing conflict. Crimea did not participate and only about 20% of voters in Donetsk and Luhansk could take part because of restrictions imposed by separatist leaders. The former president, Yanukovych, had been expelled from the ranks of Regions, which was represented by the ineffectual Mykhailo Dobkin, and Symonenko once again headed the Communists.

Petro Poroshenko, a compromise candidate for the pro-Euromaidan factions, won convincingly with 54% of votes in the first round. His nearest challenger was Yulia Tymoshenko, recently released from prison, with 12%. Dobkin received just over 3%; Symonenko 1.5%. Their votes, on the other hand, were well above those of far-right candidates Oleh Tiahnybok (Svoboda) and Dmytro Yarosh (Right Sector) at 1.16% and 0.7% respectively.[172]

---

[171] See Romanyuk, et al (2010).
[172] For the full results, see "Pozacherhovi Vybory Prezydenta Ukrainy" (2014).

The same pattern continued in the parliamentary elections, except that the Petro Poroshenko Bloc and the People's Front, the parties led by the President and Prime Minister (Arsenii Yatseniuk) dominated the vote almost equally. Together with the third-placed party – the Self-Reliance group led by former Lviv mayor Andrii Sadovyi, they controlled 244 seats out of 450 in the assembly. The Opposition Bloc led by Yurii Boyko, won 29 seats with a popular vote of less than 1.5 million.[173] Boyko is a native of Horlivka, one of the Donetsk regional mining towns at the very centre of the conflict in the east.

The elections marked the formation of a new pro-Western coalition in Ukraine, indicating that Donbas has ceased to play a pivotal role in Ukraine, for the first time in the history of the independent state. Moreover, of all the regions of Ukraine it has suffered the most, economically and socially, as a result of the war and conflicts on its territory. A mass exodus of population occurred in the second half of 2014, with over 1 million people choosing or forced to migrate to other regions, mostly to the Russian Federation, though there has been a population decline since 2004.[174]

There are a number of different ways to interpret the recent voting habits in Ukraine. On the one hand, the view adopted by many Western analysts, they appear to give Ukraine a green light to sever all ties with the Soviet period and start a new pro-Western and pro-democratic path that will take it, irrevocably, out of the Russian orbit.[175] The main parties in the parliament may disagree on the attitude to be adopted toward the larger neighbour: whether one of compromise, as suggested by Poroshenko; or of confrontation, the attitude manifested during the elections last October by Yatseniuk. There is little disagreement, however, on overall policy, which to some extent has been catalysed by the hostile attitude of Moscow, though Russian president Vladimir Putin did recognise the legitimacy of the presidential elections and the ascendancy of Poroshenko.

A second way to view events, and one adopted by a minority of Western analysts as well as Russia and its spokespersons, is that Ukraine experienced a right-wing coup from February 2014 that removed a legally elected president and established a new regime – scornfully described as a 'junta' – and that Western agencies funded these events as a means to remove Ukraine from all Russian influence.[176]

---

[173] See "Vybory do Rady-2014" (2014).
[174] Ridna kraina (2014). See also the story of Pervomaisk in Sakwa (2015).
[175] See, for example, http://www.rri.ro/en_gb/ukraine_chooses_democracy-24358
[176] The most obvious example here is the RT network, which has cited inter alia, the comments of ousted president Yanukovych: http://rt.com/news/yanukovich-statement-

Further, there have been allegations that the 'coup' resulted in a general assault on Russian-language speakers in Ukraine, necessitating the Russian annexation of Crimea, which in any case simply righted a historical wrong perpetrated by the Soviet leadership in 1954. Russia has not recognised the new regimes in the east of Ukraine (DNR and LNR), but it has supported them with weapons and personnel, and essentially prevented their destruction, despite a variety of rifts within the respective leaderships and a manifest lack of policies and infrastructure. In this way, Russia is responding to Western aggression.

A third interpretation may be closer to the truth than either of the first two. It is that in 1991, the issue of state formation had hardly been broached, and that Ukraine made progress in fits and starts, but without a clear conception of the nation, its past, and where it lay in the geopolitical space between Russia and the West. That space became more contested after the eastward expansion of the EU in 2004, which brought former Communist states and former Soviet republics into that entity for the first time. Ukraine at that time became the new frontier. The Russian side had attempted to create several integrationist formations and the Russian president took an active interest in Ukrainian elections. The differences became particularly acute under Yushchenko because of his overtly pro-Western stance, and also because of his efforts to build a new nation on the exploits of anti-Soviet heroes such as OUN leader Stepan Bandera and UPA leader Roman Shukhevych, whom he made 'heroes of Ukraine.'[177]

For Russia, on the other hand, the danger appeared to be minimal for most of the post-Soviet period. Neither Kravchuk nor Kuchma could be described as anti-Russian; both presidents were primarily concerned with domestic issues and improving the economy. Though Yushchenko and the colour revolution caused great concern in the Kremlin, the victory of Yanukovych, an old ally, in the 2010 presidential elections, brought hope that Ukraine might finally be a partner, alongside Russia, Belarus, and Kazakhstan, in the new Customs Union.

Corruption in Ukraine was among the highest of any country in Europe, thus destabilising the country, and Ukraine was dependent on Russia for imports of oil and gas. Russia could anticipate the monopolisation of power by Yanukovych for years to come, somewhat along the lines of Aliaksander Lukashenka in Belarus – at times unpredictable, but clearly an ally. That confidence was dispelled by the events that followed a meeting between Putin and Yanukovych in Moscow just prior to the EU summit in Vilnius in

---

ukraine-crimea-074/

[177] See, for example the commentary of Snyder (2010).

November 2013.

The elections of 2014 affirmed the success of Euromaidan, but also weakened Ukraine in a number of ways. They demonstrated that the multi-vectored foreign policy of Kuchma is no longer feasible. Ukraine has chosen its direction by removing its far eastern regions from the centre of power. Even without Russian intrusions, Donbas would have been disaffected. From almost complete control over Ukraine, it is now isolated and alienated. And, it is impossible to return to the past. Crimea may be lost for many years. No Ukrainian leader has come up with a strategy to facilitate its return.

Thus, the elections mark the emergence of Ukraine as a truncated state, without key industrial regions. And while Euromaidan was popular among about half of the population, and especially those under 50, it has rendered the future more uncertain time than any before in the 23 years of the independent state. Moreover, the turnout in October 2014 was the lowest of any recent election at 52%, and an estimated 50% of those who had voted formerly for the Party of Regions or the Communist parties did not take part.[178]

Is Ukraine more united today than in the past? It is difficult to answer definitively. One can suggest that voters are prepared to give President Poroshenko an opportunity to lead the country. They are concerned about the conflict, but are preoccupied even more with the economic situation, job security, and standards of living.[179] The plethora of political parties has been a feature of Ukrainian elections since 1991. Other than the Party of Regions and formerly the Communists, none has wielded massive political or economic influence. Yatseniuk's Popular Front, for example, which gained the highest overall percentage of votes in 2014, was a completely new formation, as, for that matter, was the Petro Poroshenko Bloc.[180] Voters in Ukraine do not have firm alliances or party identities. They are concerned more with individual leaders and the list of candidates that is supplied by each party prior to each election. There has also been uncertainty concerning the division of powers between the president and the parliament, though most presidents, and particularly Yanukovych, easily circumvented constitutional issues to wield more power. Today, as in Russia, it is the president's own party that has most seats in Parliament, despite finishing only second in terms of percentages of the vote.

The future of Ukraine remains uncertain because of the precarious state of

---

[178] *The Economist* (2014).
[179] See the results of the December 2014 Gallup survey in Esipova and Ray (2014).
[180] "Vybory do radi-2014 (2014).

the economy and the relative fragility of the new ruling coalition. Control over elections by a corrupt leader and his minions ended violently and contentiously. Ukraine appears to have embraced democracy, however, and its elections have always been more open and honest than those of its former Soviet neighbours like Belarus and Russia. The most pro-Russian regions have either been added to Russia or else remain in conflict.

The Soviet legacy that affected and influenced earlier elections is now, like the statues of Lenin, consigned to memory, but the new leaders will need to make broader appeals to the electorate than has been the case hitherto. Ultimately, even without the full return of Donbas to Ukraine, the electorate is centrist rather than rightist; and prefers compromise to confrontation. It remains fearful, justifiably, of further Russian encroachment, but is wary of the impact of closer association with a EU that appears, likewise, uncertain whether to fully embrace its new partner.

26

Ukrainian Parliament Legalises 'Fighters for Independence in the 21st Century'

9 April 2015

On 9 April, Rada deputy Yurii Shukhevych (Radical Party) introduced a new law to the Ukrainian Parliament 'Concerning the legal status and commemorating the memory of the fighters for Ukrainian independence in the 20th century'. It also introduced a Remembrance and Reconciliation Day on 8 May for the victims of the Second World War, as well as other laws opening access to former Soviet archives and banning Communist and Nazi symbols, all of which were accepted by a majority of deputies.

The period for the registering of the bills, authored by historian Volodymyr Viatrovych, head of the Ukrainian Institute for National Memory and others was astonishingly short given the significance of the content of these laws. Less than six days were given for discussion over issues that affect almost every facet of Ukrainian history of the 20th century. The impact may solidify national support for the current Parliament, which has been wavering, but it is unlikely to placate Ukraine's critics abroad, either in the Russian government or in Europe.

The law consists of six articles, which deal without differentiation with all so-called 'fighters for the independence of Ukraine in the 20th century' starting with the Ukrainian People's Republic of 1918 and ending with the People's Movement for Perestroika (better known as Rukh) prior to 24 August 1991, the date of the declaration of independence. Most controversial are the Ukrainian Military Organisation (UVO), the Organisation of Ukrainian Nationalists (OUN), and the Ukrainian Insurgent Army (UPA).

These 'fighters' ('strugglers' is another possible translation of this unsatisfactory noun), according to Article 2, played the chief role in the restoration of Ukrainian statehood in 1991 and are to be guaranteed social benefits, recognition, and military awards (Articles 3 and 4). Article 5 is concerned with publicising the activities of the various groups and the creation of new gravesites and memorials. Finally, Article 6 makes it a criminal offence to deny the legitimacy of 'the struggle for the independence of Ukraine in the 20th century'. Public denial is to be regarded as an insult to the memory of the fighters.

To discuss briefly the possible reactions to this bill, one can take three angles: firstly, my own, which is that of an historian; second, that of Russia, a country with which Ukraine has been at loggerheads for the past eighteen months; and third, that of the democratic West, principally the European Union and North America.

From the angle of an historian, the new law is too simplistic to be taken seriously. The various organisations are vastly different. How can one compare, for example, the intellectual leaders of the Ukrainian People's Republic (UNR) with the young hotheads of the Organisation of Ukrainian Nationalists (OUN) in the 1930s or the ruthless insurgents of the Ukrainian Insurgent Army (UPA)? Even more basic: is one supposed to assume that the state that emerged in August 1991 was a direct result of the activities of the fighters for independence? Ironically, it owed much more to reforms in Moscow begun by Mikhail Gorbachev and the former leader's reluctance to use force to prevent a groundswell of independence movements in the former Soviet republics.

In addition, the all-encompassing rejection of any facets of the Soviet legacy is troublesome. The Red Army, after all, removed the Nazi occupation regime from Ukraine in alliance with the Western Powers. Soviet leaders such as Khrushchev and Brezhnev were (respectively) raised or born in Ukraine, and there were other leaders who supported Ukrainian cultural development while maintaining a devotion to Communism, such as Petro Shelest. There were also serious Marxists who rejected Russification, such as Ivan Dziuba. Essentially this law attempts to erase from history their contributions to modern Ukraine.

Moving back further to the 1920s in Western Ukraine, perhaps a majority of politically active Ukrainians supported or joined the Ukrainian National Democratic Union (UNDO), which cooperated with the Polish Sejm and took part in its activities.

From the perspective of the Russian leadership and more militant activists in Russia, the law at one stroke provides credibility to some of their most outrageous and outlandish claims. What better evidence could there be to accusers in Moscow that extreme nationalists are now running the Ukrainian legislature? Practically overnight, the issues that caused so much trouble for former president Viktor Yushchenko have been encapsulated in law.

The question that stymied the proposed Holodomor Law of Yushchenko – making denial (in this case of Genocide) a criminal offence – has simply been overridden in the current bill. Presumably now historians can be arrested for denying the heroism of a Stepan Bandera or the father of the introducer of the bill, Roman Shukheyvch. Russian trolls operating on social networks, very prominently featured in Western media over the past week, have now acquired new and authentic ammunition for their verbal arsenals.

For the Europeans and North Americans some serious dilemmas arise, particularly in Poland, a country that has been especially supportive of Ukraine, but has long agonised over the massacre of its countrymen in Volhynia at the hands of UPA in the spring and summer of 1943 in one of the most graphic examples of ethnic cleansing of the Second World War. The veneration by Yushchenko of Bandera as a hero of Ukraine was the subject of particular venom in Polish society, as well as in the European Parliament.

In the West as a whole, friends of Ukraine will have a difficult time accepting both the wisdom and timing of such a facile and asinine decree that avoids complex problems by lumping together disparate organisations of different periods and seeks to legitimise controversial organisations (OUN and UPA) by cloaking them within general rhetoric of fighting for independence in the 20th century.

No doubt this Law has its origins in the aftermath of Euromaidan, the loss of Crimea, and separatist control of large swathes of Donbas. It may also be linked to the dissatisfaction with the new government among some of the more radical elements in society, such as the voluntary formations fighting in the east. But it is hard to escape the conclusion that its acceptance into law is a major error, even akin to a death wish vis-à-vis Donbas, where a quite different version of the 20th century prevails.

Was this crude distortion of the past really necessary? Can one legislate historical events and formations in such a fashion? The law seems inimical to the values embraced at the peak of Euromaidan.

27

Volodymyr Viatrovych and Ukraine's Decommunisation Laws

2 May 2015

In April 2015, over seventy scholars from North America, Western Europe, and Ukraine, including myself, published a letter opposing some facets of Ukraine's 'Anti-Communist Law', introduced In the Ukrainian Parliament in draft form earlier in the same month.[181] The scholars were concerned that the laws violated the spirit of scholarly inquiry by making certain subjects taboo. In May 2015, Volodymyr Viatrovych, leader of the Ukrainian Institute of National Memory, published a response in which he makes a number of unwarranted assumptions about our intentions and about Western scholarship on Ukraine generally.[182]

In his opening remarks, he comments that the letter does not analyse *the circumstances* 'under which the Ukrainian Parliament approved the decommunisation' package. Later he suggests that we did not read all the laws because we only focused on two of them. Of course, we read all the laws. The two laws to which we referred caused most concern. And, it was not the circumstances so much as their rapid path to approval without much discussion – not merely in the Parliament, but in the country generally, including among the scholarly community – that elicited our response.

Viatrovych asserts that 'similar laws were adopted by other Eastern European

---

[181] https://krytyka.com/en/articles/open-letter-scholars-and-experts-ukraine-re-so-called-anti-communist-law
[182] https://krytyka.com/en/solutions/opinions/decommunisation-and-academic-discussion

countries', a non sequitur as an explanation of the motives for adopting them in Ukraine. We were not discussing the laws in other countries. Had we focused on them we might well have reached the same conclusions as we did for those of 9 April. There is certainly no indication in our letter that we are somehow satisfied with them; they remain a topic for debate and have been roundly criticised in some forums.

Viatrovych dismisses the non-voting MPs on 9 April as pro-Russians who do not have at heart the interests of Ukraine. But are they not elected officials representing their own specific communities? Opinion polls circulating in early 2014 suggest that fear of Euromaidan was as prevalent in Ukraine as support for the protestors. But for Viatrovych all opposition to the laws is either pro-Moscow or of benefit to Moscow and thus should be dismissed and disparaged.

One can accept that there are frustrations with the legacy of the Soviet Union and one can surely remove Lenin statues, which frankly are an eyesore. Yet one cannot force people to change long-held views overnight or ignore their opinions simply because we disagree with them. If one wishes to attain such a goal, it can only be done in stages, by convincing them that a different approach should be taken.

One of the problems of the treatment of Donbas region in general by the Ukrainian authorities is that its residents are somehow backward or not 'real Ukrainians' because they do not adhere to a nationalist point of view. For Viatrovych, those in opposition are ipso facto traitors who 'confidently hit the 'yes' button on January 16, 2014' to approve the 'dictatorship laws'. Such intolerance is reminiscent of the Communist period he abhors so much.

He writes further that: 'The phrase 'criminal responsibility' does not appear in the text being criticised'. True. But much in this law is implicit rather than explicit. It is what is omitted as much as what is included that causes confusion. Public denial is considered 'derision', and 'humiliation of the Ukrainian people's dignity' is unlawful. But how does one define these phrases? What constitutes humiliation?

It is still unclear what happens to those who fall on the wrong side of these laws. Viatrovych suggests that no scholars will be punished for what they write. But one of the Ukrainian signatories to our letter to Poroshenko and Hroisman has already been harassed and threatened by his superiors, suggesting that opposition to the new laws will not be tolerated.

On UPA he seems to have a blind spot. He suggests inter alia that our comments on ethnic cleansing in Volhynia represent simply one point of view, hinting that perhaps this event never took place or that it has been misconstrued. 'It is only *one* of the opinions that has the right to exist'. It is not an opinion, however, but a fact and one that has been carefully documented by a number of scholars, including Timothy Snyder in his *Past and Present* article of May 2003. I cite this article in particular because Snyder can hardly be accused of being anti-Ukrainian and has been among the most supportive scholars of Ukraine throughout the current crisis.

Viatrovych makes the analogy of Article 2 of the Law of Ukraine on the Holodomor, which recognises public denial of the event as illegal. There is virtually no scholar alive today, however, who would deny that the Famine of 1932-33 took place and that has been the case for the past 25 years. When President Viktor Yushchenko initially brought this law forward, however, his goals went considerably further. He wished to make it *illegal to deny that* the Holodomor *was an act of genocide*, which was not accepted by the Ukrainian Parliament. Such a law would have impeded 'comprehensive study of the Holodomor'.

The use of symbols and slogans of the Ukrainian Insurgent Army (UPA) or Stepan Bandera on the Maidan – 'the Banderite 'Glory to Ukraine' became the official Maidan greeting' writes Viatrovych – also seems to me derivative and expedient rather than evidence of commitment to any sort of cause. That statement is supported by the miserable performance of far right presidential candidates in the election that followed. Participants in Euromaidan have stated to the contrary that such slogans became popular *despite* the fact that they originated with prewar and wartime nationalists. Many of those repeating the mantra did not even know its origins. On the other hand, the appearance of the red-and-black flag did seem ominous to some onlookers and Russian propaganda organs instantly exploited their appearance on the square.

Viatrovych's comment on the 1920s also seems misguided. No one is suggesting that the cultural renaissance of this decade justified what followed or the Stalin regime in general. But it did take place in the Soviet period that is universally condemned by these laws. In other words, the Soviet period was like the curate's egg in that not everything about it was universally bad and evil. In turn there were 'good' Ukrainian Communists just as there were malevolent ones, as well as Communist leaders who left a mixed legacy such as Petro Shelest.

Lastly, Viatrovych objects to certain signatories on our list whose articles on 'primordial Ukrainian collaborationism' are 'actively used by Russian propaganda'. Unfortunately, propaganda organs, Russian or otherwise, regularly exploit and distort scholarly work in this way. But Viatrovych is suggesting also that our naive trust of a group that wishes to malign Ukraine 'was a reason for the appearance of this appeal', which 'has already become an instrument in this war'.

I cannot speak for everyone who signed the Letter, but my hope is for the development of a Ukraine based on freedom of expression and thought rather than the acceptance of diktats by MPs in parliament backed up by the law courts. One cannot erase the past; one can only seek to understand it. Of course, OUN and UPA fought for the independence of Ukraine, and no doubt many of their members did so at great cost to themselves and their families. But one should not try to conceal the darker deeds or pretend that they only exist in the minds of anti-Ukrainians.

There is nothing herein that is unique to Ukraine incidentally; Americans have experienced soul-searching about some criminal acts in Vietnam; my own country, Canada, has faced condemnation for its treatment of the indigenous population; Britain has had to come to terms with many aspects of the colonial period; and more obviously the Germans have tried to atone for the Holocaust. By and large they have done so. The Turks in contrast have refused to acknowledge the genocide of Armenians a century ago, despite what to many appears incontestable evidence; just as Viatrovych refuses to accept criticism of UPA for crimes on a smaller scale.

I have no quarrel with Viatrovych's views on the moral equivalence of Hitler and Stalin's regimes. Personally, I do not agree with him because I regard the crime of the Jewish Holocaust as unique, but I have long thought that in the Baltic States and Ukraine, and perhaps also Belarus, it is logical that citizens often adopt such a perspective, including many in the Diaspora who fled from the Red Army.

The difficulty with Ukraine's past is that it is intensely contested and controversial. On many issues, there can be no definitive conclusions among scholars as the far more reasoned early 21st century debates among Ukrainian historians about OUN and UPA indicated. And the 'circumstances' to which Viatrovych refers are critical: it is precisely the reason why such laws should not be rushed through and approved at this juncture, while a war rages in the East, an economic crisis ravages the country, and the government struggles to deal with its oligarchs.

The Parliament and courts of Ukraine must be more rational and wise than the gangster regimes that preside in Donbas, or for that matter than the Communist regime that was in power for over seven decades. Perhaps, ultimately, they will be. In the West, we can write and think what we want. Our friends in Ukraine should have the same right.

28

Kyiv Revisited

3 July 2015

I first visited the Maidan over 25 years ago. At that time, members of the Green World ecological association were handing out leaflets about unfeasible industrial projects in Ukraine, several linked to the Chernobyl disaster a few years earlier. Nearby red-hatted coal miners were sitting on cobblestones, publicising the reasons for their crippling strike, which paralysed the Soviet (and especially Ukrainian) coal and steel industries. In the background was the massive monument of Lenin – the stolid Hotel Moskva on the hill in the background – like a silent and critical watchdog overlooking events.

The quarter of a century that followed was not always so eventful (I returned regularly), but the mass protests of 1990, 2004, and 2013-14 overlap the period of Soviet rule and independence, as well as defining contemporary Ukraine and the extraordinary and captivating city of Kyiv. Lenin is gone and the hotel was renamed *Ukraina* after independence. But nearby Oleksandr Skoblikov's Arch of Friendship of Peoples, marking the 60th anniversary of the USSR, and Ukrainian House, built in 1982 and featuring a Lenin museum, look strangely out of place. The city is a melange of old and new, dazzling churches and monumental excess like the 200-feet Independence Monument, which always seemed out of place.

Today the Maidan is like the aftermath of a battlefield, the casualties present in spirit and their sacrifices pervading the gloom of what is now a morgue of sorts. One can barely take a step without encountering some memory of the mass protests: the commemorations of those who died in the square, hapless victims of marksmen for the most part; the photographs at what appears like an open-air museum.

Everywhere there were people asking for money for the Ukrainian army, with ATO boxes swinging around their necks. Two were soldiers who were standing at the juncture on Instytutska Street where the memorials are displayed. Others were clearly not part of the regular army and stalked all visitors relentlessly. Some young soldiers walked between parents, home on leave from the front though as one source informed, there are not many recruits from Kyiv on the government side, most are from the areas close to the border or Western Ukraine.

In 1989, there were no mass billboards with the slogan 'Glory to Ukraine! Glory to our heroes!' There were no tridents, which now appear everywhere, most often on the t-shirts of passers-by. Residents of the capital are suddenly more assertive, determined to emphasise their national identity. It seems a defensive gesture and it probably is. Billboards talk about health and the rights of young people. But whatever the tragedies of the past eighteen months, Ukraine as a nation has been indisputably strengthened.

On my last night in town I talked with Ollie Carroll, whom I've known for several years. He gave me an account of life in the war zone, where he has been 'embedded' for the past weeks, on both sides of the border. Somehow, he has managed to keep a balance (and alive!), without commitment to either side, which is of course the essence of good journalism but found so rarely in these parts.

These battles have superseded Euromaidan, which occupied world attention for so long, and the violence is remorseless. Yet the conflict zone currently is quite well defined; thus far it has not expanded much since the Minsk-2 agreement though virtually all analysts maintain that the treaty has failed or is about to fail. As one separatist fighter put it on Vice News – and I am paraphrasing – we don't care about the agreements, we just follow orders.

Ironies abound. The only other plane at Boryspil when I arrived was a Russian Aeroflot, and despite the conflict and Moscow's ban on certain Ukrainian products, Russia remains Ukraine's largest individual trading partner, albeit at only half the rate of a year ago.[183] (The EU as a block is Ukraine's main trading partner.)

Plainly, however, relations between the two Slavic neighbours are grim and even the conciliatory Petro Poroshenko is beginning to sound militant.

---

[183] http://www.kyivpost.com/content/business/after-a-year-of-war-against-ukraine-russia-is-still-the-countrys-leading-trade-partner-392123.html

Following the de-Communisation laws introduced into Parliament in April 2015 (which have caused such a raging debate), I anticipated a rapid removal of the various signs of the Soviet past, but reflected that it has to take place in stages because the costs are prohibitive. Still, new monuments are emerging alongside old ones, some reflecting current events, and at others there are clear signs of present events.

At the entrance to the Museum of the Great Patriotic War, for example, there are Russian tanks and katyushas seized during the Donbas conflict but inside the museum itself, little has changed. The interpretation remains more or less as it was during Soviet times other than the addition of a gallery on the years 1939-41, now considered officially as part of the war years. The Jewish Holocaust is still marginalised. For that matter, there is nothing therein about OUN and UPA and anti-Soviet resistance either. One simply steps back in time.

The Holodomor Memorial National Museum nearby dates from 2008 and is quite effective, in the shape of a candle, nestling between the World War II obelisk and the Pecherska Lavra. Books of Memory for each oblast can be found inside, along with various posters citing the origins of the famine and the alleged perpetrators. The sculpture of the child at the entrance is particularly impressive; less so the inflated statement of the number of victims.

Switch to the northwest and Babiy Yar (Babyn Yar) and here also there are new memorials close to the actual site of the massacre of over 30,000 Jews in September 1941 (and over 100,000 altogether). One is a wooden cross to the nationalist underground victims created in 1991; the second a Menorah-shaped monument to Jewish victims erected on the fiftieth anniversary, the third a small monument to Jewish victims, the fourth a small monument to child victims established in 2001, and a much larger edifice planned for some time now appears to be under construction. Wild dogs have gathered at Babiy Yar – some resemble wolves, but they are passive. The Soviet edifice on the other side of the metro station dates from the 1970s in the typical style of such monuments, though it is particularly striking.

Perhaps the most lasting sentiment I took with me upon leaving was the collective failure to recognise in 1991 that the peaceful fall of the Soviet Union was only the beginning of a process that is culminating in the violence of today. We are still living in the 20th century in Kyiv; the past remains alive and only the future is unknown. Many were unhappy with the former Yanukovych regime and its excesses, but the euphoria over the Poroshenko-Yatseniuk administration has clearly ended. The popularity of the Prime Minister in particular has collapsed in a manner reminiscent of that of Viktor Yushchenko, president in 2005-10.

Ultimately, we may need to re-evaluate Belavezha, the deceptive calm of the transformation of a Communist-led government to an independent one in 1991, as well as the various treaties with Russia that took place between 1990 and 2004. More evident is the enduring failure of all Ukraine's independent governments to deal with issues specific to Donbas but partially concealed by the oligarchic control of past years. And clearly the malevolence of the post-2000 Russian leadership is always in the background reducing the space for manoeuvre.

Euromaidan has unleashed forces dormant for decades and there is no indication of an end game. The relative calmness of this beautiful city in this sense is illusory.

29

What to Do with Donbas: Phase 3

16 July 2015

On 16 July, Ukrainian president Petro Poroshenko steered the draft law to provide more autonomy for separatist-occupied areas of Donbas through Parliament and to the Constitutional Court for approval. Though the motion passed convincingly (288 votes in favour, 57 against) – it was opposed only by the Radicals and Samopomich faction, and even supported by the Opposition Bloc (composed mainly of former Regions MPs) – it represents only the first in a complex process focused on Article 11 of the Minsk-2 Agreement signed earlier this year, which will change the status of Donbas.

Providing that the court approves the law, it will be returned to parliament where it requires the support of over 300 deputies in order to become valid. US Assistant Secretary of State Victoria Nuland, who was coincidentally in Ukraine during the deliberations, supports its acceptance as do the leaders of Germany, France, and other countries of the EU. In fact, Ukraine is under intense pressure from its Western allies to accept the law in order to put the principles of Minsk-2 into operation.

There are, however, a number of disturbing issues raised by the passage of the draft law.

First of all, it contravenes the existing 1996 Constitution, which does not permit outsiders to dictate changes to the Ukrainian government. Specifically, it is stated in Article 157 that:

> The Constitution of Ukraine shall not be amended, if the amendments foresee the abolition or restriction of human and

citizens' rights and freedoms, or if they are oriented toward the liquidation of the independence or violation of the territorial indivisibility of Ukraine.

In December 1991, when a Ukrainian referendum backed the 24 August Declaration of Independence, all the countries currently pressuring Ukraine to the constitutional amendment recognised the country within its existing borders of that time. The Constitution further strengthened the notion that these borders were inviolable.

Second, Minsk-2, like its predecessor Minsk-1, gave a voice to the leaders of the breakaway 'Donetsk People's Republic' and 'Luhansk People's Republic'. The leaders of these two regions signed the document, instantly enhancing their credibility when hitherto the Western world had considered them little more than advance posts of a predatory Russia. The rebels now demand that these changes become enshrined officially in an amended Constitution of Ukraine.

Whether the DNR and LNR have any real legitimacy is a moot point. There appears to be as much infighting among their leaders as there are barbs directed at the government in Kyiv. Clearly the settlements within are disaffected, having been bombarded by the Ukrainian army over the past year and used as a refuge by the renegade leaders. The reality is that we do not really know how popular they are, and how much support they could attract were a free and fair election possible.

Third, the goals of Russia are uncertain and fluctuating. Speculation about the eleventh point in the Minsk-2 agreement, which is already nebulous, suggests that Vladimir Putin's personal advisor Vladislav Surkov, a Russian-Chechen businessman who was First Deputy Chairman of the Russian Presidential Administration for twelve years (ending 2011), inserted that particular clause, undoubtedly with the president's approval. It stipulates that Ukraine should be decentralised 'taking into account peculiarities of particular districts of Donetsk and Luhansk Oblasts, agreed with representatives of these districts'.[184]

That Russia supports more autonomy for Donbas is evident, but what are its long-term goals? The answer would seem that these goals have receded from the once triumphant (though fundamentally and historically flawed) concept of 'Novorossiya' to one of holding on to one's gains and propping up, more or

---

[184] http://www.telegraph.co.uk/news/worldnews/europe/ukraine/11408266/Minsk-agreement-on-Ukraine-crisis-text-in-full.html

less, a defunct military regime that will ultimately succumb to pressure from the Ukrainian army or collapse from within thanks to feuds and in-fighting.

The limitations of Russian ambitions are illustrated by a reluctance to escalate the conflict further and to engage in any form of physical occupation. Though propaganda against the 'neo-Nazi' government in Kyiv has been relentless – and boosted by the rash actions of the Right Sector in Mukachevo,[185] whether or not these were based on a moral crusade against corruption and smuggling – Putin himself has been strangely subdued, even extending some feelers to the West for cooperation over the crisis in Syria, while protesting the notion of an international commission to investigate the shooting of a Malaysian airliner over Donetsk region just over a year ago.

Lamentably, through the blundering of both sides, Donbas is the real victim of this protracted conflict. Economically it is a wasteland that will take years to rebuild, if indeed it can be reconstructed. It would require enormous investment, an outlay that at present is as remote from the Ukrainian reality as it is possible to be. Its more enterprising souls have fled the scene. Thousands are dead; they are victims of frequent shelling that does not discriminate between one side or another. The survivors live amid intermittent warfare, dreading the coming winter. It may well be a frozen conflict, but that conflict is for a land that one really wants.

Thus, what the Europeans and the United States are saying to Ukraine is: you must retain these devastated areas, feed them, provide them with resources, but without taking full authority over them or at least, not in the immediate future. In short, the fulfilment of this part of Minsk-2 would weaken fundamentally the Ukrainian state established in 1991. Today no one outside the country is supporting the notion of a centralised Ukraine under the rule of president or parliament. One would have to conclude that the recognition of 1991 has been abruptly violated by both friends and enemies of the country.

There are further implications for Ukraine here. The return of Crimea is not even part of Minsk-2. Further, those placing pressure on Poroshenko are not exerting similar pressure on the separatist governments, which are largely and openly ignoring the agreement, after some token gestures to comply. Most of its stipulations, like Ukraine's control over its original eastern border by the end of the year, are unenforceable. Ukraine can survive without Donbas and (especially) without Crimea, but only if they are severed permanently. At present, it cannot regain Crimea but it cannot discard the occupied Donbas, which it has treated as alien territory for some time, albeit without a blockade in place.

---

[185] http://www.radiosvoboda.org/content/news/27123021.html

Other questions will emerge, most notably the determination of where the border of the two oblasts should lie and whether Russia will permit the disarming and defeat of the two separatist regimes by ceasing the constant flow of advanced weaponry over the border and removing its 'volunteer' soldiers from the war zone. For Putin, it is a drain of resources; one suspects that for most of the Russian troops fighting in Ukraine, it is an unpopular war. The messianic phase is over but the end goal is unclear. The only certainty is that there are no winners in this conflict.

30

Ukraine at 24

23 August 2015

On its 24th anniversary, Ukraine's problems continue to multiply. First of all, the GDP continues to fall, if not as catastrophically as last year and the possibility of default in payment of debts remains high. Second, the Minsk-2 ceasefire barely holds in the east as conflict continues with the separatist 'governments' of the so-called People's Republics of Donetsk and Luhansk (DNR and LNR). Third, the government has not made much progress in eliminating the power of oligarchs. Lastly, the popularity of the pro-Western leaders President Petro Poroshenko and Prime Minister Arsenii Yatseniuk has plummeted since last year.

Underlying its problems are relations with Russia, its largest and most powerful neighbour. Over the twenty-four years the relationship has fluctuated though the debating points have invariably been the same.

First of all, the territorial divisions resulting from the breakup of the Soviet Union in 1991 remained unresolved. For the Russians, the presence of Crimea and the port of Sevastopol in newly independent Ukraine caused concern, mainly but not exclusively because of the presence and potential fate of the Black Sea Fleet. The Russian Duma, rather than Russia's first president Boris Yeltsin, flatly opposed the 'loss' of an autonomous republic that it had 'donated' to Ukraine in 1954.

Yeltsin and Leonid Kravchuk, the first Ukrainian president, held several meetings on the future of the Fleet while a noisy pro-Russian nationalist movement flourished on the peninsula. The Treaty of Friendship signed by the two presidents in 1997 appeared to have clarified most questions, with Russia retaining over 80% of the fleet, and leasing two bays in Sevastopol. Ukraine previously has abolished the position of Crimean president ending attempts to hold a referendum on the future of the region.

Second, Ukrainian independence in 1991 came with an announcement that the new state would be neutral and non-aligned. After some initial reluctance, the country relinquished its Soviet arsenal of nuclear weapons, as had Belarus and Kazakhstan before it, having been guaranteed its security by the United States, Russia, and the United Kingdom, in 1994. Ukraine never formally ratified the CIS Treaty and there was little thought of joining NATO.

Third, Ukraine found itself dependent on Russia for energy resources, first and foremost oil and gas. It provided the pipelines in turn for much of Russian gas exported to Central and Western Europe. Disputes over gas prices highlighted most high-level summits between the leaders. Russian government involvement in Gazprom dates from late 1992 when company Chairman Viktor Chernomyrdin was appointed Prime Minister of Russia. Privatisation of the company in 1993-94 ended in 2005 when the Russian government obtained a majority stake. Since that date, Gazprom and the Russian government have operated as one.

Ukraine's own gas interests run deep (including the infamous United Energy Systems of Ukraine company of the 1990s run by Yulia Tymoshenko), but it has fought hard to control its own assets by and large.

Most Ukrainian oligarchs successfully built mini business empires without intrusion from their powerful counterparts in Russia. Others, like Dmytro Firtash and his company RosUkrEnergo, made careers out of bargaining between the two, while maintaining close ties with the government leaders in Kyiv and Moscow.

Perhaps the key difference to development in Russia and Ukraine is that in the latter, the business empires were diverse and constituted separate centres of power. In Russia after 2000, though oligarchs remained very powerful, they either refrained from political aspirations or else formed close ties with the leadership. In Ukraine, the restraints were few. And once they entered the political arena, they controlled it closely. Ukraine's richest man, Rinat Akhmetov, financed the Regions Party and its leader Viktor Yanukovych, as well as running successfully for the party in the parliamentary elections of 2006. The eastern oligarchs reached the culmination point of their power in 2005 when Yanukovych became president.

Critics, correctly, have blamed Yanukovych for the mass corruption during his presidency, a time when the rule of law receded before a system of cronyism and mass aggrandisement of wealth in government circles and among deputies of parliament. The ultimate failure of the Orange Revolution manifested itself in the willingness of former president Yushchenko to work with Yanukovych, appointing him Prime Minister in 2006-07 as well as supporting his imprisonment of former Orange partner but now implacable enemy, former Prime Minister Yulia Tymoshenko.

Frequently Western media refer to Yanukovych as a 'pro-Moscow' leader. The appellation is only partially true. Yanukovych, like his patron Akhmetov, was interested first and foremost in personal success, affluence and power of the Donetsk region, and his acolytes there and in government. Vladimir Putin was a reliable friend and partner, who did not intrude in Yanukovych's fiefdom, which appeared secure and was a more dependable neighbour than under his predecessor Yushchenko. But the relationship has many facets and it is doubtful whether Putin fully trusted him, not least because Ukraine's business elite also sought closer ties with the European Union.

During the years of independence, Ukraine achieved a number of positive developments that in terms of democratic steps outpaced its Slavic neighbours. Its presidential elections have been held regularly and by and large fairly – the first round in 2004 notwithstanding – and Poroshenko is its fifth president, compared to Russia's three and Belarus' one. The composition of its parliament likewise has changed regularly. There has always been diversity of opinion, and the media, though at times restricted under Kuchma and Yanukovych, has been largely free. It has also begun to wrest itself from reliance on Russia for energy imports.

Euromaidan illustrated, inter alia, the growth of civil activism, a desire to throw off shackles of the past, and to end corruption, in what was termed a 'revolution of dignity'. Ukrainians – perhaps in the majority (and especially among those under twenty-five) –perceived the EU as an ideal that could complete and consolidate the path to a western-style democracy. That the ideal was naïve or unrealistic, or that it became contorted and itself somewhat corrupted, should not detract from the initial impressive demonstration of public will, as tens of thousands braved bitterly cold nights to remain on the Maidan.

Yet, Euromaidan brought a dramatic break with the past, the consequences of which are still being felt. Russia regards it as a pro-Western right-wing coup that removed a legitimate, if very weak, president from office. Russian troops snatched Crimea without warning, and tried to move further by backing separatists in Donetsk, Luhansk, Odesa, and other regions. But the 'Novorossiya' concept was abandoned – at least by the Russian government – within a few months.

Ukraine responded by mounting an 'anti-terrorist operation' (ATO) that was initially quite successful until direct Russian intervention halted its advance, and later by signing the Association Agreement with the EU, which Yanukovych had opted to reject, as well as the more recent banning of the Communist Party. It moved away from the careful multi-vectored foreign policy of Leonid Kuchma (1994-2004) and committed itself to a pro-Western and pro-European path, albeit one hardly strewn with roses or clear direction.

Activists of the late 1980s and of the Orange Revolution justifiably see links between the events of their eras and Euromaidan. But perhaps those connections lie more in the origins than what took place on the square. The violence of the past year has exceeded by far anything in the history of independent Ukraine, and one would need to reach back to the 1950s for any analogies in the Soviet period.

Euromaidan was also about the forming of a national identity, interpretations of the past, and visions of the future. Some critics maintain that extremists are dictating policy and trying to limit free expression. Others claim that Russia's truculence derives from Western and NATO advances rather than the Kremlin's belligerence. The situation in the disputed regions resembles in its devastation that in North Africa or Iraq and Ukraine's ATO played its own role, though the question of how one deals with an enemy holed up within major towns is one with which Western governments have also struggled to deal.

Former president Kravchuk now advocates the abandonment of the separatist enclaves, while the DNR and LNR leaders promise a referendum after local elections in the fall on 'union with Russia', a notion hardly palatable to Moscow. The alternative to voluntary relinquishment of the breakaway regions seems to be a frozen conflict, sapping the finances of Ukraine, and perpetuating the economic crisis. The imperfect analogies of Transnistria, Abkhazia, and South Ossetia are hardly a cause for optimism.

Perhaps the biggest dilemma for the Ukrainian leadership is what to do next. Many would regard any form of compromise with Vladimir Putin as a sign of weakness; yet a failure to reach some accommodation suggests intransigence. Armed battalions doing much of the fighting in the east are openly dissatisfied with the Poroshenko leadership and threaten another Maidan. Yet a wholesale government crackdown on anti-separatist/anti-Russian elements is inconceivable. The leaders can take some solace from the fact that the extremists could not win a democratic election – but they are unlikely to lay down their weapons.

In the midst of such turmoil, the questions about economic and administrative reforms appear peripheral, but they are too pressing to ignore. The formerly powerful steel industry is in deep decline; the venerable Donbas coalfield is yet another victim of the conflict and many coalmines are faced with closure, their miners often unpaid. Akhmetov's company DTEK stands accused of fuelling miners' unrest and protests, which have focused on removing Energy and Coal Industry Minister Volodymyr Demchyshyn.

The twenty-four years have shown above all, that Ukrainians wish to live in an independent state, with limited influence from and no control by outside neighbours. They would benefit if the holders of wealth invested in Ukraine rather than their own companies and interests. They would also gain by moving closer to the EU agreement but not necessarily as NATO members, following the examples of Finland (the closest case to Ukraine as part of the former Russian Empire), Sweden, Austria, Ireland, and Switzerland.

But if such a route were taken, it could only be through a binding treaty with Russia and the United States, guaranteeing its territorial integrity, possibly without Crimea (though its annexation should not be recognised) and the conflicted regions of Donetsk and Luhansk. Should Russia refuse to come to the table, NATO membership could be advanced as the only alternative. Russia in turn would have to abandon the DNR and LNR 'governments' to their fates. Internal fighting and vendettas such as the recent purge of the Cossacks will likely see their demise shortly in any case, a consequence that one suspects would be acceptable to the Kremlin but for the loss of prestige it would signify.

Lastly, on the relationship with Russia: the crass propaganda emanating from government-paid sources in that country has been unceasing for over a year. But the cacophony of anti-Russian statements and editorials on the Western side has also been sustained, if less vociferous. Yet this year marks just two decades since the abandonment of the pro-Western foreign policy by the Kremlin. Even in 1996, Western agencies were helping the ailing Russian president Yeltsin to win re-election. In short, the current situation, what some have termed a 'new Cold War', is not necessarily static.

And while full reengagement may appear far-fetched, overt hostility toward Russia on the part of the West is plainly counter-productive. Putin's cooperation with the United States in Iran shows that some avenues for dialogue exist, and several EU countries would prefer to keep the window to the east open for trade. In short there is no united front against the Russian Federation. Moreover, it is facile to blame Russia for all Ukraine's economic problems, which by some indicators were worse in 2011 than they are today.

Ultimately, Ukraine cannot choose its neighbours. Hence, it has to coexist with them one way or another. The same can be said of its relations with opposition political parties, and former Regions-era oligarchs. As long as they wish to work for and within the country, it would be difficult to make progress without using the assets of its business elite – including those who were missing-in-action during Euromaidan. The country also needs a period of stability that may depend on rapprochement between the Western powers and Russia, but which can be catalysed by its own actions.

All these requirements suggest that Ukraine's 25th year might be best spent in seeking solutions and compromises to the problems that engulf the state: working with the EU while improving relations with Russia; ensuring that oligarchs, if they are to remain, work with the government and not in their own interests; improving the training and equipping of the army; implementing economic and administrative reforms; and using foreign loans to offset the financial impasse.

31

Peace at Last in Ukraine? Analysing Russian Goals

30 September 2015

As we await the form of the local elections in the areas of Donbas occupied by the so-called Donetsk and Luhansk People's Republics (the DNR and LNR), there is much speculation in the Western media whether the Minsk agreement will be upheld. Much revolves around Russia's intentions, as well as the attitude of the militant separatist leaders who wish to use the elections to remove their fiefdoms from Ukraine.

Over the past days according to the reports of the OSCE and other sources, overt conflict in the separatist regions seems to have ended and some of the separatist leaders have either been removed or else appear to have migrated, at least for now, to the Russian Federation. Vladimir Putin is reluctant to remain involved in a war that is going nowhere, but costing Russia sorely in terms of commitment of weaponry and manpower, and even more in terms of alienation from Europe and the United States.

Some observers have noted a sustained build-up at Tartus, Russia's military base in Syria in support of the forces of President Bashar Al-Assad. Predictably, Russian Foreign Minister Sergey Lavrov denies any increase in Russian forces and maintains that it is little changed from earlier.

Nonetheless, that Russia has increased its commitment to Syria while reducing that to the territories of 'Novorossiya' in Donbas is evident. It is unclear whether in the event of a Ukrainian attempt to regain its former territories there would be much opposition in the Kremlin. Rather, as almost occurred in the summer of 2014, Russia might prefer to abandon the separatist regimes and leaders to their fate.

How can such a move be equated with the apparent commitment to Ukrainian separatists and the construction of 'Novorossiya'?

Some reasons can readily be dismissed, such as the decisive impact of Western sanctions. Sanctions have had some effects, but there is no indication that they have had a serious impact on Putin's popularity or Russia's ability to withstand prolonged recession.

Instead, more important are the following. First, the annexation of Crimea has proven extremely costly, and has become more a symbolic triumph than an act of wise statesmanship. True, many Crimeans may have supported it. But providing services to Crimea is difficult, and the peninsula, other than providing bases for the Russian Black Sea Fleet, has little to offer. Russia is not about to give up Crimea but it cannot take on the even more onerous load of the separatist areas of Donetsk and Luhansk.

Second, the militants, unsurprisingly given their dearth of ideas and commitments, have failed to attract support of the populations in the areas they control. A case in point is Aleksandr Zakharchenko, the leader of the DNR, who continues to make bellicose statements as the peace process makes advances. Though there are many important distinctions between the DNR and LNR, both require conflict to make advances rather than periods of stability. Both require the continued investment of Russian troops, equipment, and personnel that Moscow is no longer prepared to offer so freely given the remote chance of long-term success.

Third, and related, Russian-speaking Ukrainians outside the small separatist enclave have no interest either in joining Russia or supporting a prospective full-scale Russian invasion. Even Sergey Aksyonov, the appointed leader of Crimea, would make little headway in a free election, as was evident in the last pre-annexation elections when his party achieved less than 5% of the vote. When pro-Russians failed in their attempted takeover of cities like Kharkiv in the late spring of 2014, it was evident that Vladimir Putin had misinterpreted the signs of support in Ukraine.

In short, opposition to Euromaidan did not necessarily signify pro-Russian sentiment or separatism. Most opponents of the protests in Ukraine would, given the choice, put up with the new government, particularly if it secured economic stability, just as they endured the turbulent years of the Yushchenko presidency, or for that matter the corruption of the Yanukovych years. Insofar as the concept of 'Novorossiya' existed, it was limited to a small coterie of gunmen and Russian idealists who for a time had the backing of the Kremlin.

Fourth, Russia has moved on. One of the few identifying aspects of the Putin leadership, as with his personal image, is the need for instant triumphs without sustained commitment, images over concrete achievements. That requires foreign policy manoeuvres that might enhance the prestige of the regime and allow it to maintain profitable contacts with the Western world. Rhetoric aside, and there has been much of it, Moscow prefers to keep the lines open to the markets of the West while adopting the role of a major player in international affairs.

As far as Syria is concerned, perhaps the logic is that by maintaining Assad in power, Russia can persuade the West that it is better to keep it as a partner rather than an adversary. Just as in 2001, Moscow and Washington can join forces against terrorists, in this case the Islamic State. That is not to say that such a policy will receive much sympathy in Washington, which perceives such intervention as exacerbating the conflict.

Another theory is that by intervening in Syria, Russia will bring the West to the negotiating table, with an agreement that if the Russians keep out of that conflict, they might be given a free hand in Ukraine. But as argued above, that is not what they are seeking at present. Rather the goal is to be recognised as a significant power – in short, it is alienation that rankles rather than sanctions. Russia would like to return to the G8 and believes that there is a possibility of doing so.

Where does that leave Ukraine? Over 8,000 have died in the Donbas conflict to date and over a million residents have left the region. Analysts in the West continue to debate whether there is a civil war or a Russian war in Ukraine. The correct answer is probably a little of both. But the fact remains that the rebels would not survive for long without Russian support. Once they lose it, and given the Kremlin's current acceptance that an invasion would be highly unpopular both in the area and at home, the likelihood is that DNR and LNR will once more come under Ukrainian control.

None of the above should lead to a conclusion that the Russian government recognises the territorial integrity of Ukraine. Rather it prefers to wield influence from afar, to ensure that in terms of security interests, both Ukraine and Belarus are in the Russian sphere. A new accommodation with the West would then, in theory, lead to the return of economic growth, decreased commitment of military personnel and equipment, and assurance that there should be no further build-up or expansion of NATO.

There is also herein an assumption that there must be some logic to Russia's latest policy moves, an apparent commitment to the peace process of Minsk as well as to the government of Syria. In reality, such moves may be no more than feelers to elicit the reaction of Western powers. Still, Russia is clearly dissatisfied with the status quo, in Ukraine and elsewhere. And that is bad news for the leaders of the DNR and LNR.

32

Communist Heroes of Ukraine

4 November 2015

In a recent interview cited in *The New York Times*, Volodymyr Viatrovych, head of the National Institute of Memory of Ukraine and an author of the 'decommunisation' laws approved by President Petro Poroshenko in May, equated Lenin statues with 'totalitarian propaganda' and a sign of the presence of 'polite people', by which he signified troops of the Russian Special Forces, in Ukraine.

The May 2015 laws remain controversial, particularly their implicit and now actual ban on all forms of Communist propaganda and ultimately on the former Communist Party of Ukraine as a legal entity. Lenin is an obvious focus given the plethora of Lenin statues throughout the former Soviet republics but as far as Ukraine is concerned he is among the least relevant.

The Law of Ukraine (2015, No. 25, 190) 'On the legal status and honouring the memory of fighters for the independence of Ukraine in the 20th century' is a long one, but notable by the absence from it of any former Communist parties. By definition, Communists could not have been struggling for the independence of the republic, but operating only on orders from Moscow. Today streets named after former Communist leaders such as Mykola Skrypnyk (1872-1933) are being renamed.

Yet denying Communists any positive role in the 20th century history of Ukraine is simply distortion, if not outright denial of historical events. Skrypnyk, no doubt, was a committed follower of Lenin, but even he recognised the threat of 'Great Russian chauvinism' and became a pioneer of 'Ukrainisation' of culture and language in the 1920s. He was also determined to maintain the ethnic unity of Ukraine, resisting efforts by Russian Bolshevik leaders to form a Donetsk-Kryvyi Rih Soviet republic in 1918. Disillusioned by

Stalin's centralisation, and by the arrival of Pavel Postyshev to take over the leadership (in practice, though he was in fact Second Secretary) in January 1933, Skrypnyk committed suicide.

Perhaps even more notable than Skrypnyk are two other Ukrainian Communists who merit the status of 'heroes' just as much as the leaders of the parties mentioned in the May 2015 decree: Mykola Khvliovyi and Oleksandr Shumskyi. Khvyliovyi, who was born in Kharkiv region in 1893, was a prominent writer who joined the Communist Party in 1919, and he is best known for his romance stories and prose and his activity within the Free Academy of Proletarian Literature. By the mid-1920s he was speaking out against Russian oppression in what became a series of pamphlets culminating in his slogan 'Away from Moscow!'

Stalin was quick to respond to such 'bourgeois nationalism', even though it was a natural outcome of the new focus on all things Ukrainian. Khvlyiovyi was forced to recant his views though he continued to publicise them in unofficial sources. Like Skrypnyk, he was dismayed by the arrival of Postyshev and even more so by the mass famine of 1933, and committed suicide in May of this year. Notably many of the political positions enunciated at the Maidan in 2013-14 echo the writings of Khvyliovyi. But like that of Skrypnyk, his part in the Ukrainian renaissance and the 1991 independence of Ukraine is to be erased.

Third, there is the remarkable national Communist Oleksandr Shumskyi (1890-1946), a former Commissar of Internal Affairs and Commissar of Education of the Ukrainian SSR, who joined the Communists by an indirect route: an alliance of the *Borotbisty*[186] and the Communist Party of Ukraine (CPU) that resulted in a full merger in March 1920. Like his two contemporaries, Shumskyi wished to deepen Ukrainisation and have Ukrainians appointed to leading positions in the party. By 1925, the phenomenon of 'Shumskyism' was at its peak within the CPU.

By 1927, however, the Soviet leadership had removed Shumskyi and moved him to Moscow. He was denounced as a 'nationalist deviant', and accused of causing problems not only in the Soviet Ukrainian party but also the Communist Party of Western Ukraine (KPZU) in Poland. Both parties underwent severe purges and in 1938 the Comintern dissolved the KPZU on Stalin's orders. Shumskyi was arrested in the same month that Skrypnyk committed suicide (January 1933) and given a 10-year Gulag

---

[186] *Borotbisty* or The Strugglers, were nationally oriented Communists, allowed to flourish as a result of Lenin's dictum that Soviet republics could be socialist in content and national in culture.

sentence. After the war, he tried to return to Ukraine from the Russian city of Saratov, but never arrived in Kyiv. His death, like so many of those during Stalin's rule, remains unexplained.

These three biographies all pertain to individuals who were committed both to Communism *and* the future of Ukraine, and they are likely the best known of the Ukrainian leaders of the 1920s. But there were many others. They were characterised precisely by their concern for their native land and lack of subservience to the leadership in Moscow. Yet they served a party that does not feature in the long list of those 'fighting for the independence of Ukraine' in the May Laws. That list includes incidentally even the Hetmanate under Pavlo Skoropadskyi, which requisitioned grain from Ukrainian peasants to feed the Imperial German army in the latter stages of the First World War.

Their omission from Law No. 25, 190, not only politicises the decommunisation procedures; it represents an unfortunate and selective manipulation of the past by the authors of the decree, including the director of the Institute of National Memory. None of this is to suggest that the Communist leadership did not commit crimes in Ukraine; only that there were meritorious Communists in Ukraine who died for their beliefs and love of their country well before the Second World War broke out.[187]

---

[187] For further reading on this topic, see Mace (1983), Palko (2014), and Shkandrij (1992).

33

The DNR, 'Grisha Phillips', and Speaking the Truth

14 November 2015

The Ukrainian conflict has been characterised by propaganda on both sides. Perhaps that is unsurprising in a military situation. But what is of note is that observers and analysts who would not appear obliged to take on partisan positions have sometimes done so. This article focuses on one such journalist whose name is instantly recognisable such is his reputation for outspokenness and prodigious activity in eastern Ukraine in particular.

In a recent interview, the leader of the 'Donetsk People's Republic' Aleksandr Zakharchenko declared his desire to add the remaining parts of Donetsk Oblast – a larger area than the current DNR – to the republic. The comment clearly undermines the Minsk Protocol, which foresaw complete Ukrainian control over the original Ukraine-Russian border by the end of the year.

The comment portrays the transparent ambitions of one of the main separatist leaders in Ukraine that, if fulfilled, would fundamentally undermine the peace process. The territories sought could only be captured by violent assault since they lie outside the DNR territory. The DNR, like the leadership of the Luhansk People's Republic (LNR), maintains that it is Ukraine that is intent on further aggression and violating the Minsk Protocol. But Zakharchenko's naked ambition suggests otherwise and indicates a goal to expand his area of control and enhance his own power. Other motives are hard to perceive.

Yet one journalist from Western Europe identifies almost totally with such views, and specifically with the now outdated and historically flawed concept of 'Novorossiya' and has for all intents and purposes 'gone native'. This is Graham ('Grisha') Phillips, a Scottish-born English patriot from Nottingham, who produces You Tube reports from Donbas and edits an on-line magazine called *The Truth Speaker*. He has incensed many Ukrainians by his wholesale advocacy of the Russian perspective, as well as his collusion with the separatists, even to the extent of taking part in battles (he was featured, for example, in the victory celebrations after the Battle of Ilovaisk in August 2014) and his zealous interviews of wounded POWs.[188]

To cite just one example of a Phillips posting: on 12 November, and not for the first time, Phillips made reference in his Twitter account to 'Ukrainian-occupied Mariupol'. There were no qualifying or explanatory remarks. The comment surely leads directly to a question: when did this occupation begin? The city has recently been at the forefront of the DNR's attention, and the Ukrainian leaders recognise its vulnerability. But some background is useful if we are to explain its place or lack of it, in the 'Russkiy Mir'.

Since 1997 in its Treaty of Friendship with Ukraine, the Russian Federation has formally recognised Mariupol as an integral part of the latter country. How is it possible for Ukraine to occupy a city that is part of its territory and moreover has been so since the declaration of independence? Even prior to 1991, Mariupol was part of the Ukrainian Soviet republic. Earlier, before 1774, the area was under the control of the Crimean Khanate for over three centuries (during part of that period, the Khanate was under the rule of Ottoman Turkey).

Russian annexation was thus a relatively recent phenomenon in historical terms, and came about largely as a result of a series of wars with the crumbling Ottoman Empire. For most of the Soviet period the city was called Zhdanov, after the dour Leningrad party boss who imposed cultural uniformity under Stalin in the early postwar years. It has a long and chequered history though it was largely destroyed during the German-Soviet war. To claim that it is part of 'Novorossiya', i.e. an area that 'belongs' to Russia historically, is a gross simplification of past events – though that is not unusual in the polemics over the Ukrainian conflict.

Alongside Phillips' Twitter reference were some photographs of damaged buildings in Mariupol, which he contrasted with 'peaceful' Donetsk. The reader is asked to stretch credibility even further by the implicit conclusion that the destruction was caused by Ukrainian shelling. So from where did the

---

[188] See, for example, https://www.buzzfeed.com/maxseddon/how-a-british-blogger-became-an-unlikely-star-of-the-ukraine?utm_term=.rla6w8y1y#.dnjPyj2e2; and Shaun Walker's article on Ukraine's detention of Phillips in the spring of 2014: https://www.theguardian.com/world/2014/may/21/british-journalist-graham-phillips-detained-east-ukraine

shells emanate? Was the Ukrainian army bombing its own citizens in a city it allegedly occupies? What would be the point? Why not acknowledge that in the case of Mariupol the shelling came from separatists armed and supported by Russia?

I dwell on these postings because they are patent examples of distortion, as well as indicating an unquestioning acceptance of the version of events propagated by the Russian media and separatist leaders. They present a picture of a Donbas population striving for change, to be part of Russia, a country to which they are connected by ethnic origin and language. Phillips, as an analyst with access both to Russian and Western media, should know better. It is one thing to criticise Ukraine; quite another to swallow wholesale all information emanating from Moscow – particularly when there are numerous surveys from reliable sources demonstrating that even in Donetsk oblast over 60% of the population prefers to reside in a unified Ukraine.

If there are true believers in Novorossiya today, they are few in number. Most separatists are motivated by other factors. Some cling to the view that without this industrial power base, Ukraine cannot survive. Yet, Donbas generally has been in decline since the 1980s when Soviet leaders opted to reduce investment into a coalfield beset by accidents, methane gas explosions, and reckless exploitation and transfer resources to the Siberian coalfield of the Kuznetsk Basin. The steel industry also is in need of reconstruction and modernisation.

Around this same time incidentally (1984-85), Margaret Thatcher, British Prime Minister, was closing similar coalfields in Phillips' home area of Nottinghamshire, as well as in neighbouring counties. The mines were no longer considered profitable. Donbas in more recent years has been exploited ruthlessly by local oligarchs for its steel and coal, and the civilian population is depleted by the war. Today the famous economic heartland of the former Russian Empire, founded on Western investment, needs help.

Where Phillips, and some others, err is in thinking (perhaps hoping) that the Russian leadership has embarked on some sort of ideological or messianic mission to free Ukraine from 'tyranny'. In reality, the Russian motives are much more straightforward: to keep Ukraine in the Russian orbit, to prevent it joining the EU or NATO, and to ensure that its government is friendly toward Moscow. True, that is not the reason why Igor Girkin/Strelkov initially entered eastern Ukraine to lead the rebels, espousing rhetoric that would have made Aleksandr Dugin proud, but his faith in the Russian government dissipated once it failed to support his mission, something already evident by August

2014.

For the DNR leader Zakharchenko, admittedly, the position is complex. He is backed neither by Russia nor much of Donetsk. He struggles to rule a region that is not self-sufficient, has been abandoned by Ukraine in terms of supplies and investment, and lately neglected by Vladimir Putin. The speed with which Putin transferred Russian interests from Donbas to Syria demonstrates the transience of Russian foreign policy, which essentially is a series of gambits, some of which succeed, and many of which have failed. There is no room here for esoteric and meaningless concepts like Novorossiya, especially not when oil prices continue to fall and Western sanctions remain in place.

Graham Phillips' comments about Mariupol illustrate the folly of only examining one side of a conflict and reducing motives to visionary concepts and ideology rather than Kremlin *realpolitik*. In turn, such opinions necessitate a perception of the Ukrainian post-Euromaidan leadership as a pro-Nazi cartel. That is not to say that there are no extremists within the ruling circles in Kyiv, but the vast majority are outside them and increasingly resentful.

While Putin's policies are often cynical, the leaders Phillips is ostensibly following – Zaharchenko, Mikhail Tolstykh (Givi), Arseniy Pavlov (Motorola), and others – have little to offer other than violence and demands for more territory. The DNR is less a government than a band of armed gunmen. Its survival depends on more violence but it lacks the power to go far without either external support or, more critically, the backing of the local population it claims to represent. It is to date not recognised, even by the Russian Federation. Only South Ossetia has offered formal recognition, and that region itself is an artificial creation.

The Minsk Protocol represents its potential death knell, which is why it will soon be broken, but the future of the DNR looks very limited, as does the future of Graham Phillips if he has truly abandoned his profession to become an activist in this flawed yet ruthless enterprise.

34

Russians as Terrorist Victims

23 November 2015

It is important to answer the following question in the context of the prolonged conflict in Ukraine. Should the Russian leaders and their policies dictate our responses to civilian catastrophes, and particularly the one brought about by ISIS?

World Terrorism and Russian Leaders

The commemoration of the tragic events in Paris by states, cities, and at high-level sporting events in Europe and North America has been affecting, and an example to follow. Strikingly, the shooting down of the Russian plane over Egypt on 31 October, which cost the lives of 224 passengers, has been treated almost in silence.

What explains the contrasting responses? Do they derive from the viewpoint that Russia's behaviour in Ukraine or in Syria does not warrant sympathy for its residents? Or that Russia's alleged responsibility for the destruction of Malaysian Airlines flight 370 over eastern Ukraine negates any such solidarity? Or do we in the West simply regard Russians differently, as the 'natural enemy' from the Cold War Years?

Much attention on media and social media has been focused on Russian president Vladimir Putin, a figure of great loathing in some circles, but seemingly highly popular in Russia. To a lesser extent Foreign Minister Sergey Lavrov has also attracted opprobrium. But should the Russian leaders and their policies dictate our responses to civilian catastrophes and particularly one brought about by ISIS, which has openly claimed responsibility?

Terrorism in Independent Russia

Russia has been dealing with terrorist actions since the late 20th century (as well as much earlier in its history if one goes back to the People's Will movement of the late 19th century) and on a similar scale to the atrocities conducted in Paris by ISIS. The terrorism in its earlier phase was a reaction to the initially disastrous intervention in Chechnya, authorised by first Russian president Boris Yeltsin in December 1994. Several bombs exploding in apartment blocks in distant parts of Russia in 1999 were never satisfactorily explained. A common opinion is that they were carried out by the FSB to encourage support for a renewal of the assault on Chechnya, which took place in late 1999.

In September 2001, after the 9/11 attacks in New York and Washington, Russia's president offered a united front with the United States in a common cause against terrorism: Chechens were linked to the extremists that carried out the attacks on the World Trade Center. At that time, President George W. Bush had claimed to have looked into Putin's eyes and got 'a sense of his soul'.

The following years brought horrific attacks by Chechen terrorists. In October 2002, forty terrorists led by Movsar Barayev held hostage a packed house of 912 at the Dubrovka Theatre in Moscow, with women clad in back carrying suicide bombs on their waists. Russian security forces responded by pumping gas into the theatre. The result was the death of all the terrorists but also of 130 hostages. The response was conducted in such secrecy that ambulances could not approach the theatre to assist the victims because of cars parked throughout the neighbourhood.

An even more savage attack took place in September 2004 in the North Ossetian town of Beslan, this time at a school on the first day of term. The attackers were under the leadership of Chechen warlord Shamil Basayev (1965-2006), who demanded the removal of Russian forces from Chechnya. The siege lasted three days, with terrified schoolchildren and their teachers held captive.

Once again Putin authorised extreme force, with security forces storming the school, backed up by tanks and sections of the Russian army. Of the 1100 hostages, 385 were killed, roughly half of whom were children. The escape of Basayev and other terrorists further marred the operation. Subsequently, Moscow was put into the sort of lockdown that took place in Brussels over the weekend of 20-22 November 2015 as the authorities mounted a frantic search for terrorists.

The Russian response appeared to carry a clear message: no concessions to and no agreements with terrorists. The violence may be equated with the personal methods of the president, which were mirrored by the Russian army's ruthless tactics in the recalcitrant republic. The subsequent alliance with Ramzan Kadyrov, who took over the Chechen presidency in 2007, brought together two like-minded leaders and reduced, though it did not end, the attacks on civilians.

Russian Citizens as Victims

After the disappearance of the Russian airliner over Egypt, the Russian leadership appeared reluctant to acknowledge a terrorist act, perhaps because such a revelation would bring back memories of an earlier era in which the government had appeared largely helpless to prevent such assaults. Prior to the event, Russian air strikes over Syria had targeted militants directly adjacent to the area still under the control of the Syrian government rather than those occupied by ISIS.

Western reports criticised Russia for its defence of President Assad, but were largely bemused by the sudden switch of priorities in Moscow from eastern Ukraine and Crimea to the Middle East. Yet it is not illogical. Russia has been an ally of Syria (albeit in its Soviet guise) since the 1950s. The potential loss of a reliable ally was seen as another Western intrusion into areas Russia considered within its purview. Moreover, there seemed to be possibilities of forming a common cause against ISIS that might appeal to the West and bring an end to the sanctions imposed on Russia because of its actions in Ukraine.

Throughout the 21st century, Russian citizens have been the main victims of the government's policies. Whether they are reluctant army conscripts fighting in an area they considered fraternal, or hostages of terrorist attacks, or passengers on a civilian airliner, they have borne the brunt of Putin's hardline approach to politics. The macho image that the president likes to perpetuate – even to the extent of including the very non-macho Prime Minister Dmitry Medvedev at a weightlifting session in late August – pervades foreign policy: the notion of being strong and defending one's own, however narrowly that may be defined.

He has survived to date because the image of masculinity, though sometimes ridiculed, has been mostly successful. It is the perception of a powerful state that prevails rather than the reality, but the latter is in any case shrouded in ritualistic propaganda about the devious manoeuvres of the West, and how the US controls and even chooses the Ukrainian government.

But outside Russia, its citizens are often linked directly with the government. One synopsis is that if Russians love Putin, then they must support his policies; that comment falls short on several fronts, not least an understanding of the nature of Russian foreign policy, which is precisely its indefinability.

An authoritarian state, which is an appropriate way to describe the Russian Federation since 2000, must convince its residents that the dangerous world necessitates extreme measures: the advance of NATO into the former Communist East, Western intrusions into Ukraine, EU approaches to Ukraine that exclude Russia, and of course terrorist attacks. Enemies are everywhere. As a result, Russians must support a strong leader and be prepared to make sacrifices.

In reality, however, Russia has no clearly defined policy. Without doubt it has moved far from the pro-Western stance of the early 1990s. Yet it is easiest to perceive its recent activities as kneejerk responses to problems as they arise, which was the case with the sudden takeover of Crimea, following Ukrainian protesters that resulted in the flight of President Viktor Yanukovych in February 2014.

Western Sympathy

None of this should preclude Western sympathy for the victims of Metrojet flight 9268. The victims of terrorism are not responsible for crimes, real or perceived, of their government, particularly one over which they have little or no control, and which has no moderating influences in Parliament or the courts.

Likewise, the perception of Russians per se as intrinsically linked to the government in Moscow is also a false one. They are not inherently imperialist or chauvinistic. Moreover, the handful of oligarchs aside, for the past quarter century they have been subjected to bewildering transformations that have undermined their security, depleted savings, impoverished the majority, and left them wanting only stability and an opportunity to live and raise families in peace and with the means to do so.

The destruction of the Russian airliner is a clear indicator that even under the current regime Russians are still vulnerable to random attacks. Yet many still place faith in Putin as the only leader who can offer some semblance of order, in contrast to the fumbling Yeltsin who left the country in financial crisis, or for that matter, Mikhail Gorbachev whose leadership ended with the Soviet empire in ruins.

Democracy and the pro-Western policies of the late 1980s and early 1990s are seen as an unhappy failed experiment, and kowtowing to Western demands. And while many Western analysts think Putin is not the answer, many Russians have to be convinced otherwise. If we are ever to co-exist in peace and with mutual understanding, we could begin by mourning the victims of flight 9268 as a signal that Russian victims are no less important than others.

35

Decentralisation: Pros, Cons, and Prospects

25 January 2016

The reform process in Ukraine introduced after the Euromaidan protests has a number of facets. One of the most critical falls under the headline 'decentralisation'. This paper explores what is meant by this term in the context of contemporary Ukraine. It also examines the prospects for the success of the reform, its benefits and drawbacks and whether or not it can be applied realistically to the areas of Donbas currently occupied by the rebel regimes of the Donetsk and Luhansk 'People's Republics' (the DNR and LNR).

The need for such reform predates the events of 2013-15. The last major reforms of Ukraine's administrative structure occurred in the 1930s and caused numerous problems by empowering new oblast administrations that, at least initially, had little contact with the districts ('raions') over which they governed. The present changes respond to the inequities of the old Soviet administrative system that was hierarchical in nature, with enormous powers resting in the central bodies in Kyiv. They virtually dictated policies at the oblast level, which in turn did the same to the raion organisations. In this way a 'diktat' from the republican centre (which itself emanated from Moscow prior to 1991) might have little relevance to the real situation in the regions to which it was applied. It also meant that the regions had few financial resources and limited possibilities of decision-making.

The Stipulations of the Minsk-2 Agreement

Ukraine's particular case is complicated by a civil conflict that has involved the intervention of a foreign power – the Russian Federation – and the participation and the encouragement of the European Union and the United States on the side of the new government led by President Petro Poroshenko and Prime Minister Arsenii Yatseniuk.

Two 'armistices' were held in Minsk, Belarus (September 2014 and February 2015) under the auspices of the OSCE, which tried to provide a solution to the conflict in Donetsk and Luhansk oblasts, with the participation of the representatives of the two 'governments' of those regions, along with the OSCE, Germany, France, Ukraine, and Russia, with the mediation of the Belarusian president, **Aliaksandr Lukashenka**. The resulting agreement, it can now be said with some certainty, placed certain obligations on Ukraine that will be difficult to fulfil.

The Minsk Agreements stipulated that decentralisation would mean special status for the two eastern regions and for three years they would receive some form of autonomy.[189] These new powers, however, would only come into force with an end to the fighting, the withdrawal of all foreign (Russian) troops and the Ukrainian 'Anti-Terrorist' forces from the scene, along with heavy weapons, and Ukrainian control over the border area by the end of 2015. That has not happened, though the serious fighting has abated and both sides have desisted from major campaigns.

The granting of autonomous status must also be preceded by local elections, which did take place in the rest of Ukraine, but are expected in Donbas' occupied and some unoccupied areas only by the spring of this year and according to the Agreement, they must be held under the supervision of Ukraine rather than the rebel authorities. Already, Aleksandr Zakharchenko, the Prime Minister of the DNR, has declared that the Ukrainian authorities ignored both the breakaway governments in drawing up the new laws, thus violating the accords signed in Minsk.[190] The position of the DNR and LNR forms an important background to the discussion of decentralisation and is now the principal question on the agenda.

The Main Ideas of Decentralisation

Decentralisation signifies local powers over certain areas of decision-making, but the Ukrainian leaders stress that it does not mean federalisation. One of the sentiments behind the new laws is that federalisation may give birth to separatism, and hence the influence of the local authorities must have some

---

[189] See http://ria.ru/world/20150212/1047311428.html
[190] http://novorossia.today/kiev-regime-s-decentralization-reform-is-a-joke-zakharchenko/

limits.[191] Whereas federalism would create new power bases in the regions, decentralisation would allow local bodies more initiative and financing to carry out governance in areas such as health care, education, basic (as opposed to specialised) health care, cultural institutions, public works – such as roads and street cleaning, and others. The transfer of resources to the regions has to be embedded in the revised Constitution of Ukraine. The Ukrainian authorities emphasise that there will be 'constructive dialogue' on issues such as use of the local language.

In place of the former system of 'oblasts' and 'raions', the new law will apply a three-tier system: oblasts, raions, and communities (hromady). Regional governors, who held vast powers under the former system, are to be replaced by 'prefects' in the oblasts and raions who monitor the decisions of local assemblies and hold executive powers in the localities. They are to be state employees but apolitical and not members of the local political elite.[192]

The local self-governments are now responsible for budgets and attracting investment, and will answer to their own local voters. But the important fact is the devolution of authority to the communities, rather than the oblasts or raions. And since Ukraine comprises many small villages and hamlets (over 12,000), these are asked to unite voluntarily into larger bodies to form grassroots organisations with enough power to make their own decisions on local affairs without having to answer to former bosses at the oblast level.

The authorities in Kyiv maintain that the reform will provide incentives for economic development and business, removing much of the present bureaucracy and central control. The central authorities essentially will be sharing power with the regions, and the main goal is to return 'a sense of dignity to the people', one of the tenets of Euromaidan. In addition, since the regions of Ukraine are so diverse, the reform will take place with a sensitive and careful approach to the particular characteristics of the local region. The newly merged communities in this way will be rendered 'sustainable'.

The ostensible model for the reform is Europe, and specifically Poland, where a similar local-government reform was carried out after the removal of the Communist authorities, despite major economic difficulties at the time, along with a high inflation rate. The Poles were persistent and, in the long term, decentralisation proved successful. It should be added that Poland does not share Ukraine's ethnic diversity.

---

[191] http://decentralization.gov.ua/en
[192] http://decentralization.gov.ua/infographics/item/id/28

Assessments of the Reform

When the first reading of the law on decentralisation was passed by the Ukrainian Parliament on 31 August 2015, it was accompanied by violent protests, involving supporters of the far-right Svoboda party and some members of the Radical Party, and resulted in the deaths of five policemen and injuries to hundreds of people gathered outside the assembly after several grenades were thrown into the crowd.[193]

The opponents of the law declared that the law was a 'sell out' to the separatists, and a betrayal of the principles for which Euromaidan had fought. They did not, however, represent a substantial segment of public opinion.

Elsewhere some activists protested more peacefully, arguing that the reform's creation of the figure of the 'Prefect' (see below) would in reality augment rather than reduce state power in the regions. Still, the reform process went ahead, and as noted by the Carnegie Endowment's 'Ukraine Reform Monitor', the number of communities is anticipated to drop from 11,000 to 1500 larger bodies.[194] The report did comment, on the other hand, that 'perceptions of poor communication and coordination' among the various parties conducting the reform was 'suffering from a lack of strategic direction'.

A critic of the Ukrainian government, Halyna Mokrushyna of the University of Ottawa, has outlined some other defects of the reform. First of all, as far as Donetsk and Luhansk are concerned, the 'special order' for these regions is to last only three years, and thus Ukraine has avoided the issue of granting permanent autonomy to Donbas. These regions also are subject to a separate law, implying that this latter document will not be part of the Constitution of Ukraine. The idea of special status, she also notes, is opposed strongly by two factions of the Parliament, namely the Radical Party led by Oleh Lyashko and Samopomich, headed by Oleh Berezyuk, as well as former Socialist Party leader Oleksandr Moroz.[195]

From a different perspective Halyna Coynash has questioned whether the authorities in the occupied parts of Donetsk and Luhansk will even permit Ukrainian parties to take part in the elections (Zakharchenko confirmed this on 24 January in a DNR news report). She notes also the conciliatory position (in this respect at least) of Russia, which has suggested possible

---

[193] http://euromaidanpress.com/2015/09/01/ukraines-decentralisation-and-donbas-special-status-what-you-need-to-know/
[194] http://carnegieendowment.org/2015/10/05/ukraine-reform-monitor-october-2015/iik7
[195] http://www.counterpunch.org/2015/08/28/decentralisation-reform-in-ukraine/

replacements of the current leaders (Zakharchenko and Igor Plotnitskiy) in order for more open contests.[196]

On the other hand, in mid-January, Boris Gryzlov, Russian Representative to the Contact Group for Ukraine, visited Kyiv, and also stressed the need to coordinate the amendments to the Constitution, including those for decentralisation, with the representatives of Donbas. Without them, he stressed, the Minsk Accords cannot be fulfilled.[197]

Mokrushyna also rails against the activity in Kyiv of American functionaries such as Assistant Secretary of State Victoria Nuland and former US Ambassador Geoffrey Pyatt, and believes that the decentralisation laws were rushed through the assembly in their first draft to satisfy the West.[198] Whether or not they were hasty, they certainly lack clarity. And the fact that they were introduced at the top of the hierarchy for application at the local level appears to undermine one of the ideas behind them, namely grassroots or local initiatives for change. Regarding US involvement, it has occurred with other reforms such as the formation and training of the new police force.

Another critic of the Decentralisation Laws is Oleksandr Slobozhan, representative of the Association of Ukrainian Cities, who maintains that the propose state subventions to the regions do not meet the minimal needs for education and health care and the new laws serve to raise the financial burden in the regions as areas formerly covered by the centre now must be paid through the local budget. He also noted that the state still collected local taxes and he feels generally that there is still too much government control over local affairs.[199] The critique is perhaps hasty in that one could not anticipate completion of decentralisation overnight.

Concerning the role of the Prefect, Berezyuk, leader of the Samopomich faction, maintains that it constitutes a form of dual power at the local level, alongside oblast or city councils. Others, especially in the Opposition, complain about the lack of discussion of the bill beforehand with the leaders of Donetsk and Luhansk.[200]

Interestingly the authority of the Prefect is to be applied to oblasts (this old Soviet term is to be abolished in favour of *rehiony*) and raions, but not to the

---

[196] http://khpg.org/en/index.php?id=1453675878
[197] http://rbth.com/international/2016/01/18/gryzlov-significant-progress-possible-in-fulfillment-of-minsk-agreements_560107
[198] http://www.counterpunch.org/2015/08/28/decentralisation-reform-in-ukraine/
[199] http://www.epravda.com.ua/rus/columns/2015/12/16/572561/
[200] http://www.counterpunch.org/2015/08/28/decentralisation-reform-in-ukraine/

hromady. The real powers of the latter are not clearly delineated. In essence, the law seems to reduce considerably the former authorities of the raion, but the oblast appears to retain some important functions, such as regional economic programmes.

Unsurprisingly there is even harsher criticism from the separatist representatives, particularly on prefects. Thus, the blog of Pavel Gubarev, the former Governor of Donetsk Region, states that they are government appointees and are only responsible to the President and that if a Prefect comes into conflict with local self-administration, the President may impose temporary direct rule until the conflict is forwarded to the Constitutional Court for resolution. He perceives the prefects as 'some sort of feudal lords' with enhanced powers.[201]

The bill for decentralisation, and to give the breakaway eastern regions special status, passed its first reading, though not with a very substantial majority (265 votes in favour), but its subsequent passage faces difficulties since it needs a minimum of 300 votes to be accepted ('a constitutional majority'). First it will go to the Constitutional Court for approval before returning for an anticipated decisive vote in Parliament in February 2016.

Still, changes are already taking place. On 17 January, the first elections were held in the territorial hromady with the election of 30 starosty (village elders).[202] At this same time, 159 communities were already elaborating their own budgets. Chair of Parliament Volodymyr Hroisman stated that the biggest challenges would be training new personnel and for the communities to understand that they, rather than the centre, are now responsible for decision-making.[203]

Prospects

Various opinion polls, including one sponsored by the government of Canada,[204] in recent months provide a clear picture of sentiment in Ukraine toward the leadership, the current batch of reforms, and priorities of the public. Without doubt, there have been changes in outlook in Ukraine, the residents of which are now better disposed toward democracy, joining the NATO alliance, and toward the European Union.

---

[201] http://novorossia.today/pavel-gubarev-o-popravkah-v-konstitutsiyu-ukrainy-zhestkaya-tsentralizatsiya/
[202] http://www.pravda.com.ua/news/2016/01/17/7095681/
[203] http://rada.gov.ua/news/Top-novyna/122891.html
[204] http://www.pravda.com.ua/news/2016/01/13/7095267/

Conversely, Ukrainians are much more wary than hitherto about Russia and its designs, and a majority in all regions supports the retention of Donetsk and Luhansk regions in a unified Ukraine. At the same time, there is strong opposition to the current leaders, especially toward Yatseniuk, whose popular standing is now lower than that of Viktor Yushchenko in the 2010 presidential elections, but also toward Poroshenko.

All polls show weariness and disillusionment with the fight against corruption, and the most popular political figures are outsiders parachuted into positions in Ukraine, like Odesa governor and the former President of Georgia Mikael Saakashvili. Poroshenko, in particular, has remained very cautious in taking on some of the more controversial figures in his administration, not least Prosecutor Viktor Shokin, who has shown a marked reluctance to bring any cases of corruption to court and Interior Minister Arsen Avakov, whose televised confrontation with Saakashvili dominated social networks for a period late last year.[205]

Underlying the anti-government sentiment are a number of factors, not least the apparent unwillingness of the coalition to deal decisively with corruption, which is a fact of life for residents of Ukraine and the continuing economic difficulties. And in the background is the lack of resolution of the status of the occupied parts of Donetsk and Luhansk regions. The government cannot offer a definitive resolution; hence it has assigned a temporary status to these areas, but even that concession has provoked much anger among its critics. Some argue that this is not the time to introduce decentralisation, and that there needs to be time for the economy to recover from its lengthy crisis first. The opinion polls cited above all demonstrate that the conflict remains a leading concern for most residents of Ukraine, but it is not something that offers any easy solutions.

The Poroshenko government implicitly accepted the existence of separatist governments when it signed the Minsk Agreements with them. The Agreements now hang over Ukraine like the Sword of Damocles. Not only Vladimir Putin's Russia but also the EU is anxious to see them implemented. Reports suggest that former president Leonid Kuchma, who represented Ukraine in Minsk, finds the Accords so unpalatable that he has requested his role be taken over by his predecessor, Leonid Kravchuk.[206] Decentralisation and the Minsk Accords appear inseparable, and Kuchma does not wish to be the one signing away–apparently–the unified Ukrainian state within the borders it possessed at independence in 1991.

---

[205] https://www.youtube.com/watch?v=GXk6GLqQdIU
[206] http://www.day.kiev.ua/en/article/topic-day/minsk-ii-how-trap-works

Conclusion

The Decentralisation Bill is today opposed not only by the opposition, which is gaining in support, but also by current and former members of the ruling coalition, as well as by the Batkivshchyna faction in the parliament led by the former Prime Minister Yulia Tymoshenko. Yatseniuk's solution to the prospects of an embarrassing coalition defeat in Parliament for a second reading of the bill is a nationwide referendum on the proposed constitutional changes.[207] But such delaying tactics are highly unpalatable to Ukraine's friends abroad. Russia faces equal problems: first decentralisation eliminates its own preferred solution of a federal structure for Ukraine; and second, it forces Putin's hand in either abandoning his Donbas allies, or forcing them to comply with the Minsk Accords.

The main solace for Ukraine is that if the Accords were actually fulfilled, there would be no border issues and Ukrainian control over its eastern boundaries, by definition, means that the DNR and LNR would become part of Ukraine, albeit with some special status. The elections in these territories in the coming months in that regard may provide clarification whether the local self-appointed leaders are prepared to accept Ukrainian control in return for autonomous status and even whether they can survive at all (especially if deserted by Russia, which seems to have withdrawn from any wholehearted commitment to the two 'republics'). Such status should also be made more permanent as it would meet the desires of most of the local population, which supports autonomy but not separation.

One hopes the current coalition can remain in power long enough and have the will to complete this complex process. To do so it will need to be bold and uncompromising, qualities it has not always exhibited hitherto.

---

[207] https://www.kyivpost.com/article/opinion/op-ed/timothy-ash-ukraines-constitutional-reform-conundrum-406630.html

36

The 'Imminent Collapse of Russia': A Response to Alexander J. Motyl

29 January 2016

Alexander Motyl's most recent commentary on the imminent demise of Vladimir Putin's Russia[208] provides a now familiar synopsis, based on broad simplifications, innuendos, and precious little hard analysis. Almost exactly one year ago, he provided a similar offering[209] and in mid-December another editorial in which he described Russia as a 'failed state' in contrast to Ukraine's progress toward a 'normal Western market democracy' (a concept he chooses not to define).[210]

Here is a direct quotation from the opening of the current article:

> Last year, Russia was basking in the glow of its annexation of Crimea and aggression in the Donbas. The economy, although stagnant, seemed stable. Putin was running circles around Western policymakers and domestic critics. His popularity was sky-high. Now it is only his popularity that remains; everything else has turned for the worse. Crimea and the Donbas are economic hellholes and huge drains on Russian resources. The war with Ukraine has stalemated. Energy prices are collapsing, and the Russian economy is in recession. Putin's punitive economic measures against Ukraine, Turkey, and the

---

[208] *Foreign Affairs*, 27 January 2016: https://www.foreignaffairs.com/articles/russian-federation/2016-01-27/lights-out-putin-regime
[209] https://www.foreignaffairs.com/articles/russia-fsu/2015-02-05/goodbye-putin
[210] http://www.worldaffairsjournal.org/blog/alexander-j-motyl/putin-steering-russia-collapse

West have only harmed the Russian economy further. Meanwhile, the country's intervention in Syria is poised to become a quagmire.

If one delves a little further into the sources of the above statements, one finds that 'economic hellholes' and 'huge drains' on Russian resources are both derived from the German tabloid *Bild*, hardly a reliable source of information and not one a scholar would normally cite. All the others are based on comments in earlier articles in *Foreign Affairs*. They in fact offer very little evidence to support the sweeping statements made in the article, the purpose of which appears to be to create an image of Russia as a state on the verge of collapse.

It is true that Russia's GDP declined last year. But the decline of 3.7%[211] was far below its peak crisis years of -7.8% in 2009 and -5.3% in 1998, a year of financial collapse, a sharp fall in the values of the rouble, and a run on banks. Even in those two years there were no signs of state collapse. Most analysts anticipate modest growth in 2016.[212]

Admittedly Russia has opted to wait out the economic downturn caused by the fall in world oil and gas prices by relying on its foreign exchange reserves. Yet according to the IMF and other sources, it still ranks seventh in the world in reserve holdings, well ahead of the United States (18th), and local neighbours Ukraine (66th) and Belarus (95th), which are suffering from related problems.[213]

As for the areas that have 'turned for the worse', it rather depends on the object of the exercise. Clearly the initial concept of 'Russkiy Mir' indeed failed to materialise, mainly because it was based on a fundamental misreading of sentiment in the cities and towns of eastern and southern Ukraine, and perhaps partly in Donbas as well. Such misreading was evident much earlier, prior to the Orange Revolution, when Putin failed to comprehend Ukraine beyond the familiar canards of a common history and religion.

Yet the adaptation to the status quo on the part of Russia has been relatively painless. Two military victories at Ilovaisk (August 2014) and Debaltseve (February 2015) that owed more to the incompetence of the Ukrainian High Command than Russian efficiency have in fact placed Russia in a strong

---

[211] http://www.ft.com/fastft/2016/01/25/russian-gdp-contracted-3-7-in-2015/

[212] See the analysis by Martin Gilman of the IMF: http://www.themoscowtimes.com/opinion/article/can-russias-economy-recover-in-2016-op-ed/553709.html

[213] https://www.imf.org/external/np/sta/ir/IRProcessWeb/data/rus/eng/currus.htm

position in terms of achieving more basic objectives. Ukraine signed the Minsk Accords with Russia and the separatist 'states', thereby committing itself to drastic revisions in the Constitution to accommodate the special interests of Donbas, as well as decentralisation generally.[214]

Neither Poroshenko nor Yatseniuk can be sure of their political futures, no matter whether or not the Decentralisation bill passes its second reading later this year. If it passes, more radical sources have threatened a 'third revolution' against abandonment of the ideals of the Euromaidan protests;[215] if it fails, they will likely fall with it. Putin is under no such domestic pressure.

In turn, the Russian commitment to the so-called Donetsk and Luhansk republics is relatively low, provided that they remain within a unified Ukraine where they can be a source of endless headaches to the Kyiv government. Putin can in fact pose as a mediator, sacrificing if necessary the nondescript leaders of these republics if needed.

Professor Motyl appears to be on sounder ground in his remarks on the costs to Russia for the invasion of Crimea. But this factor has to be qualified by the removal of the considerable costs for the rental of the two bays in Sevastopol in Ukraine, confirmed by the Kharkiv Accords of 2010, at around $4 billion annually and not due to expire until 2042.[216] Moreover, as yet we do not know the true values of Crimea's offshore hydro-carbon assets, other than that they are considerable.[217] Crimea also has a valuable wine industry as well as potential tourist dollars if it is ever demilitarised. In short, Crimea is hardly an 'economic hell hole'.

Ironically, Motyl does acknowledge what is perhaps the most vital factor in the survival of the Putin presidency, namely the popularity of the president himself. The sources of such popularity are regularly debated – from the president's physical prowess and strength to the image of a leader fighting against the odds, or reversing the 'losses' incurred at the end of the Cold War. Whatever the illusions of the population and the role of propaganda, the fact remains that presidents anywhere with ratings of over 80% rarely are removed from power (at least from within) – in Putin's case the rating is closer to 90%.[218]

---

[214] http://news.liga.net/news/politics/5077595-polnyy_tekst_soglasheniya_podpisannogo_kontaktnoy_gruppoy_v_minske.htm
[215] See for example Deputy Speaker Oksana Syroyid's comments at http://gazeta.dt.ua/internal/sche-raz-pro-osoblivosti-osoblivostey-samoupravlinnya-_.html
[216] http://www.km.ru/news/teksty_soglashenij_ukrainy_i_ros
[217] http://expert.ru/south/2014/24/shelfovyij-prirost/
[218] http://www.bbc.com/russian/international/2015/10/151022_putin_highest_approval_rating_list

In the case of Putin, though he has been in power (albeit with a short hiatus as Prime Minister) for over fifteen years, the population can still recall the anarchy and insecurity of the Boris Yeltsin years, with a president mainly confined to the sanatorium after 1996, and the perceived failures of Western-style democracy when applied to Russia. Even Putin's support for a tyrant like Bashar al-Assad of Syria indicates that unlike Yeltsin's Russia, the current regime does not abandon its friends.

None of this is to say that one should not criticise a leadership that has dropped any pretence of respect for human rights or international borders. But that is a far cry from making unwarranted statements about Russia's imminent collapse, based on very little, if any, real evidence.

37

Poroshenko, Polls, and the Rise of the 'Gas Princess'

8 April 2016

The past week has seen a veritable media circus around the revelations of the Panama Papers, in which, among many others, the name of Ukrainian president Petro Poroshenko appears, accused of opening an offshore account while his country suffered its worst defeat in the war against Donbas separatists in August 2014. What is Poroshenko's current standing and how long can the government headed by Prime Minister Arsenii Yatseniuk last in office?

Responses to the Panama Papers came rapidly. While the leader of the Radical Party, Oleh Lyashko, immediately called for the president's impeachment, several analysts rushed to the president's defence. Poroshenko understandably insists that he has done nothing wrong. In another setback for Poroshenko, who at the time was on a state visit to Japan, the non-binding Dutch referendum voted against the EU Association Agreement with Ukraine, decisively, albeit with low voter participation just above the 30% minimum threshold.

At present, few analysts can ascertain much from the limited information available on Poroshenko's activities. Upon taking office, he promised to sell his chocolate company Roshen, but failed to do so, claiming that there were no offers during a time of military conflict initiated, in his view, by the leadership of the Russian Federation. That claim might be valid: the principal client for Roshen products prior to 2014 was Russia, but that country promptly banned all imports from the company after Euromaidan. Nonetheless, that situation was already evident at the time of the election, since it followed directly the Russian annexation of Crimea.

For Poroshenko and the ruling coalition in Parliament, these events come at a difficult time, in a number of respects. Some European states have been sceptical of the leadership's failure to deal with corruption or respond to critiques from friendly sources. Though Parliament opted not to move to early elections, there are nonetheless generally negative sentiments toward the government of Arsenii Yatseniuk, and the only difficult question is with whom to replace him. Poroshenko appears to have settled on the most palatable choice for himself, namely the Parliamentary Speaker, Volodymyr Hroisman, the former mayor of Vynnytsia, rather than a technocratic reformer such as Finance Minister Natalie Jaresko. Neither it seems would win the overwhelming approval of the general population (see below).

I have suggested in earlier writings that Poroshenko at present is the least problematic leader of Ukraine, a compromise candidate during a period of polarised politics, economic problems, and constitutional issues such as decentralisation, Donbas autonomy, and decommunisation. It is evident, however, that the coalition in parliament is fast disintegrating and new challenges are emerging for the leadership of both the assembly and the office of president. The population generally seems supportive of a concept like decentralisation but dissatisfied with current policies, their own situations, and the lack of progress on eliminating deep corruption in society.

In an opinion poll conducted by the Razumkov Centre in mid-February, three parliamentary blocs were more or less evenly divided in popular support – the Opposition Bloc at 11.3%, Self-Reliance at 11.2%, and the Poroshenko Bloc at 11.1%. Yulia Tymoshenko's Batkivshchyna was slightly behind at 9.1% – based on responses to the question how respondents would vote were an election to be held on the coming Sunday (28 February, 2016). Also, just above the 5% threshold were the Radical Party of Liashko at 6.6%, and a party that does not yet exist in any tangible form, the Party of Mikheil Saakashvili at 5.8%.

Among the parties that would fall below the threshold for seats in the Rada were Svoboda at 3.7%, the Ukrainian Association of Patriots (UKROP) at 2.7%, the Civil Position of Anatolii Hrytsenko at 2.9%, and, distantly, the Popular Front of Prime Minister Yatseniuk at 2%. To the analogous question on presidential elections, Poroshenko was ahead with 14.7% followed by Tymoshenko at 9.5%, and Andrii Sadovyi, the mayor of Lviv, at 8.9%. The poll was based on over 2,000 respondents over the age of 18 in all areas of the country excluding Crimea and the occupied territories of Donetsk and Luhansk.

Another poll conducted along similar lines (over 2,000 respondents across unoccupied Ukraine) almost immediately afterward by the Kyiv Institute of Sociology (23 February-8 March) offered somewhat different ratings that may indicate an emerging trend rather than contradictory results, i.e. momentum may be building for a new leadership at both levels of government. According to this poll, had the elections for Parliament been held in mid-March, 9.5% would have voted for Batkivshchyna, 6.7% for the Opposition Bloc, 5.8% for the Poroshenko Bloc, and 5.5% each for Self-Reliance and the Radical Party. As with the earlier poll, all the other parties would be well below the 5% threshold, and the Popular Front reduced to just 1%.

Concerning the position of Prime Minister, linked in social media discussions in recent months with Hroisman, Saakashvili and Jaresko, Tymoshenko has now emerged as the most popular candidate, at 12.9%, with Saakashvili at 9.9%, Lyashko at 6.5%, Sadovyi at 5.9%, and Yatseniuk at 5.6% – with only 3.2% for Jaresko and no scores listed for Hroisman. The figure for Yatseniuk is surprisingly high, given that 33.2% of respondents held him responsible for the 'deterioration of the socio-economic situation in Ukraine over the past two years'; 24.2% blamed Poroshenko and 11.1% the Cabinet of Ministers generally.

On 17 February, Batkivshchyna left the ruling coalition, after Yatseniuk had survived a vote of no confidence. Tymoshenko and her party appear to have benefited from that move. Moreover, Tymoshenko's support is the most committed of all candidates and she is the only candidate other than Opposition leader Yurii Boiko to have broad support in Donbas as well as leading all candidates in Western Ukraine. In the Kyiv International Institute of Sociology (KIIS) poll, she also led Poroshenko in a potential presidential poll (10.9% to 9.3%) and would win a theoretical second round against the incumbent president (a reversal of what happened in 2014).

The intriguing question that emerges from these polls – and following the Panama Papers revelations and Dutch referendum – is whether Tymoshenko can revive a career that appeared to have ended at least twice: following her imprisonment during the Yanukovych years; and her rather ignominious comeback after her release from prison during Euromaidan and the 2014 presidential elections. With her party now in opposition in the assembly, she can distance herself from both the passivity of the government on dealing with corruption and her onetime political partner but now unpopular rival, Yatseniuk. If she were to eventually emerge as the new Prime Minister, or even President, it would be an event comparable to the resurrection of Lazarus.

Notably, in the KIIS poll over 56% of respondents did not support the 'appointment of foreigners to important government positions in Ukraine', implying that the alternatives as Prime Minister of either Saakashvili or Jaresko may not be palatable to most voters. For Western analysts who support reforms in Ukraine, the Jaresko candidacy was especially appealing but may no longer be feasible.

Thus, among the more obvious questions today are the following: would Tymoshenko and Batkivshchyna provide a strong reformist government? Could Poroshenko work with a Tymoshenko government (it provided a particular problem for Viktor Yushchenko in 2005)? And could a Tymoshenko government form a working coalition either with the more radical blocs in the Parliament or with the Opposition, should there be no obvious alternative? Ukrainians seem reconciled to the fact that even if Poroshenko stays, Yatseniuk's time in office is limited.

Based on her past record, a coalition on similar lines to the former one built after Euromaidan appears improbable. Yet the alternatives are increasingly slim. Moreover, the road to Europe, if not blocked, is hardly wide open, whatever the background of and questions raised by the Dutch referendum; the position of the Russian Federation remains unfriendly if not outright hostile; yet the Russian-backed Minsk Accords brokered with the separatists under OSCE auspices remain for most Ukrainians the best possibility of ending the impasse with the two separatist regimes in Donetsk and Luhansk – 66% of respondents to the KIIS poll supported this statement.

As for Poroshenko, the re-emergence of Tymoshenko will stir memories of their past rivalries from 2005-06 when they clashed repeatedly during Yushchenko's presidency and traded bitter accusations of corruption. Likely there are few political figures less appealing to him as a partner though their business backgrounds are not dissimilar. Both are senior political players who have been prominent in leadership positions over the past decade. He may concur that she would be preferable as a Prime Minister than yet again a rival for the presidency. But if the groundswell of popular support continues to rise, she is unlikely to be satisfied with the lower-ranking prize.

38

Ukraine and Russia: Rewriting Histories

2 June 2016

The 2016 commemorations of victory in World War II illustrate the growing divide between Russia and Ukraine, one that mirrors their current conflict over Crimea and parts of eastern Ukraine. Whereas Russia celebrated the traditional 9 May Victory Day with ceremony and military swagger, in Kharkiv, Ukraine, clashes broke out between pro-Russians and young Ukrainian nationalists.[219]

A rift between Ukraine and Russia has been growing for the past two years. Opinion polls show that attitudes towards Russia have changed markedly for the worse even in regions of Ukraine, traditionally friendly and Russian speaking. The change of attitude is largely a result of Russia's annexation of Crimea and its role in the conflict in eastern Ukraine, but it is also about interpretations of the past and defining national identity. World War II figures prominently as an area of acute dispute and propaganda, on both sides.

Below I will discuss Ukraine's relations with Russia by analysing the decommunisation campaign in Ukraine that is under the control of the Ukrainian Institute of National Memory (UINM). The ostensible goal is to eradicate any vestiges of Communist influence in Ukraine but the programme has taken on a distinctly anti-Russian hue that will clearly have an impact on bilateral relations.

The underlying question is: Could Ukraine sever relations with Russia completely, which appears to be the theme of the current changes embraced

---

[219] http://www.dw.com/en/russian-victory-day-prompts-clashes-in-kharkiv-kyiv/a-19244215

by the March 2015 'Memory Laws' and the enforced abolition of leftist political parties that originated in the Soviet period or shortly thereafter? And if so, what would be the chances of success in building a new pro-European path? Is decommunisation a valid, or even advisable route to take?

The Start of Decommunisation

Ukraine has embarked on a campaign to fulfil the so-called Memory Laws introduced in March 2015[220] to eliminate all vestiges of Communism and Nazism in Ukraine. This 'crusade', pioneered by Volodymyr Viatrovych, head of UINM, might be dismissed as secondary to the actual conflict, but the way in which it has been implemented seems guaranteed to exacerbate problems with Russia and divide Ukraine.

Indeed, decommunisation is intrinsically and unabashedly directed against Russian influence in Ukraine. When the parliament passed an updated decree 'On renaming some settlements and districts' on 4 February 2016, Andrii Parubyi, Deputy Speaker of Parliament (he is now Speaker) referred to the decree on his Facebook page as 'exorcising the demons of Russkiy Mir'.[221] Communist names, in his view, are symbols of 'humiliation and enslavement of Ukrainians'.

Viatrovych has claimed that the demand for name changes, as well as the dismantling of Soviet-era statues, first and foremost those of Lenin, is linked to changes of interpretation of the past, and particularly the perception of 'heroes' such as the Organisation of Ukrainian Nationalists (OUN) and Ukrainian Insurgent Army (UPA), cited in the Memory Laws as among the builders of an independent Ukraine.[222] The leaders of these organisations, particularly Stepan Bandera (leader of an extreme faction of the OUN from 1940), are to acquire streets in their names in all major cities of Ukraine.

For example, in Kyiv, the new Bandera Street will replace Moskovskyi Avenue (it also houses the Russian Embassy!). The avenue of General Mykola Vatutin, who was assassinated by Ukrainian nationalists, is to be known as Roman Shukhevych Avenue, thereby commemorating the leader of the assassins. The anti-Russian symbolism of the change could hardly be missed. Viatrovych insists that disputes over the past between Ukraine and Russia are not simply arguments but military confrontations because 'today's

---

[220] http://www.memory.gov.ua/laws/law-ukraine-legal-status-and-honoring-memory-fighters-ukraines-independence-twentieth-century
[221] http://www.radiosvoboda.org/a/27532795.html
[222] http://www.memory.gov.ua/laws/law-ukraine-legal-status-and-honoring-memory-fighters-ukraines-independence-twentieth-century

Russia is built on imperialism'.

At the same time, the local role is limited to discussing names proposed by UINM, not alternatives or retention of the original name. The UINM encountered a problem with Kirovohrad (named after Sergey Kirov, who was leader of Leningrad until he was assassinated in late 1934), where according to a poll of April 2016[223] a majority of citizenry (56.9%) prefers to keep the current name, 30.6% want the former name of Ielysavethrad (after Saint Elizabeth, i.e. former Empress of Russia and thus offensive to Viatrovych), and only 4.2% back Kropyvnytskyi, the name recommended by the profile committee of the Parliament.

One of the suppositions of decommunisation is that in a few areas of Ukraine, and especially Donbas, a *'sovok'* mentality prevails. The term is derogatory and refers to those people indoctrinated by the Soviet Union that have retained the former Soviet mindset. By implication it is an 'incorrect' attitude, and Viatrovych and others regard it as something that needs to be eradicated. Haran and analyst Sviatoslav Pavliuk agree that: 'sovok dwells not in monuments to Lenin, but in our motivations and actions'.[224]

Interviewed on Ukraine's Channel 5 (3 May 2016), Viatrovych declared that: 'occupied Donbas is an island of *sovok*, and *sovok* is the main reason behind the war that happened there.' He believes that Donbas is a successful example of the Soviet-era attempts to create a 'Soviet Man'. Donbas and Ukraine represent two different worlds, in his view: one that tries to live in the 1970s and 1980s and one that has returned to its 'national, religious, and European roots'. The isolated community of *sovok* in Donbas presages the 'beginning of the end of Russia in its present form'.[225]

It would be difficult to find a more emphatic dismissal of a region that only four years ago was Ukraine's most powerful economic sector, the leaders of which comprised most of the Cabinet of Ministers. Even in the late Soviet period, however, Ukrainian leaders, who were starting to assert their authority, recognised the importance of autonomy in Crimea and Donetsk region in particular (for example the presidential candidate I.R. Yukhnovskyi in Donetsk in October 1991).[226] It is facile to assert that Donbas is simply representative of the Soviet past or that the views of some residents should be dismissed outright.

---

[223] http://www.pravda.com.ua/news/2016/04/18/7105908/
[224] http://www.radiosvoboda.org/content/article/27710695.html
[225] https://www.youtube.com/watch?v=yfAUlrUazZE
[226] See Anatolii Yeremenko, "Nashli vzaymoponimanie," *Pravda Ukrainy*, October 12, 1991, p. 2.

Defects of Decommunisation

On 24 February 2016, German historian Karl Schloegel commented that the dangerous aspect of the Ukrainian approach to decommunisation was the monopolist position of the Ukrainian Institute of National Memory, which has too much control over a process that should be pluralistic and involve the general public, historians, and academic institutions. It is essential in his view 'not to turn decommunisation or desovietisation into a battleground for political games and not to enforce it from top to bottom'.[227] Yet that is precisely what appears to be happening, with threats increasing to those mayors (including incidentally Kyiv's Vitalii Klychko) who make arguments in favour of the retention of monuments of artistic value.

On a broader level, decommunisation has resulted in a ban not only on the Communist Party, which failed to gain representation in Parliament in the most recent elections, but also the Socialist Party (only created in late 1991 after the Communist Party was banned) because of alleged violations of the law banning totalitarian symbols, which were the subject of an analysis by a commission of the Ministry of Justice. The Commission reached the conclusion that the party programme falls within the new regulations, but the party symbols, which include the hammer and sickle, represent a violation. The conclusion was based on the 'expertise' of the Ukrainian Heraldic Society headed by Andrii Hrechylo.[228]

Finally, it is stating the obvious to assert that the campaign is removing some items of artistic value, which are linked irrevocably to the history of 20th century Ukraine, however tragic that history may be. Vandalism and destruction have superseded reason and discussion.[229] The equation of Soviet Communism with German National Socialism, including in the Memory Laws of May 2015, signifies that only the complete eradication of memory is contemplated. The naïve premise appears to be that by removing the symbols and remnants of Soviet power, popular memories will be eradicated. They are to be replaced by monuments, city and street names of heroes, including 1930s and wartime integral nationalists, the very names of which are anathema to Ukrainians in some regions.

Critics, internal and external, are not to be tolerated. One response to the Open Letter to Poroshenko and Hroisman – which implored the Ukrainian authorities to reconsider acceptance of the Memory Laws because of the

---

[227] http://www.dw.com/uk/ (24 February 2014).
[228] http://novynarnia.com/2016/04/22/min-yust-ne-zatverdiv-komunistichnu-simvoliku-rozkolotoyi-sotspartiyi/
[229] https://www.facebook.com/soviet.mosaics.ua/posts/897752127003905

potential threat to historical inquiry – was to accuse the signatories (in a letter to Education Minister Serhii Kvit) of being agents of the Russian Secret Service.[230] Another, from Viatrovych himself in the online *Krytyka*,[231] maintained that other states in former Communist Europe had taken similar measures and that the opponents of the laws were in close harmony with the Russified leaders of the DNR and LNR, and thus did not merit a vote.

Such sensitivity borders on the neurotic, as does a recent ban by Ukraine on foreign journalists who received accreditation from the leaders of the breakaway regimes in order to report the conflict.[232] Without their reporting it is doubtful whether news about the war would have reached the Western media. At a similar level was the overreaction to former Soviet leader Mikhail Gorbachev's support for the Russian seizure of Crimea – a five-year ban from entering Ukraine.[233] Gorbachev is 85 years of age and has made public statements both for and against the Putin presidency, but he has little influence in Russia where he remains highly unpopular. Authoritarian measures are sometimes justifiable in a time of warfare, but neither the reporters nor Gorbachev pose threats to Ukraine.

Conclusion

At this stage of the Viatrovych-led programme, an observer might question the methods used to introduce changes, which are imposed from above, with minimal discussions, and as historian Georgiy Kasianov notes,[234] reminiscent ironically of the way in which Communist names were imposed earlier. One goal, which is frequently stated explicitly, is to move Ukraine away from Russia and eliminate any vestiges of symbols of cooperation, with perhaps the sole remaining exceptions being the Rodina-Mat (Motherland) monument and the Museum of the Second World War. Another is to glorify two nationalist movements representative of a small area of western Ukraine – the imposition of a regional narrative to the entire history of the country, which is both misleading and divisive. Regions of Ukraine have their own singular histories and what is lacking is a unifying narrative and common 'heroes' during a time of prolonged crisis.

The discipline of history, also, has never been black and white; there is no

---

[230] http://foreignpolicy.com/2016/05/02/the-historian-whitewashing-ukraines-past-volodymyr-viatrovych/
[231] https://krytyka.com/en/solutions/opinions/decommunisation-and-academic-discussion
[232] https://cpj.org/2015/09/ukraine-bans-41-international-journalists-and-blog.php
[233] http://www.pravda.com.ua/rus/news/2016/05/27/7109860/
[234] http://life.pravda.com.ua/society/2016/05/7/211912/

single correct version of events, and the attempt to construct one, depicting Russia as the evil 'other', represents a mode of thinking ironically as one-sided as the earlier Soviet interpretations. Whereas Russia is conducting a hybrid war against Ukraine, UINM has responded with a propaganda war that not only attempts to cleanse the country of all Soviet remnants, but also, it now appears, anything linked to Russia.

Decommunisation is thus a means to take Ukraine out of the Russian orbit and to create and infuse a new nationalist mind-set. It is not unique, since similar practices have taken root in Poland and the Czech Republic, and other states. But it will of necessity alienate many residents of Ukraine who do not share the new official views about the past. Moreover, the anti-Russian framework is expressly linked to the current conflict in the east rather than a carefully constructed programme that takes into account the diverse strands of modern Ukrainian identity. In this respect, it is dangerously narrow.

One other aspect needs to be emphasised in conclusion. Removing Nazi symbols and monuments after 1945 helped to foster democratic changes in a Europe that was predominantly fascist or authoritarian. Removing Communist symbols in Ukraine in 2015-16 might have a similar intent, but not if the end result is to construct heroes out of leaders of the OUN, which was highly authoritarian, emphasised a 'Ukraine for Ukrainians', and followed a figure in Bandera who adhered to these principles long after the war had ended. This is not the path to democracy or the European Union but a reversion to the ideology of the 1930s and 1940s. It failed then as it will fail today. In short, it is a 'road to nowhere'.

39

The Donald on Crimea

1 August 2016

Donald J. Trump's co-chairman, Sam Clovis, maintains that the presidential candidate 'was thinking about something else' when he made his comments on Crimea to ABC network's 'This Week' programme.[235] Yet they are consistent with his astounding lack of knowledge about all parts of the world beyond the borders of the United States.

For the record, the key part of the interview was the following:[236]

> GEORGE STEPHANOPOULOS: Why did you soften the GOP platform on Ukraine?
>
> DONALD TRUMP: I wasn't involved in that. Honestly, I was not involved.
>
> STEPHANOPOULOS: Your people were.
>
> TRUMP: Yeah. I was not involved in that. I'd like to — I'd have to take a look at it. But I was not involved.
>
> STEPHANOPOULOS: Do you know what they did?
>
> TRUMP: They softened it, I heard. But I was not involved.

---

[235] http://www.politico.com/story/2016/08/trump-crimea-ukraine-sam-clovis-226501
[236] https://mediamatters.org/research/2016/08/01/trump-s-fact-free-comments-russias-annexation-crimea-roundly-condemned/212070

STEPHANOPOULOS: They took away the part of the platform calling for provision of lethal weapons to Ukraine to defend themselves. Why is that a good idea?

TRUMP: It's, look, I have my own ideas. He's not going into Ukraine. OK? Just so you understand, he's not going to go into Ukraine. All right? You can mark it down. You can put it down. You can take it any way you want —

STEPHANOPOULOS: Well, he's already there, isn't he?

TRUMP: OK. Well, he's there in a certain way, but I'm not there. You have Obama there. And frankly, that whole part of the world is a mess under Obama. With all the strength that you're talking about and all the power of NATO and all of this. In the meantime, he's going away, he takes Crimea. He's sort of, I mean–

STEPHANOPOULOS: But you said you might recognise that.

TRUMP: I'm going to take a look at it. But, you know, the people of Crimea, from what I've heard, would rather be with Russia than where they were. And you have to look at that also.

Several points are worth contemplating further. First of all, Trump appears to condone military aggression and equates Putin and Russia as if they are synonymous. 'He's there in a certain way' signifies the complete annexation of a territory that Russia had recognised, both implicitly and explicitly, in several international treaties. It suggests that Trump perceives the leader as ipso facto the voice of the state, and one who is free to determine the policies and image of that state.

Second, he implies that under a Trump presidency the invasion would not have happened. One is left to assume, indeed he states overtly as well, that President Obama is to blame for Russian actions, and by deduction, for Ukraine's Euromaidan uprising (the direct cause of the invasion) as well. But the United States is not omnipotent. It does not control international politics and it has considerably less influence in Ukraine than, say, in countries that are part of the NATO alliance.

Third, he states that from what he has heard, the people of Crimea prefer to be under Russian rule 'than where they were'. Does that statement signify faith in a referendum conducted under military occupation? It is true that a slight majority of residents of Crimea are ethnic Russians and perhaps many of them sought more autonomy from Ukraine. Since 1992, there had been occasional protests toward rule from Kyiv.

Of far more importance, and ignored by Trump, is the fate of the Crimean Tatars, who lived here for several hundred years before Russia invaded in 1783. Crimea has a lengthy and colourful history, but perhaps the Tatars above all residents have the strongest claim to a homeland. There is no evidence they were discontented under rule by Ukraine after 1991. There are, on the other hand, disturbing revelations about how they are treated today that are too numerous to ignore.[237] They are of course Muslims, which may explain the silence on the part of the Trump campaign.

Lastly, Trump says he did not know about the softening of the GOP platform on aid to Ukraine. Why not? Does it mean that his campaign manager Paul Manafort, who formerly worked for the disgraced former president of Ukraine Viktor Yanukovych, decides Republican foreign policy? Does it mean that a Trump presidency would move closer to Russia under Vladimir Putin?

Trump has already hinted strongly that he might recognise Russia's annexation of Crimea (even though Putin is 'not going into Ukraine'). He sees Putin as a fellow 'strong man', someone who attains power by denigrating his rivals and openly lying about his actions. Trump's disdain for minorities (Mexicans, Muslims) is evident as is his enormous faith in himself. He lacks Putin's erudition and knowledge but recognises a kinship in terms of attitude and disdain for the rights of small powers.

Below the rhetoric lies a dichotomy between two worldviews. One holds that Putin's Russia is simply asserting itself in response to NATO expansion and Western influence in territories that were formerly part of Russia's neighbourhood. The annexation of Crimea by this token symbolises Moscow fighting back after 25 years of retreat and kowtowing to US and Western European demands.

The other view is that of Russian aggression to establish a 'Russkiy Mir' in its region, meaning that the independence of countries such as Ukraine and Belarus, or even the Baltic States, must fall into question. In the absence of a protector, Russia can use force when needed, as has been the case in

---

[237] http://www.aljazeera.com/indepth/opinion/2016/03/russia-continues-oppress-crimea-tatars-160308054208716.html

Georgia in 2008 and Ukraine in 2014.

Admittedly these statements represent a gross simplification of a complex problem that also entails the future and role of the European Union, various political actors, and not least US policy in a world in which it may no longer be the key economic player, but remains by far the chief military one. There is some truth in both worldviews. Certainly, there were times in the late Soviet period when it appeared that most of the concessions – not least a reunited Germany within NATO – were coming from Moscow.

Prior to the invasion of Crimea, nonetheless, there was a more stable, and largely peaceful environment in geographical central Europe. That event changed the situation radically and led directly to the conflict in eastern Ukraine that has clouded the situation ever since. If one accepts the annexation of Crimea, it offers a green light to more powerful regimes to take over territories of weaker ones (one recalls Iraq's invasion of Kuwait in 1990). Without the US, NATO becomes a severely weakened force and European divisions would become accentuated.

Russia's main 'excuse' for its actions has been that a 'neo-Nazi regime' took over in Kyiv in the spring of 2014, ousting the legitimate president. It has also maintained it has no presence in eastern Ukraine's Donetsk and Luhansk regions, where breakaway regimes are in power. But the decisive battles to date (Ilovaisk, Debaltseve) have been fought mainly by regular Russian troops. Left to their own devices these 'republics' could not survive even though many residents are disillusioned by rule from Ukraine – and more importantly the destruction of their homes and livelihood as a result of Ukraine's Anti-Terrorist Operation.

Moreover, Russia has taken no steps to help re-establish Yanukovych as president. On the contrary, he is derided as a man who refused to defend his domain against an extremist insurgency, a weak leader undeserving of support. It is hardly far-fetched to see deeper motives here, the exploitation of an opportunity to change the status quo in Ukraine.

If Trump becomes president, will he offer Russia the freedom to assert control in the former Soviet republics? Would he support a NATO response to an incursion into the Baltic States, for example? Would the United States stand by an ally like Ukraine? It doesn't appear so, to the extent that he has given any thought to the situation. Together with Russia, he believes, the US could defeat ISIS while retreating into isolationism behind walls and economic protectionism. By way of compensation, Russian military power can prevail over morality and human rights.

It is small wonder that the analogy of fascism in the 1930s appears in so many analyses of the Trump campaign. It has many similar features: demagoguery, false creation of internal enemies as the source of all problems, autarky, isolation, mass propaganda, and a bombastic leader. The difference is that unlike Italy and Germany, the United States did not suffer military defeat and a harsh peace treaty in a world war. The images of a state maligned and deprived of its rights are based on illusions. But they do ally with similar self-images of post-Cold War Russia.

Over the next few months of the election campaign, it is to be hoped that the Western media will question Trump further on his intentions. The quoted comments are disturbing in many ways. Not only do they reveal an alarming ignorance of world affairs – something well established by now from other interviews – but they also suggest should he win the election a dramatic change of American foreign policy direction and a lack of recognition for the rights of smaller nations, particularly in Europe.

40

Death of a Separatist Leader

9 February 2017

The death of Mikhail Tolstykh (1980-2017), commander of the Somali Battalion of the 'Donetsk People's Republic' (DNR) better known by his nickname Givi, was affirmed on 8 February by Aleksandr Zakharchenko, the Prime Minister of the 'Donetsk People's Republic' (DNR), a separatist enclave within Donetsk Oblast of Ukraine.

Tolstykh died when a bomb exploded in his office around 6am. Zakharchenko accused the Ukrainian authorities of carrying out a terrorist attack and vowed to carry out revenge. In turn Ukraine's Security Service (SBU) denied responsibility and attributed the assassination to internal disputes within the DNR.

Tolstykh is the latest of several rebel commanders to die during the conflict that has now lasted almost three years. On 16 October 2016, the commander of the Sparta Battalion, Arsen Pavlov (1983-2016), better known as 'Motorola', was also killed when a bomb exploded in the elevator of his apartment block in Donetsk. Zakharchenko himself has survived several assassination attempts, illustrating the precarious existence of prominent separatist leaders.

The group includes two others who were especially prominent in 2014, the time of the pivotal battles at Ilovaisk and Donetsk Airport that saw separatist successes with the aid of the Russian army ('volunteers', according to Russian president Vladimir Putin): Pavel Gubarev from Severodonetsk and Igor Girkin from Moscow. Girkin in fact, based on his regular Twitter feeds, has returned to Donetsk, though evidently not in a leadership role.

Tolstykh and Pavlov were quintessentially men of action with few scruples.

Tolstykh, who served initially in the Ukrainian army, maintained in an interview that his only ambition in life was to be a soldier. He was an overt admirer of Putin and his style of leadership, a supporter of Russia and a self-acclaimed patriot of Donbas, the place of his birth – he was born in Ilovaisk. Girkin and Pavlov, on the other hand, were born in Russia, and in the case of the former prominent on several battlefronts that involved Russian intervention, including in Bosnia and Crimea.

Tolstykh and Pavlov were guilty of abusing prisoners of war, and even appeared in several YouTube videos beating captured Ukrainian soldiers. In one chilling clip, Tolstyk interrogates four prisoners, hitting them, and then taking out a knife, removing their epaulettes and forcing the Ukrainians to eat them. During this process, he abuses them with foul language and threatens to kill the main officer. Pavlov confessed to killing personally fifteen POWs and maintained consistently that Donbas was Russian territory.

Both justified their savage treatment of prisoners, which violated the Geneva Convention, by stating that the captured troops were responsible for the deaths of women and children in the city of Donetsk during the Ukrainian government's Anti-Terrorist Operation (ATO) bombardment of the city. In fact, the location of the separatist troops in Donetsk was a result, ironically, of Putin's abandonment of Girkin's army, formerly based in Slaviansk. Rather than submit to capture and execution, Girkin led the remnants of his army into Donetsk, knowing that any Ukrainian attack would inevitably result in hundreds of civilian deaths (a classic tactic also pursued by ISIS incidentally). There they have remained despite the removal of Girkin as commander.

Givi gave several interviews in 2014-16, some taken by the freelance British reporter Graham Phillips, who has unequivocally supported the separatist cause. Many are grim, others more convivial, such as dancing in fatigues with two similarly clad women to the former Soviet group Kino during an elaborate party for Givi's 35th birthday in Donetsk.[238]

In another, Givi conceded that most male residents of Donetsk had taken no part in military activities, adding to the reporter that: 'We must agree that they are not men'. He cited the example of several women who were commanding separatist battalions but the impression given was that he and his fellow soldiers represented a minority of citizens.

In contrast to the better-educated and more intellectual Girkin, it was always

---

[238] See Phillips' tribute to Givi, 8 February 2017: https://www.youtube.com/watch?v=V7OqBdNonJQ

hard to comprehend his life goals – and he must have known that his time was limited given the deaths of more than twelve fellow separatist leaders over the course of the past two years. He appeared to represent that nebulous phenomenon of a Soviet man, disillusioned by events in Ukraine that heralded change, Western ideas, and threats to the quasi-Soviet lifestyle he embraced.

In Ukraine, few tears will be shed for the charismatic Givi, and the separatist cause is now bereft of leaders with his commitment to the cause of the DNR and the neighbouring 'Luhansk People's Republic'. Neither can survive without Russian support but what they are receiving is spasmodic and uncertain. The sudden breakout and attack on Avdiivka seems to have receded with new Russian air attacks in Syria and perhaps because of stubborn Ukrainian resistance.

The apparent cordial relationship between Putin and new US president Donald Trump also brings uncertainty. Putin might perhaps refrain from further aid to the two separatist regimes if Russian control over Crimea is not contested in The White House (though it clearly would be elsewhere in the US administration). And there have been few clear signs that Russia wishes to annex the regions under separatist control. On the contrary, they represent an unsustainable burden during tough economic times.

Thus, the eventual return of the separatist enclaves to the government in Kyiv appears plausible, albeit in some autonomous or decentralised federal structure. Very few people are talking about Novorossiya in February 2017. That is not to doubt the sincerity of a figure like Givi, the archetypal brave but ruthless fanatic, who ultimately failed to attract fellow citizens to his cause.

41

The Destruction of 'Colonial Remnants'

22 February 2017

In late November 2016, Radio Svoboda held a programme on Ukraine's 'post-colonial status' that featured comments from supporters and practitioners of decommunisation. Its most notable feature was the sentiment that in spite of the progress made in 2016, many Ukrainians remain ignorant of their own history and trapped in a colonial mind-set imposed during the Soviet period.

Before examining the comments in more detail, the current progress of the campaign to decommunise Ukraine is worth noting. First of all it appears to be quite popular. Information provided on the Facebook site of the Ukrainian Institute for the Future reveals that over 54% of Ukrainians – one wonders if this is distinct from residents of Ukraine – supports the process being conducted by the Ukrainian authorities.[239]

In the year 2016, as part of this campaign, 1,320 monuments to Lenin were dismantled and 51,493 streets renamed. A further 1,069 monuments linked to other Soviet figures were also removed and 987 towns and villages renamed.[240] Thus the face of Ukraine has undergone a remarkable transformation, so much so that Volodymyr Viatrovych, the head of the Ukrainian Institute of National Memory (UINM), was able to report that 'the past year was the year of Ukraine's total decommunisation' and the completion rate is 90%.[241]

---

[239] http://apostrophe.ua/news/society/2016-12-29/opublikovanyi-dannyie-ob-otnoshenii-ukraintsev-k-dekommunizatsii/82084
[240] http://www.radiosvoboda.org/a/news/28199678.html
[241] http://apostrophe.ua/article/society/2016-12-29/dekommunizatsiya-v-golovah-kuda-zaydet-borba-s-sovetskim-proshlyim/9192

Seemingly not everything went smoothly. The biggest remaining Lenin monument, following the destruction of the one in Kharkiv city centre, was in Zaporizhzhia, which was almost 20 metres in height. Several protesters, described as 'mostly pensioners' tried to defend it and were accosted by Ukrainian activists who pelted them with eggs. It finally fell on 17 March.

The changing of the name of the city of Kirovohrad went through several stages, entailing six months of public debates, and the local administration missed the 21 November 2015 deadline to submit its proposals to the Ukrainian Parliament. As a result, explained UINM's Serhii Riabchenko, the Parliament stepped in and chose one of the names under discussion, Kropyvnytskyi.[242] In Riabchenko's view, the arguments opposing the new name are emotional rather than legal and the decision is unlikely to be reversed.[243]

In eastern Ukraine, 76 renamed settlements are under the control of separatist rebels, as is also the case for 75 in Crimea, and thus these changes remain on paper only. There is also the question of funding for a programme that entails changes of address for thousands of businesses at a cost of 'billions of hryvnia'. This issue is practically ignored by the UINM, since the expenditure devolves to local councils, which have to come up with ways of finding the money. Evidently some have funded the changes brought by decommunisation by selling off the removed Lenins to the highest bidder.[244]

Radio Svoboda's discussion, as noted, was less a debate on the merits of decommunisation than a series of comments on the mentality of Ukrainians today by supporters of the process. It cites initially the comment of the former political prisoner (and one-time Ukrainian Ambassador to Canada) Levko Lukianenko that 'Ukraine is a post-genocide, postcolonial nation – for 340 years Russia murdered Ukraine, russified it'. [245] Such a sweeping statement hardly contributes to reasoned debate.

A more sophisticated approach is that of writer Mykola Riabchuk, who

---

[242] It is to be named after the 19th century writer and playwright Marko Kropyvnytskyi (1840-1910) who was born near the city, originally called Yelysavthrad (Elizabeth's city). That name was a candidate for a replacement for the name Kirovohrad as well. The city was the birthplace of leading Bolshevik Grigoriy Zinoviev (Hirsch Apfelbaum), executed during the Great Purge of 1936.
[243] http://www.radiosvoboda.org/a/28206004.html
[244] http://apostrophe.ua/article/society/2016-12-29/dekommunizatsiya-v-golovah-kuda-zaydet-borba-s-sovetskim-proshlyim/9192
[245] http://www.radiosvoboda.org/a/28148649

distinguishes Ukraine from Asian and African colonies because the difference 'between dominant and subordinate groups was linguistic and cultural, not racial in nature'. Currently the country is building a new nation that 'recognises and honours the Ukrainian ethno-linguistic and cultural core of the political nation'. That indeed is what is happening, which appears to indicate the end of any attempt to construct a civil society.

The reasons for such an approach, one that is in line with the goals of the UINM, are encapsulated by the founder of the historical society Kholodnyi Yar, Roman Koval. He argues that unless Ukraine takes steps to change the educational system and de-Russify the country, millions of Ukrainians will remain mired in the Soviet past. Koval was horrified by his visits to schools in Odesa and Mykolaiv, especially in rural areas, which demonstrated to him that a generation of children and their teachers were completely ignorant of their own history.

Vasyl Filipchuk of the International Centre for Policy Studies also believes that the 'post-colonial syndrome' dominates the minds of Ukrainians, which he attributes to 'several hundred years' of control by foreign empires, and most significantly the USSR. Ukraine is thus living in a state of 'alternative reality' that distinguishes it from other developed countries. Thus, this colonial remnant must be eradicated.

There are different approaches to decommunisation, which is being treated by the authorities as a social form of economic shock therapy: at breakneck speed and without much discussion, particularly among professional historians. In this respect, Viatrovych's role is that of state propagandist rather than one who is seeking some sort of objective analysis of the past based on primary sources. But likely there would be little chance of success otherwise – one recalls the lengthy debates on the Organisation of Ukrainian Nationalists (OUN) and Ukrainian Insurgent Army (UPA) in the early years of the 21st century that essentially went nowhere in practical terms.

Yet it is likely that the new transformation will suffer the problems of the Soviet commemoration of the past, namely a refusal to examine events in depth, including the good and the bad, in an attempt to construct this alternative reality. Supporters of decommunisation generally look to Poland or the Czech Republic for models. One can suggest that these are not ideal – the political situation in Poland is beginning to resemble an anti-Communist witch-hunt. Wiser examples would be the countries of North America, which are still coming to terms with their pasts, particularly the treatment of aboriginal peoples.

Is decommunisation the end point of Euromaidan or the Revolution of Dignity? That is likely the ideal, but instead it may represent yet another failed attempt for Ukraine to emerge from its Soviet past. Riabchuk cites three examples: 1991, 2004, and 2014. Viatrovych is looking more to 1918 as evidence that Ukrainian independence is not something that suddenly happened after the collapse of the Soviet Union.

One issue is that the Revolution of Dignity was not only about ending Communist links. It was also about eliminating corruption, a topic that has a distinctly home base quite separate from that of Russian oligarchs and business empires. The subject is intrinsic to Ukraine's future economic progress and more difficult to resolve than the so-called sovok mindset among some Ukrainians. It is the reason why some frustrated radicals now threaten a 'Fourth Maidan' that will target the Ukrainian leadership under Poroshenko, to add to previous presidential targets Leonid Kuchma and Viktor Yanukovych.

Ultimately one can depend too much on interpretations of history in nation building and state consolidation, especially events that still remain in popular memory. More enduring historical myths could be built on writers and thinkers: Shevchenko, Drahomaniv, even Shumskyi and Dziuba, who would be less divisive than Mazepa or Petliura, and far less so than Bandera or Shukhevych.

The most unifying event of the Soviet period, and rightly so, is the Famine-Holodomor of 1932-33. And here there are no heroes, only villains. It remains a cornerstone of the modern Ukrainian nation and yet we still have much to learn about it as all Famine scholars acknowledge. In this respect, the Memorial established under the leadership of Ukraine fourth president Viktor Yushchenko was a starting point.

Finally, even some Ukrainian scholars perceive the question of historical memory as a sideshow during a time of intense conflict. That may be correct. But it is also one reason why the conflict developed and why it has proven so difficult to resolve, aside from the roles of international players like the EU and the United States. Enshrining individuals or events as part of a national ethnos detracts from their study in greater depth and with absolute freedom to reach independent conclusions. And that question is surely unique to Ukraine of all post-Soviet states.

One should not belittle Ukrainian achievements. Its media is relatively free, and its elections are generally fair, in contrast to those of its two counterparts Russia and Belarus. Its 25 years of independence are a similarly impressive achievement, particularly given recent Russian encroachments and threats. These factors should all be borne in mind when dwelling on its corruption and bitter infighting.

Bibliography

References

Arefev, A.L. (2013). "Russkiy yazyk v Ukrainskoy respublike." *Demoskop Weekly*, 14-31 October. http://demoscope.ru/weekly/2013/0571/analit03.php .

Cohen, Stephen F. (2014). "The Silence of American Hawks About Kiev's Atrocities." *The Nation*, 7 and 17 July. http://www.thenation.com/article/180466/silence-american-hawks-about-kievs-atrocities#

Colton, Timothy J. (2011). "An Aligning Election and the Ukrainian Political Community," *East European Politics and Society*, Vol. 25, No. 1 (February): 4-27.

Darden, Keith (2013). "Colonial Legacies, Party Machines and Enduring Regional Voting Patterns." Paper prepared for the Post-Communist Workshop, The George Washington University, Washington, D.C., 7 October.

Esipova, Neli and Julie Ray (2014). "Ukrainians Ratings of Their Lives, Country, Hit New Low," 19 December. http://www.gallup.com/poll/180269/ukrainians-ratings-lives-country-hit-new-low.aspx

Katchanovski, Ivan (2010). "Terrorists or National Heroes? Politics of the OUN and UPA in Ukraine." Paper prepared for presentation at the Annual Conference of the Canadian Political Science Association, 1-3 June. http://www.cpsa-acsp.ca/papers-2010/katchanovski.pdf

Kochura, Ilona V. (2012). "Coal Market of Ukraine: Analysis and Development Background," *GeoScience Engineering*, Vol. LVIII, No. 1, pp. 17-23, http://gse.vsb.cz/2012/LVIII-2012-1-17-23.pdf

Kulyk, Volodymyr (2011). "Language Identity, Linguistic Diversity, and Political Cleavages: Evidence from Ukraine," *Nations and Nationalism*, Vol. 17, No. 3, 627-648.

Kuzio, Taras (2015). "Vigilantes, Organized Crime, and Russian and Eurasian Nationalisms: The Case of Ukraine," in David R. Marples and Frederick V. Mills, ed. *Euromaidan: Analyses of a Civil Revolution*, forthcoming ibidem Verlag (Stuttgart), pp. 57-76.

Mace, James E. *Communism and the Dilemmas of National Liberation: National Communism in Soviet Ukraine, 1918-1933.* Cambridge, Mass: Harvard Ukrainian Research Institute, 1983.

Nuzhdin, Serhii, Yetenko, Maksym, and Ivan Halenda (2013). "Evromaidan-2013: khto ta za shchto protestuvav?" (Euromaidan-2013: who is protesting and what for?) https://www.academia.edu/8955785/ ЄВРОМАЙДАН-2013_хто_та_за_що_протестував

Palko, Olena, "Ukrainian National Communism: Challenging History," *Journal of Contemporary Central and East Europe*, Vol. 22, No. 1 (2014): 27-28.

"Pozacherhovi Vybory Prezydenta Ukrainy 25 travnya 2014 roku" (Extraordinary Elections of the President of Ukraine 25 May 2014) (2014). http://www.cvk.gov.ua/info/protokol_cvk_25052014.pdf

Riabchuk, Mykola (2012). *Gleichschaltung: Authoritarian Consolidation in Ukraine, 2010-2012.* Kiev: K.I.S.

Ridna kraina (2014). "Viina na Skhodi mozhe dokorinno zminyty demohrafichnu kartu Ukrainy" (The war in the east may radically alter the demographic map of Ukraine), 25 June. http://ridna.ua/2014/06/vijna-na-shodi-mozhe-dokorinno-zminyty-demohrafichnu-kartu-ukrajiny/

Romanyuk, A.S., Skochylyas, L.S., et al. (2010). "Elektoral'na karta L'vivshchyny u mizhrehional'nomu zrizi (Electoral map of Lviv region and interregional units). L'viv, TsPD. http://www.lnu.edu.ua/faculty/Phil/El_karta_knyzka/el_hystory_ukraine-2004.htm

Sakwa, Richard (2015). "Ukraine's forgotten city destroyed by war." *The Guardian*, 7 January.

Shkandrij, Myroslav, *Modernists, Marxists, and the Nation: the Ukrainian Literary Discussion of the 1920s.* Edmonton: Canadian Institute of Ukrainian Studies, 1992.

Snyder, Timothy (2010). "A Fascist Hero in Democratic Kiev." *The New York Review of Books*, 24 February. http://www.nybooks.com/blogs/nyrblog/2010/feb/24/a-fascist-hero-in-democratic-kiev/

State Statistics Committee of Ukraine (2001). *National Composition of Population.* Kyiv. http://2001.ukrcensus.gov.ua/eng/results/general/nationality/

The Economist (2014). "Good voters, not such good guys," 1 November. http://www.economist.com/news/europe/21629375-poll-results-were-promising-future-ukraine-dauntingly-difficult-good-voters

"Vybory do Rady-2014: povni spysyky kandidativ vid usikh partii" (Parliamentary Elections 2014: full register of candidates from all parties) (2014), 30 September 2014. http://tvi.ua/new/2014/09/30/vybory_do_rady_2014_povni_spysky_kandydativ_vid_vsikh_partiy

Further Reading

Åslund, Anders. *Ukraine: What Went Wrong and How to Fix It* (Washington, DC: Peterson Institute for International Economics, 2015).

Bachmann, Klaus and Igor Lyubashenko, *The Maidan Uprising, Separatism And Foreign Intervention: Ukraine's Complex Transition* (Frankfurt am Main ; New York: Peter Lang GmbH, Internationaler Verlag der Wissenschaften, 2014),

Bedritsky, A.V., Kochetkov, A., and Stanislav Byshok, *Ukraine after Euromaidan: Democracy Under Fire* (Moscow: Narodnaia diplomatiia, 2015).

Black, J.L. and Michael Johns, *The Return Of The Cold War: Ukraine, The West And Russia* (London ; New York: Routledge, 2016).

Boyd-Barrett, Oliver. *Western Mainstream Media and the Ukraine Crisis: A Study In Conflict Propaganda* (New York, NY: Routledge, 2017).

Czuperski, Maksymilian. *Hiding in Plain Sight: Putin's War in Ukraine* (Washington, DC: The Atlantic Council of the United States, 2015).

D'Anieri,, Paul J. *Understanding Ukrainian Politics: Power, Politics, and Institutional Design* (Armonk, N.Y.: M.E. Sharpe, Inc., 2007).

Dragneva-Lewers, Rilka and Kataryna Wolczuk, *Ukraine between the EU and Russia: The Integration Challenge* (Houndmills, Basingstoke, Hampshire; New York, NY: Palgrave Macmillan, 2015).

Fedor, Julie, Portnov, Andriy, and Andreas Umland, *Russian Media and the War in Ukraine* (Stuttgart: Ibidem-Press, 2015).

Gardner, Hall. *Crimea, Global Rivalry, and the Vengeance of History* (New York, NY: Palgrave Macmillan, 2015).

Grant, Thomas D. *Aggression Against Ukraine: Territory, Responsibility, And International Law* (New York: Palgrave Macmillan, 2015).

Grigas, Agnia. *Beyond Crimea: The New Russian Empire* (New Haven: Yale University Press, 2016).

Hale, Henry E. and Robert W Orttung, *Beyond The Euromaidan: Comparative Perspectives On Advancing Reform In Ukraine* (Stanford, California: Stanford University Press, 2016).

Herpen, Marcel van. *Putin's Propaganda Machine: Soft Power and Russian Foreign Policy* (Lanham: Rowman & Littlefield, 2016).

Herpen, Marcel van. *Putin's Wars: The Rise Of Russia's New Imperialism* (Lanham: Rowman & Littlefield, 2015).

Hill, Fiona and Clifford G Gaddy, *Mr. Putin: Operative in the Kremlin* (Washington, D.C.: Brookings Institution Press, 2015).

Horbulin, V.P. *Donbas and Crimea: Return at What Price?* (Kyiv: National Institute for Strategic Studies, 2016).

Judah, Tim. *In Wartime: Stories from Ukraine* (New York: Tim Duggan Books, 2016).

Kadri, Liik, and Andrew Wilson, *What Will Happen With Eastern Ukraine?* (London: European Council on Foreign Relations (ECFR), 2014).

Kalb, Marvin L. *Imperial Gamble: Putin, Ukraine, and the New Cold War* (Washington, D.C.: Brookings Institution Press, 2015).

Kent, Neil. *Crimea: A History* (London: Hurst & Company, 2016).

Kolstø, Pål and Helge Blakkisrud, *The New Russian Nationalism: Imperialism, Ethnicity and Authoritarianism 2000-15* (Edinburgh: Edinburgh University Press, 2016).

Koshiw, J.V. *Abuse of Power: Corruption in The Office Of The President* (Reading, Berkshire, England: Artemia Press Ltd, 2013).

Kuzio, Taras. *Democratic Revolution in Ukraine: From Kuchmagate to Orange Revolution.* (Hoboken: Taylor and Francis, 2013).

Kuzio, Taras. *Ukraine: Democratization, Corruption, and the New Russian Imperialism* (Santa Barbara, California: Praeger Security International, 2015).

Kuzio, Taras. *The Crimea: Europe's next flashpoint?* (Washington, DC: Jamestown Foundation, 2011).

Legvold, Robert. *Return to Cold War* (Malden, MA: Polity, 2016).

Leitch, Duncan and Andreas Umland, *Assisting Reform in Post-Communist Ukraine 2000-2012 The Illusions of Donors and the Disillusion of Beneficiaries* (Stuttgart: Ibidem, 2016).

Lendman, Stephen. *Flashpoint in Ukraine: How the US Drive for Hegemony Risks World War III* (Atlanta, GA: Clarity Press, Inc., 2014).

Luciuk, Lubomyr Y., ed. *Jews, Ukrainians, and the Euromaidan* (Kingston, Ontario: Kashtan Press, 2014).

Lutsevych, Orysia. *Agents of The Russian World: Proxy Groups in The Contested Neighbourhood (*London: Chatham House, 2016).

Marples, David R. and Frederick V. Mills, eds. *Ukraine's Euromaidan: Analyses of a Civil Revolution.* Stuttgart: Ibidem Verlag, 2015.

McNabb, David E. *Vladimir Putin and Russia's Imperial Revival* (Boca Raton, FL: CRC Press, Taylor & Francis Group, 2016).

Moser, Michael, and Andreas Umland. *Language Policy and Discourse on Languages in Ukraine under President Viktor Yanukovych* (Stuttgart: Ibidem, 2015).

Onuch, Olga. *Mapping Mass Mobilization: Understanding Revolutionary Moments in Argentina (2001) and Ukraine (2004)* (Houndmills, Basingstoke, Hampshire; New York, NY: Palgrave Macmillan, 2014).

Pantti, Mervi. *Media and the Ukraine Crisis: Hybrid Media Practices and Narratives of Conflict* (New York: Peter Lang, 2016).

Pikulicka-Wilczewska, Agnieszka and Richard Sakwa, eds. *Ukraine and Russia: People, Politics, Propaganda and Perspectives* (Bristol: E-International Relations Publishing, 2015).

Pinkham, Sophie. *Black Square: Adventures in Post-Soviet Ukraine* (New York: W.W. Norton & Company, 2016).

Plokhy, Serhy. *The Gates of Europe: A History of Ukraine* (New York: Basic Books, 2015).

Pylynskyi, Yaroslav and Viktor Stepanenko, *Ukraine after the Euromaidan: Challenges and Hopes* (Pieterlen Lang, Peter Bern 2014).

Rajan Menon, Rajan and Eugene B Rumer, *Conflict in Ukraine: The Unwinding of The Post-Cold War Order* (Cambridge, MA: The MIT Press, 2015).

Rose, Gideon, ed. *Crisis in Ukraine* (Tampa, Florida: Council on Foreign Relations, 2014).

Sakwa, Richard. *Frontline Ukraine: Crisis in The Borderlands* (London: I.B. Tauris, 2016).

Stepanenko, Viktor and Yaroslav Pylynskyi, *Ukraine After the Euromaidan: Challenges and Hopes* (Switzerland: Peter Lang, 2015).

Wilson, Andrew. *Ukraine Crisis: What It Means for the West* (New Haven: Yale University Press, 2014).

Wood, Elizabeth A., Pomeranz, William E., and E Wayne Merry, E. Wayne, and Maxim Trudolyubov. *Roots of Russia's War in Ukraine* (New York; Woodrow Wilson Centre Press / Columbia University Press, 2015).

Williams, Bryan Glyn. *The Crimean Tatars. From Soviet Genocide to Putin's Conquest* (London: Hurst & Company, 2015).

Wood, Elizabeth A., Pomeranz, William E., Merry, E. Wayne, and Maxim Trudolyubov. *Roots of Russia's War in Ukraine* (Washington, D.C: Woodrow Wilson Centre Press, 2015).

Yekelchyk, Serhy. *The Conflict in Ukraine: What Everyone Needs to Know* (New York, NY: Oxford University Press, 2015).

Note on Indexing

E-IR's publications do not feature indexes due to the prohibitive costs of assembling them. If you are reading this book in paperback and want to find a particular word or phrase you can do so by downloading a free PDF version of this book from the E-IR website.

View the e-book in any standard PDF reader such as Adobe Acrobat Reader (pc) or Preview (mac) and enter your search terms in the search box. You can then navigate through the search results and find what you are looking for. In practice, this method can prove much more targeted and effective than consulting an index.

If you are using apps (or devices) such as iBooks or Kindle to read our e-books, you should also find word search functionality in those.

You can find all of our e-books at: http://www.e-ir.info/publications

www.ingramcontent.com/pod-product-compliance
Lightning Source LLC
Chambersburg PA
CBHW071236080526
44587CB00013BA/1643